GRACE DARLING

Grace Darling
Victorian Heroine

Hugh Cunningham

hambledon
continuum

Hambledon Continuum is an imprint of Continuum Books
Continuum UK, The Tower Building, 11 York Road, London SE1 7NX
Continuum US, 80 Maiden Lane, Suite 704, New York, NY 10038

www.continuumbooks.com

First published 2007

British Library Cataloguing-in-Publication Data
A catalogue record for this book is available from the British Library.

ISBN 978 1 85285 548 2

Typeset by Egan Reid, Auckland, New Zealand
Printed and bound by MPG Books Ltd, Cornwall, Great Britain

Contents

Illustrations

Acknowledgements

Queen Victoria's journal in the Royal Archives is reproduced with the permission of Her Majesty Queen Elizabeth II. Material from the papers of the Trevelyan family is cited by permission of the Trustees of the Trevelyan Papers at the Robinson Library, University of Newcastle upon Tyne; from the Collections of Manuscripts at Alnwick Castle by permission of the Duke of Northumberland; and from Catherine Sharp's paper by permission of Gloucestershire Archives.

For guidance on archives, I am indebted to Elaine Archbold at the Robinson Library, University of Newcastle upon Tyne, Clare Baxter at Alnwick Castle, Christine Bell at the Grace Darling Museum, Diana Coke at the Royal Humane Society, Barry Cox, Carolyn Anand and Derek King, Maureen La Frenais at the RNLI archive in Poole, Olive Graham at Newcastle City Library, Rod Hamilton at the National Sound Archive, Erika Ingham at the National Portrait Gallery, Joan Jones at Royal Doulton, Mrs J. M. Kavanagh and Julie Snelling at the BBC Written Archives Centre, Mrs J. Kelsey at the Royal Archives, Julie Anne Lambert at the Bodleian Library, Geoff Smith at Ohio State University (Jessica Mitford archive), Lynne Ritchie at the National Maritime Museum, Captain Hamish Robertson, archivist of the Fraternity of Masters and Seamen in Dundee, Kitty Ross, Curator of Social History and Costume at the Abbey House Museum in Leeds and Mrs S. Wood at the Northumberland Record Office at Gosforth. All have been unfailingly helpful, as have the librarians at the Templeman Library, University of Kent and the British Library.

For help with a wide range of other issues, my thanks to Malcolm Andrews, Keith Armstrong, Tony Benn, Grace Brockington, Mark Connelly, Kirsty Cunningham, Janet Davis, Michael Duffy, William Fortescue, Rebe Freeman-Thomas, John Gardiner, Nicola Gordon Bowe, Joan Graham, Stephen Heathorn, Nicholas Hiley, Louis James, Masahiro Kawamoto, Brenda and Edgar Knight, Mary Lovell, Bryan Lewis, Sarah Moss, Jim Murray, Katrina Porteous, Myrna Schkolne, Martin Sheppard, Shurlee Swain, Jenny Uglow, Linda Wilson and Pete Yeandle. My wife, Diane, has been a constant source of encouragement, my eBay researcher, and has lived uncomplainingly with Grace Darling for rather longer than she reckoned on.

Introduction

I can't remember exactly where and when I first heard the story of how Grace Darling had rowed out with her father to rescue survivors from the wreck of the *Forfarshire* in 1838. Perhaps it was at home in the Scottish lowlands, perhaps at school at Dunbar, on the east coast, not many miles north of Grace's Bamburgh. Her story came for me to be inextricably linked with other stories that constituted something which would eventually become history: Alfred and the burnt cakes, Robert the Bruce and the spider, Florence Nightingale and her lamp. These stories of persistent endeavour and courage were an essential early childhood ingredient of what was still thought of as 'Our Island Story'.

Others of my generation (born 1942), boys, it seems, as much as girls, remember more precisely how they learned of Grace. Many say that they can 'see' her. 'What do you see?' I ask, and they act out, or describe to me, a picture of Grace sitting in the coble, grasping both oars in a stormy sea, her father airbrushed away. This was how she appeared in Arthur Mee's *The Children's Encyclopedia*. Boys learned of her in the pages of the *Eagle*. For girls brought up on books of heroines, the story of Grace was often the favourite, perhaps because it was easier to relate to her than to some of the more imposing champions of philanthropic endeavour whose life-stories padded out such books.

If most of my contemporaries encountered the story of Grace in some form, this is even more the case of an older generation. Many remember the 'Grace Darling song'. Kenneth Williams, brought up in the slums of north London, could re-enact his grandmother singing it (her only song). At the other end of the social scale, the famous Mitford sisters stood round the piano singing the song, which their mother loved: and from the Mitford home in Gloucestershire it was to travel to California, whose restaurants in the 1970s and 1980s reverberated with Jessica's loud renditions of it.[1] Others learned the song at school. When I met Rebe Freeman-Thomas, who had been a schoolgirl at Whitby in the 1920s, she immediately launched into:

> Twas on the Longstone Lighthouse,
>   There dwelt an English maid:
> Pure as the air around her,
>   Of danger ne'er afraid.

> One morning just at daybreak,
>   A storm toss'd wreck she spied;
> And tho' to try seemed madness,
>   'I'll save the crew!' she cried.

But ask anyone aged between about twenty and fifty outside the north east of England, and the words 'Grace Darling' are likely to draw a blank. She disappeared from the school syllabus and from the stories thought suitable for young readers. There was a 'Graceless' generation. But recently things have changed. In the early twenty-first century the story of Grace Darling has embedded itself in the 'Key Reading Stages' of the national curriculum. Children can encounter her, for example, in a Channel Four programme with an accompanying booklet written by Christine Moorcroft and Magnus Magnusson, featuring 'Famous People'; there she is in company with, among others, Cleopatra, Boudica and Leonardo da Vinci. Grace Darling herself was astonished at her fame – some think it killed her. She would have been even more astonished if she had known that over a century and a half later her name was still remembered, and that there was a museum dedicated to her deed attracting 40,000 visitors a year. My aim in this book is to describe and explain why an act of courage should have had such resonance.

'Grace Darling (1815–1842), heroine ...' So starts the entry on Grace Darling both in the old nineteenth-century *Dictionary of National Biography* and the new *Oxford Dictionary of National Biography*. In the latter, and probably in the former, she is the only 'heroine' *tout court*. Other 'heroines' there are, nine of them, but they are a 'Jacobite heroine' (Flora MacDonald), or 'royalist heroines' (Lady Fisher and Charlotte Stanley, Countess of Derby), or a 'nurse and war heroine' (Edith Cavell), or a 'tragic heroine' (the obscure Irish queen, Gormlaith, who died in 948). The ten heroines are matched by ten heroes, but no fewer than six of these are either 'legendary heroes' or 'folk heroes'. Of course there are entries that describe heroism of action or character, but the people who earn that accolade are soldiers or sailors, missionaries or martyrs. Grace Darling alone is defined purely by her heroism.

Grace Darling risked her life to save life. Her act was, on any definition, heroic. But many other people have risked life, or given life, to save others. Before she was born, the Royal Humane Society had been founded to give recognition to people who saved others from drowning. More recently, the George Medal has been conferred on civilians who have displayed exceptional courage in lifesaving. But most of us would be hard put to name the recipients of the Society's awards or of the George Medal. Why did Grace Darling's deed stand out from the rest and achieve national and international recognition?

It was in large part because she was a woman. Had her brother been at the lighthouse on the night of 6 September 1838, he would have rowed out to the rescue with their father, and the deed would soon have faded from memory. Heroes were commonplace, heroines rare. Her deed was, in the alliterative words of a contemporary, 'unexampled in the feats of female fortitude'.[2] As such, as we shall see, it attracted intense attention. And in the later nineteenth and first half of the twentieth centuries, when her fame was at its height, many writers speculated on what lessons her life held for contemporary women.

Heroines are of two kinds. There are those who in real life perform heroic deeds, and there are those who are the leading female characters in fiction or on stage. Carry out a text search for 'heroine' in the *Oxford Dictionary of National Biography*, and you find the word 420 times. The vast majority are 'heroines' in the form we normally encounter them, the heroines of fiction or drama. Grace Darling, instantly a heroine in the first sense, was almost equally rapidly a heroine in the second. The first four books with her name in the title, published between 1838 and 1840, were fictions – three novels and a play. 'Grace Darling' was little more than a peg on which to hang an improbable tale. There was in truth little to say about Grace Darling the real life heroine. She was the daughter of a lighthouse keeper, living an isolated life on the rocky Longstone Island, and then she became a heroine. Perhaps fiction offered a way of understanding Grace. When William Howitt visited the Farne Isles in 1840, one of a stream of visitors keen to gaze at the heroine, he turned to a fictional heroine to describe Grace: 'She is to me more completely a Jeannie Deans than I could have conceived or can express'.[3] The heroine of Walter Scott's *The Heart of Midlothian* needed no introduction to Howitt's readers. Fact and fiction interweave themselves in the story of Grace Darling and of the perpetuation of her memory, the most distinguished recent example being Jill Paton Walsh's *Grace* (1991).

Grace Darling, the heroine, quickly became also Grace Darling, the celebrity. The speed with which the contemporary media took up her story and the prominence they gave to it is astonishing. Before the 1830s were out, she was the subject of books, plays, panoramas, songs and pottery figurines. Painters and sculptors had broadcast their images of her. Few could have been unaware of her name and her deed when she died of consumption in 1842. In her lifetime people wanted bits of her – her hair, her clothing, her handwriting – and she carefully distributed them to a chosen few. After her death, these became 'relics', preserved, exchanged, their authenticity sworn to or denied, like the relics of saints. Anything associated with her acquired a value, and to associate anything with her conferred value on it. Many girls at birth, perhaps particularly in the United States, were given her name, just as in the twentieth century they would be given the names of Hollywood film stars. And in the consumer boom of the late nineteenth century, advertisers used her name and image to sell goods. There was, with a degree of inevitability, a Grace Darling rose, and many other products were associated with her: chocolate, soap, pens, and so on. Celebrity can mean simply that a person becomes the focus of media attention, and this certainly happened to Grace. There is also a second order of celebrity which not all achieve, but Grace did: in this, a name or image floats free of what originally brought it to prominence, and is used to add value to something with which it has no intrinsic connection. Grace in the nineteenth century became a celebrity in this second sense.

The potent combination of heroism and celebrity gave Grace Darling relatively easy access into the ever-changing story of the past, and in particular the past of the nation. She was constantly compared with and measured against other famous women from biblical times to the present, her deed normally singled out for the purity of her motivation as well as her courage. She became embedded in the history of 'Northumbria', of the nation, and of the world, admired in Europe, the United States, Australia and Japan. People might not know much about her, they might confuse her with Flora MacDonald and her rescue of Bonnie Prince Charlie, but at some level they registered her as part of a past of which one could be proud. And there was an assumption that her deed was part of a national memory chest, something you could refer to in conversation or print knowing that your listeners or readers would know her story in the same way they would know about 1066, or Henry VIII and his wives, or Florence Nightingale. Take two examples from twentieth-century fiction. In Evelyn Waugh's *Brideshead Revisited* Anthony Blanche, after reciting passages from *The Waste Land* to 'the sweatered and muffled throng that was on its way to the river', declares that 'All b-boatmen are Grace Darlings to me'. And in P. D. James's *Innocent Blood*, Maurice has a prized collection of Staffordshire figures: Nelson, Wellington, Victoria and Albert, and 'a lighthouse rising from a turbulent sea of unchipped waves, with Grace Darling straining on her oars'.[4] There she is, the daughter of a lighthouse keeper, alongside the most famous people in nineteenth-century British history. How she got to be there is one question that this book will try to answer. But, also to be noted, is the assumption of Waugh and James that their readers will know about Grace Darling, that she is (or was) part of national memory.

In France, Pierre Nora has explored what he calls 'les lieux de mémoire', which in English translation has become 'realms of memory'. Nora, I suspect, instinctively knew a realm of memory when he came across one, but, pushed to define his term, he came up with 'any significant entity, whether material or non-material in nature, which by dint of human will or the work of time has become a symbolic element of the memorial heritage of any community'.[5] Realms of memory, with their symbolic meaning, have a capacity for metamorphosis, for change: what they mean for one generation may differ substantially from what they mean for another. In seven influential volumes published between 1984 and 1992 Nora and his collaborators explored the realms of memory of France. They studied not only buildings, say the Louvre or the Eiffel Tower, but also the

Marseillaise, the tricoleur, a popular book, food and wine, and Joan of Arc.

Across the Channel, Grace Darling, 'the Maid of the Isles', was instantly seen as the British equivalent of Joan of Arc, 'the Maid of Orleans'. Like Joan, she was and is a realm of memory, carrying a symbolic weight, and likely to mean different things to different generations. You can encounter her on the ground in material form, in memorials, monuments and a museum, literally in places of memory. But she is to be found also in objects of everyday consumption, in fiction, and in that residue of events and personalities in history that constitute national memory – Nora's 'the memorial heritage of any community'.

History in hindsight can often seem to be foreordained, inevitable and even natural. It is in fact highly improbable, and 'the advantages of hindsight' which historians invoke are rarely that. We need, in Nora's words, 'to restore the original strangeness of the subject'.[6] The fame accorded to Grace Darling and its perpetuation is one of the minor improbabilities of history. In telling the story of how it has happened, I hope to contribute to our understanding of heroism, of celebrity, and of the formation of national memory.

2

Grace's Deed

The *Forfarshire*'s fateful voyage began in Hull at 6.30 p.m. on Wednesday 5 September 1838. John Humble, her captain, had taken command in May 1838.[1] After serving his apprenticeship on one of the collier sloops trading between Shields and Newcastle, he had risen to be in command of the steamer *Neptune* that sailed between Hull and Newcastle. On this last journey on the *Forfarshire* his wife was with him. Besides the Humbles, there were sixty-one people on board, twenty of them cabin passengers, nineteen steerage or deck passengers, fourteen seamen, four firemen, two coal trimmers and two stewards. The passengers included Ruthven Ritchie, a farmer, of Hill of Ruthven in Perthshire, the Reverend John Robb, minister of Dunkeld, aged forty, who was hoping that a sea voyage would improve his health, Mr Bell, factor to Lord Kinnoul, Mrs Allison from York (or perhaps Dundee) with her son and grandson, Miss Martin of Aberdeen with a child (and with three hundred sovereigns in her dress), Mr and Mrs Allen and a child who had come from Russia, John and William Grant of Louth in Lincolnshire, Mr Scott of Dundee and his seven-year-old son, Mr Brown of Perth, James Preston and John Mcleod from Glasgow and Mrs Patrick, the wife of a Hull captain.[2] We know their names because, with one exception, they were all to die. The steamer also carried a cargo of 'superfine cloths, hardware, soap, boiler-plate and spinning-gear'.[3]

The *Forfarshire* was a paddle steamship, built by Thomas Adamson in Dundee in 1836, and registered on 7 May in that year. Dundee had developed as a port and centre of shipbuilding after the Napoleonic Wars, most of the ships built there being engaged in the coastal trade. The *Forfarshire* was 132 feet long, 20 feet in breadth, with a burthen or carrying capacity of 192 tons. Fully loaded, and with the weight of the steam machinery, she weighed 366 tons. She was powered by three boilers and carried two masts – as with all early steamships, sail was still available when needed. Owned by the Dundee and Hull Steam Packet Company, she carried goods and passengers on a route between Dundee, her home port, and Hull, making one and sometimes two trips a week; between the beginning of July and the end of December in 1836, for example, under the command of James Kidd, she made thirty-nine voyages to Hull and back to Dundee.[4]

Steamships had developed rapidly in the years since the *Comet* had sailed the twenty-two miles on the Clyde between Glasgow and Greenock in 1812. Though used mainly on rivers and in estuaries, by 1818 steamships were crossing the sea from Glasgow to Belfast, and the coastal routes were increasingly given over to steam. The 1830s and 1840s were the 'halcyon years' of coastal services, before the railways were fully established and when a sea passage was faster than a land one. In 1839 a government report stated that 'Nearly the whole of the passenger, and no inconsiderable portion of the merchandise coasting traffic of the British Isles, is carried on by steam-vessels'. Of the 766 steam vessels of which they could find a record, most were for estuary use, but 282 were being used on the open seas. In 1843, for example, 18,000 passengers travelled by sea between Leith and London.[5] The technology of steamships was also fast improving, so much so that 1838 saw the beginning of a commercial steamship service across the Atlantic. The *Forfarshire* represented this moment of hope in the history of steamships. Her owners built her to carry both cargo and passengers, their planning and publicity putting most emphasis on the latter. For the saloons and cabins, 'everything is to be done that expense and ingenuity can devise to make them splendid and convenient'. There were four four-berth 'state-rooms', their panels adorned by paintings commissioned from Horatio McCulloch. The mantelpieces were of marble and each piece of the dinner service carried a picture of the *Forfarshire*. The cabins were 'airy, commodious and elegant'. There was excellent accommodation 'for horses, livestock, carriages, etc.', but perhaps rather less so for those who travelled on deck, designed for 'common soldiers and sailors'.[6] The Directors of the Dundee and Hull Steam Packet Company were of course keen to promote their ship and to make her sound the ultimate in luxury and technology. She was sufficiently grand to persuade John Ward to paint her leaving Hull, black smoke funnelling over the port, but in reality there were bigger and more luxurious steamships in service.

Before the *Forfarshire* sailed, there had been an inspection of the boilers and a leak in the centre boiler had been repaired by Messrs Barrett and Sons. The boilers were constructed of hand-riveted iron plates. Under stress the rivets tended to work loose, and repairs of this kind were common.[7]

The *Forfarshire* passed Flamborough Head at 4 a.m. on Thursday 6 September. It was probably about then that the starboard boiler was found to be leaking. Two of the furnaces had to be drawn so that a repair could be carried out. Two hours later, the furnaces were relighted. The *Forfarshire* then made reasonable progress through the day, sailing at an average speed of eight knots.[8] She passed Bamburgh at 6 p.m., as usual taking the inner passage between the shore and the Farne Isles, and reached as far north as St Abbs Head, beyond Berwick. But by then the boiler was leaking badly again and the pumps were unable to deal with the quantity of boiling water sloshing around. The fires had to be put out, and the fore and aft sails raised. Captain Humble aimed to draw the vessel away from the land and its dangerous coastline, but two factors conspired to make this difficult. The wind turned to north-north-east, driving the cumbersome *Forfarshire*, with her paddle-boxes projecting eight feet on either side, in towards the coast. Then the tidal stream shifted from north to south, making onward progress all but impossible. At this point, perhaps around 1 a.m., or a little later, on Friday 7 September, Humble must have decided that the safest course was to go with the wind and tide and seek shelter in the lee of the Farnes.

The Farne Isles number between fifteen and twenty-eight, depending on the state of the tide. They had once been an extension of the mainland, but had eroded away to form a reef stretching five miles out into the North Sea, a haven for bird life but a constant danger to shipping. The normal course was to sail between the coast and the Inner Farne Isles, and this was what Humble had done on his journey north. Alternatives were to go out further to sea, taking care to avoid the notoriously dangerous Knavestone, the outermost Farne Isle, or to try to navigate a passage through the Farne Isles.

There were two lighthouses on the Farne Isles, one on the Inner Farne Isles, the second on the Longstone, the largest of the Outer Farnes and the home of Grace Darling. Faced with the Farnes ahead of him, Humble may have lost control of his ship. James Duncan, the mate, claimed that the wind drove the ship towards the shore, not responding to an attempt to steer a course through the Farne Isles. Equally possible, on a night that was 'very thick and foggy', Humble may have made a fatal error in confusing the two lights, if indeed he could see them at all. If he thought he was seeing the Inner Farne light on his port side, he would have assumed he was on course between the Inner Farnes and the coast. In fact, if he was seeing any light, it was the Longstone and he was heading straight for the rocks. At about 4 a.m. the *Forfarshire*, driven by wind and sea, struck the west point of Big Harcar. She lifted and struck again, with wave after wave, and finally broke up. The bow was caught high on the rock and the stern, where most of the passengers were, was swept into the sea.[9]

Shipwreck was a serious problem and attracted much attention. In 1836 a Select Committee of the House of Commons 'into the Causes of Shipwrecks' reported that in 1833–5 there were 1,573 vessels stranded or wrecked and another 129 missing or lost. The number of persons drowned in these mishaps was 1,714. And these figures, the Committee insisted, were an underestimate. An 1839 government 'Report on Steam Vessel Accidents', prompted in part by the loss of the *Forfarshire*, detailed ninety-two accidents over ten years, twenty-two of them in the previous fifteen months.[10] Aside from these formal investigations, there was a popular literature about shipwrecks. In 1838, the very year that the *Forfarshire* went down, the London Statistical Society investigated the holdings of ten Westminster lending libraries: shipwreck narratives, with 136 volumes, came second in popularity to 'Sir Walter Scott and his imitators'.[11] There were huge compilations like the three volumes of Sir John Graham Dalyell's *Shipwrecks and Disasters at Sea or Historical Narratives of the Most Noted Calamities and Providential Deliverances which Have Resulted from Marine Enterprise*, published anonymously in Edinburgh in 1812. Pamphlets on particular wrecks perhaps reached a wider readership. A famous recent wreck was described in heart-rending detail, accompanied by suitably uplifting religious reflections, in Sir Duncan McGregor's *Loss of the Kent, East Indiaman*, which went through many editions from 1825. Even more relevant to the loss of the *Forfarshire* was *Narrative of the Total Loss of the Rothesay Castle, Steam Vessel, on the Dutchman's Bank, August 17, 1831, on her Passage from Liverpool to Wales*, for, as with the *Forfarshire*, there were accusations that the vessel was in poor repair.

There were three national institutions with a responsibility for reducing the number of wrecks and the loss of life: Trinity House, which was playing an increasingly active role in the erection and maintenance of lighthouses; Lloyd's of London, the experts in marine insurance, with a clear interest in reducing the number of shipwrecks and the loss from them; and the National Institution for the Preservation of Life from Shipwreck, the forerunner of the Royal National Lifeboat Institution, which was pioneering efforts to improve rescue from shipwreck.

England's lighthouses were increasingly under the control of Trinity House of Deptford. Lighthouses first began to be constructed in the fourteenth century. Trinity House was incorporated as a seamen's guild in 1514, dispensing alms to retired or destitute seamen and their dependants. In the course of the sixteenth century it acquired more extensive powers to regulate pilotage and to provide navigational aids on land and at sea. If a lighthouse was needed, Trinity House applied for the patent, but then leased the rights to the light to a private individual in return for an annual rent. The importance of lighthouses, and the potential profit to be gained from them, grew with the expansion of trade, and, as leases ran out, Trinity House began to take more of them on itself, and to build new lighthouses. In 1820 there were twenty-five lighthouses controlled by Trinity House, with twenty-two still in private hands. By 1832 fifty-five of the seventy-one lighthouses were under Trinity House control. The move towards Trinity House control over England's lighthouses resulted from a concerted campaign by merchants and shipowners, with free trade allies in Parliament, to reduce costs on shipping. Private ownership of lighthouses, it was claimed, and the fixed dues owners were able to charge, amounted to an unfair charge on shipping: the public interest demanded that private property in lighthouses be brought to an end. By the 1830s Trinity House had in effect become the approved government body for the erection and maintenance of lighthouses in England. It was not directly controlled by government, and some reformers would have preferred the Admiralty or the Board of Trade to have control of the lights, but Trinity House had proved itself to be a responsible body by reducing rates.[12]

Lloyd's began to compile a register and classification of shipping in the 1760s. In 1834 it and a rival register united to become 'Lloyd's Register of British and Foreign Shipping'. Lloyd's had agents placed at key points round the coast. In 1825 they appointed Bartholomew Younghusband as their agent at Bamburgh. He had to 'furnish prompt and regular advice of the arrival and sailing of Vessels; of accidents or other circumstances of danger or distress that may occur; ... and generally such information as may be of importance to the Subscribers to Lloyd's'. Strict procedures were laid down in the case of a wreck, designed primarily to reduce charges to the insurers.[13] If there was a wreck on the Farne Isles, there were two national institutions, Trinity House and Lloyd's, who would soon hear about it.

The north east was the key location in the attempts, dating back to the 1780s, to build 'unimmergible boats' to carry out sea rescues. 'The Gentlemen of the Lawe House', who met in a building overlooking the Tyne, advertised in the *Newcastle Courant* a prize of two guineas for a plan or model of a boat capable of riding the stormy seas at the mouth of the Tyne. As an outcome of this, a boat, the *Original*, built by Henry Greathead, was launched at South Shields in 1789. The Duke of Northumberland funded two further boats. Then, in 1802, Lloyd's voted £2,000 for building lifeboats. By the end of 1803, Greathead had built thirty-one boats, eighteen for England, five for Scotland, and eight for foreign countries. By 1825, with Lloyd's assistance, lifeboats had been established at twenty-six stations and were subject to regular inspection. But from then onwards Lloyd's efforts were supplemented and largely supplanted by those of the National Institution for the Preservation of Life from Shipwreck in which the driving force was Sir William Hillary from the Isle of Man. The new institution was launched in London in March 1824, with the Archbishop of Canterbury in the chair, William Wilberforce moving one of the resolutions, the Prime Minister, Lord Liverpool, as first president and royal patronage assured. This glittering array of the elite promised more activity than subsequently ensued. Hillary himself was actively involved in some dangerous rescues off the Isle of Man, but in the 1830s and 1840s what was to become in 1854 the RNLI was not the well-known institution of later years.[14]

These three national institutions had their part to play in the aftermath of the wreck of the *Forfarshire*, but they were outshone by a purely local one, the Crewe Trustees at Bamburgh Castle. In the early seventeenth century the castle had come into the possession of the Forster family. In 1715 Tom Forster linked his fortunes with the Jacobites, and ended up in Newgate. He was rescued by his sister, Dorothy, who, according to one account, dressed him up as her maid. But the Forsters were now in dire financial difficulties. Rescue came in the shape of Nathaniel Crewe, Lord Bishop of Durham, who in 1699 at the age of sixty-seven married another Dorothy Forster, forty years younger than her husband, and bought the castle. The couple had no children, and, on his death in 1721, Crewe bequeathed his immense fortune to charitable purposes. Five trustees, the Dean of Durham, three prebendaries of Durham, and the Rector of Lincoln College, Oxford, were charged with the onerous task of ensuring that Crewe's wishes were carried out. Crewe's charity, yielding over £8,000 p.a. in 1830, extended to Oxford, Northamptonshire and Leicestershire, and included money for establishing and maintaining schools, subsidizing poor clergy, paying for apprentices and numerous other good causes. But at the heart of the Crewe Trustees' operations lay Bamburgh Castle.[15]

In the eighteenth century, largely through the efforts of Dr John Sharp, one of the trustees, Bamburgh Castle became the epicentre of an extraordinary charitable enterprise. In it were established free day schools for boys and girls, where 'all the children of poor persons in the parish of Bamburgh are admitted', boarding facilities for twelve poor girls to train them for service, shops for the sale of flour, cheese and groceries at subsidized prices, and a dispensary, surgery and the services of a midwife. The Crewe Trustees also provided facilities for the prevention of shipwrecks, and for the rescue of people and ships that were wrecked. On stormy nights the shoreline for eight miles was patrolled on the lookout for ships in distress. If such a ship was seen, a gun was fired to summon help. There were facilities in the Castle for up to thirty shipwrecked sailors, numerous chains, blocks and tackles for raising stranded ships, store rooms for cargo that might otherwise be looted, premiums for fishermen who went out to the rescue, and free coffins and funerals for those who died. Dr John Sharp had renovated part of the partially-ruined castle to make it suitable for residence for the trustees, and their concern about shipwrecks 'principally induced them to make Bamburgh Castle a place of occasional residence'.[16] So, at least in summer, one or more trustees would be visible. William Howitt, who visited Bamburgh in 1840, could not contain his enthusiasm: 'Thus, like a mighty guardian angel, stands aloft this noble castle, the Watching Spirit over these stormy and perilous seas; and this godlike charity lives, a glorious example of what good a man may continue to do upon earth, for ages after he has quitted it' – and so on for another page and a half. As a more cynical contemporary of Lord Crewe put it, 'Nothing in his life became him so well as his leaving of it'.[17]

It was in Bamburgh that Grace Horsley Darling was born on 24 November 1815. As her biographers noted, it was the year of Waterloo, the coincidence of battle and birth presaging some future national role for the baby. None of this would have been apparent to her parents. William and Thomasin Darling had married in 1805, he nineteen, she twelve years older. William's father, Robert, had followed the path of many Scots and emigrated. But he did not travel a great distance. From Duns, in Berwickshire, to Belford, in Northumberland, not far from Bamburgh, was a little over thirty miles. In Belford Robert Darling made a living as a cooper. In 1769 he married Elizabeth Clark. The couple had eight children, William, born in 1786, the youngest. In 1795 Robert was appointed keeper of the lighthouse on Brownsman Island, one of the Outer Farne Isles. William was nine years old at the time of the move to Brownsman Island, and, as he grew up, doubtless helped around the lighthouse. In 1812 he was officially appointed assistant keeper to his father at the Brownsman light, and, on his father's death in 1815, keeper. What he was doing between his marriage and 1812 is uncertain. When his first son was born in 1806, the father is described in the baptismal records as a 'labourer' in Bamburgh. By 1810, his own father by then in his sixties, William was certainly working at the Brownsman, the entry in his journal for 1 November of that year reading, 'The first regular Journal kept at Brownsman, by Robert and William Darling'. The bride who accompanied her young husband to Brownsman Island was the eldest child of Grace and Job Horsley, her father being the gardener to the Crewe Trustees, who owned Bamburgh Castle. The Horsleys had once been a great family in Bamburgh, but their fortunes had been in decline since the seventeenth century.[18]

No one has been able to cast any light on what, in terms of age differences, must have seemed an odd match, a teenager marrying a woman in her early thirties. The bride's relatively advanced age did not stand in the way of a large brood of children, nine in all, all of them surviving to adulthood. William, the first born, came promptly, nine months and five days after the wedding. Others followed: a first set of twins, Thomasin and Mary Ann in 1807; Job (who died at the age of twenty) in 1810; Elizabeth Grace (Betsy) in 1811; and Robert in 1814. When Grace was born her mother was forty-one, and it must have seemed to everyone that she was destined to be the baby of the family, spoilt by her elder siblings, doted on by her parents. So it was for nearly four years. But then, in August 1819, the mother now forty-five, came a second set of twins, boys this time, George Alexander and William Brooks.

As the elder children grew up, they left the lighthouse to seek jobs or marriage ashore. William helped his father at the Brownsman light until he was sixteen, then was apprenticed to a joiner in Alnwick. In 1839 he was recommended by the Duke of Northumberland to become keeper of the new Coquet lighthouse, south towards Newcastle. In the 1860s he succeeded his father at the Longstone light. Mary Ann married George Dixon Carr; Thomasin set herself up as a dressmaker in Bamburgh; Betsy married John Maule, a draper in North Sunderland (the modern Seahouses); and Robert in 1831 was apprenticed to a mason in Belford, the town to which his paternal grandfather had migrated from Scotland.[19]

The Darlings' family life falls into two parts. Until 1826 they were based at the light on Brownsman Island. There was space, and soil, on the island for a garden and for the grazing of sheep and goats. Severe gales and high tides were all too likely to wreak destruction on the garden, but there was room to move around, and relative proximity to the mainland.[20] But the Brownsman light failed to give ships warning of the hazards further out to sea, and there were all too many wrecks, particularly in 1823–4. The Brownsman light was leased by Trinity House of Deptford to the Blackett family, and this may have prevented an earlier move to the Longstone. Trinity House, a Select Committee of the House of Commons reported in 1834, had 'most injudiciously' granted leases to a number of lighthouses, including the Farne Isles, and had then, in December 1824, had to buy out the remaining fifteen years of the lease for £36,446, 'a large sum for their inconsiderate conduct in leasing these Lights'. Whatever the merits of this criticism, once in control, Trinity House immediately set to work to move one of the lights from the Brownsman to the Longstone. The Longstone was a bare rock with scant vegetation, only a few feet above water at high tide, and in exceptional tides and gales under water.[21] What sort of lighthouse could be built in such exposed conditions? The prototypes were the Eddystone built by John Smeaton in 1759, and, more recently, Bell Rock Tower, eleven miles out to sea south of Arbroath, the work of Robert Stevenson in 1808–11. The new Longstone light, constructed at a cost of £6,000, was ready for use in February 1826. It was built of masonry, circular and smooth, and nearly a hundred feet high.[22] A new phase in the Darlings' life opened. Compared to the Brownsman light, Longstone was spacious, the rooms inevitably circular. A large kitchen and living room on the ground floor gave way to bedrooms, of decreasing size as they got higher, and then to the light itself at the top. William Darling brought some sand over to encourage the terns to breed, but this can have done little to relieve the bleakness of the surroundings of the Darlings' new home.

William Darling was employed by Trinity House. His duties were set out in Trinity House's 'Instructions to Light-keepers'. He had to light the six lamps 'at sun-setting, and keep them continually burning, bright and clear, till sun-rising'. One person had to keep watch till midnight, another till dawn. On watch, the Trinity House Instructions insisted, everything had to be kept spotlessly clean, and the wicks trimmed every three hours. The keeper had to keep a journal 'of all occurrences and observations, and to be particular in describing all circumstances attending them, and to communicate the same once a quarter, or oftener if necessary'.[23] Central to these activities was the maintenance of the light. Oil lamps had long replaced coal fires, and Ami Argand's invention in the 1780s of a cylindrical wick with a double current of air, and paraboloidal reflectors of highly polished metal, increased the power of the lights. An Argand light, rotating by clockwork, had been fitted on the Brownsman in 1810. The Longstone's Argand lamps in parabolic reflectors, encompassed by a catedioptric lens, were state of the art, costing £1,441.[24]

William Darling received a salary of £70 a year from Trinity House, his employers, supplemented by a gratuity of £10 for satisfactory service, and bonuses paid by the Crewe Trustees for help with wrecks.[25] There were bonuses for sighting a wreck, for putting out the first boat to the rescue, for saving life, and for recovering dead bodies. In addition, if goods were salvaged, a proportion of the value of the goods saved was paid as a bonus. William Darling's journal is silent on the topic of bonuses, though there is very occasional mention of income from salvage. On 23 December 1824 he picked up four logs of timber, which 'sold for £14 and I received for salvage £1 10s. 0d.'. In 1829 he received £1 for salvage from a Leith boat.[26]

The Darlings could supplement what they received from Trinity House with other sources of livelihood and income. The sea provided fish, and the journal records major catches. In 1814, for example, 'Codlings very plentiful all winter and a few summer. Caught four score at Longstone south point New Year's Day'. In 1817 '15 score' of haddock were caught upon one line. Visitors to the Darlings often came away with gifts of dried fish, but doubtless many of these catches found their way to market. Duck were shot, a careful annual tally being kept, for example, 'This winter I got 48 mallards [wild duck], 10 Blue Nebs [widgeon], and 39 teal'. Often these were despatched as gifts to acquaintances on the mainland, a kind of exchange economy in operation, for the Darlings would receive back tea and other groceries. Seal were another catch. On the day after Grace's birth, 'Mr James Blackett myself and T. Fender caught four old seals in waterhole, middle of Northenhairs'.[27] Blackett came from the family who had the lease of the lights, and Fender was the Bamburgh doctor.

Very little is known with any certainty of Grace's childhood. After she became famous, a correspondent in the *Liverpool Courier* recorded a visit to Brownsman Island when Grace was about five, and remembered her 'as one of the sweetest children I ever saw'. Grace had taken charge of a nesting eider duck, which allowed her very near, but not others unless they had 'the protection of her sweet countenance and the shelter of her mild clear eye'. Grace collected sea shells and birds' eggs, the former presented to Berwick Museum, and made much of in a paper read at the Berwick Natural History Society in 1852, the latter preserved way into the twentieth century. Grace herself described her upbringing to a correspondent who asked her about her life: 'I have been brought up on the islands, learned to read and write by my parents, and knit, spin and sew ...'[28] 'Our books', she wrote, 'are principally Divinity; the authors, Bishop Wilson, Willison, Boston, Milton, Hervey, Bunyan, Ambrose, Newton, Marshall, Cowper, Flavel, Baxter and others, with a good many of the Religious Tract Society's Publications; and Geography, History, Voyages and Travels with Maps, so that Father can show us any part of the World, and give us a description of the people, manners and customs, so it is our own blame if we be ignorant of either what is done, or what ought to be done.' Life was purposeful and busy.

I have no time to spare, but when I have been on the Main I am quite surprised to see people generally after what they call getting their day's work done, they sit down, some to play at cards, which I do not understand, perhaps as well, for my father says they are some of the Devil's books; others to read romances, novels and plays, which are books my father will not allow a place in our house, for he says they are throwing away time.[29]

One can begin to get a sense of the family dynamics. Father was the dominant figure, mother rarely mentioned. It was father who taught geography, who exercised censorship over reading, who set the moral tone with his disapproval of cards. But William Darling, recalled his daughter Thomasin, 'was far from morose and Pharisaical'. He liked singing and dancing, he played the violin, and he was an ardent admirer of Robert Burns, writing poems in imitation of him. The age disparity between husband and wife apparently in no way lessened what would have been seen at the time as the natural authority of the male. The children were at pains to make this clear. 'He ... was master in his household', wrote Thomasin, 'and had the respect of his family as well as their affection. In any domestic question that arose his conclusion was decisive.'[30] The only female artist to depict the Darlings, Miss Laidler from Edinburgh, placed Mrs Darling in the centre of the family with her spinning wheel, father to the right, and Grace and her brother to the left. 'Mrs Darling', wrote a journalist, 'may be found engaging three parts of the day at least at her spinning wheel.'[31] But it seems unlikely that Mrs Darling or her spinning wheel were at the emotional heart of the family. In one portrait we have of her, painted by Henry Parker in 1838, she looks kindly, shrewd but not forceful. She was very large – twenty stone, it was claimed – and rarely descended the steps from her kitchen in the lighthouse.[32] Numerous letters of her children and husband survive, none of hers. William Darling, by contrast, in the portraits of him, by Henry Parker and T. M. Joy, has a firm, determined set to his face, his body straight and erect, his eyes alert. He wears a Trinity House cap, and looks every inch the loyal and trustworthy servant of a prestigious organization, a man of experience and judgement. He was fifty-two in 1838, and often referred to as 'old Darling', but he had another twenty-two years of work ahead of him on the Longstone. In 1838 he was fit and strong, in many ways in his prime.

The isolation of life on the lighthouse may have been compounded for the Darlings by an unwillingness or inability to establish close relations with people of their own social rank on shore. Catherine Sharp came from a prominent Bamburgh family – she was related to John Sharp who had set up the remarkable charity at the castle. After the wreck of the *Forfarshire* she wrote to the Darlings advising Grace to fulfil 'faithfully the Duties of her Station'.[33] In reply, far from resenting this unsolicited advice, William Darling was 'at a loss to find words to express my gratitude ... for the many kind favours I have received from you', and particularly that she should 'give herself so much trouble about us poor foreigners ...' He went on to mention the death of a close friend of twenty years. 'Dear Madame,' he wrote, 'I do not know whether you was acquainted with the lady but hopes you will forgive this digression as you know we have few we can ease our mind to.'[34] Why should Darling think of himself and his family as 'foreigners', why should there be so 'few we can ease our mind to'? William Darling seems to have enjoyed good relations with his social superiors, but perhaps stood aloof from others. Here may lie the seed of something that dogged the family life for years after the wreck: the accusation by others that the rescue had amounted to nothing at all.

The move to the Longstone in 1826 when Grace was ten marked a considerable break in family life for it coincided with the departure of her elder brothers and sisters. There is every sign from the scattered letters from sons to parents and between siblings that family relationships were maintained, and there were family Christmases at the Longstone. But at some point, particularly when her younger brothers began to find a place for themselves in the wider world, it must have dawned on Grace that she was likely to fulfil the familiar destiny of the youngest daughter in a large family, to stay at home and look after her parents.

Of her siblings, Grace was probably closest to Thomasin, who was seven years older than Grace. In her youth Thomasin faced an agonizing problem. Facially disfigured, with a hare lip, she perhaps resigned herself to spinsterhood and life in Bamburgh. Trained as a dressmaker – her mother, in this instance, surely her teacher – she set up business in Bamburgh. In 1831, when she was in her early twenties, a friend wrote to her that the advice she had had in Newcastle was that 'the cut in your lip would entirely prevent you from obtaining a situation and she told me by all means to advise you to have it sewed. Now my Dear Thomasine I do advise you to have it mended immediately – Mr Davison told me that it would not require more than three stitches and the pain would be very trifling.' Thomasin, it seems, rejected the advice. Perhaps her priority was to stay near her family – the friend, Margaret Ker, refers to Thomasin's distress at not being able to see her brother Job in his last illness the previous year, and at how good it was that she had been 'at home to attend your friends in their illness and it was a great Mercy they all recovered'.[35] And when George was ill in 1837, 'with a pain in his inside ... connected with the pain in his head', it was Thomasin who kept an eye on him, reporting to her anxious parents.[36] As the eldest daughter, and with something of her father's determination in her character, Thomasin was perhaps a kind of second mother to her younger siblings, especially to Grace.

There has been speculation that Grace for a time attended a school kept by Bessie Crawford at Spittal, near Berwick. Two people told Constance Smedley, Grace's biographer in the 1930s, that this was the case, but no member of the family was able to confirm it. The circumstantial evidence lies in the fact that

Grace appeared to have better writing and a better command of English than her siblings. There was another school closer at hand which was perhaps once considered. William Darnell, one of the Crewe trustees, seemed to remember offering to 'place her in the Castle school. He [William Darling] declined from the idea that if he accepted of any Charity, the Trinity Board might remove him from his place.'[37] Probably William Darling was displacing onto the Trinity Board a concern for his own reputation and self-esteem – he did not want to be dependent on charity, and Grace because of this seems to have missed out on an opportunity for some schooling. Whatever the reason, she did not go to school. 'I never was at any school', she wrote in a draft letter, and, as we have seen, it was her parents who taught her to read and write.[38] Grace lived all her life on the Farne Isles, with, of course, visits to what she called the Main. These may, indeed, have been frequent. According to James Young of Newcastle, 'She used to pull her boat from the Longstone to Bamburgh once a week, bringing back with her groceries and other articles that might be required in her island home'. Certainly, according to William Wylie, she 'was a good rower – as good, in fact, as many men. I have rowed with her many a time'.[39]

Shipwrecks were all too common an occurrence on the Farne Isles even after the Longstone Lighthouse had been built. In the period covered by William Darling's journal from 1795 to 1860, no fewer than 107 wrecks are recounted. One of these loomed particularly large in the Darling family memory. The family had gathered at the Longstone for the Christmas of 1834. On 27 December William Darling's journal records that the sloop *Autumn*, carrying coals from Sunderland to its home port of Peterhead, struck the Knavestone at 11 p.m. in a gale, and sank. The Knavestone lay further out to sea than the Longstone, and was the scene of many disasters. In this case, of the crew of three, 'two lost, one saved by the light-keeper, and three sons, viz. William, Robert and George, after a struggle of three hours. Having lost two oars on the rock, had a very narrow escape'. The man they saved, James Logan, had been ten hours, 'part on the rock, part on the mainland; the mate lying dead beside him on the rock the last three hours, having perished from cold'. Logan had been spotted by Grace at about eight o'clock in the morning, when she was putting out the lights, and the four men had set off for the rescue. The two accounts we have of what ensued differ in particulars but agree that the real danger was when they approached the rock. In one account Robert Darling, 'an able and daring swimmer' (and remember that it was 27 December), swam to the rock, fastened a rope round Logan, who was hauled into the boat, and then had to get back himself. In the other, Logan leapt into the boat, but the oars broke in the attempt to get it off the rock, and Robert and George both went into the sea to help her off. It was, said George in retrospect, 'a miracle that the boat was not destroyed when all five must have perished'.[40]

There is no contemporary documentation that describes Grace, a young woman of twenty-two, in the months before she was catapulted to fame. Everything has to be inferred from what she wrote and how she behaved after her fame, or from recollections of those who knew her. The recollections go little beyond the commonplace. 'She was a most kind-hearted girl before any applause was given her', wrote her brother George, in some distress in 1892 when doubt was being cast on the dangers incurred in the rescue.[41] What is well established is her love of nature, her familiarity with boats, and her full participation in the day-to-day work of running the lighthouse, all of which make it likely that she was more reconciled to life on the Longstone than her siblings – and perhaps made a positive choice of it. In appearance, she was in no way exceptional: a little over five foot tall, if anything slight in build, she had a pleasant face, reddish-brown hair, a rather prominent chin, and lips that were often drawn tight. She was probably shy in social contacts outside her family, and ill at ease among crowds, but everything indicates that she had a firm set of principles, rooted in a simple Christianity, to guide her thoughts and behaviour. Beneath the trappings of a conventionally dutiful daughter lay an individuality and a determination, well-known to her family, but only to be revealed to an astonished world by the wreck of the *Forfarshire*.

The Longstone lighthouse was a good hour away from the mainland, but not on that account isolated from its influences. The Darlings' elder children, as we have seen, all sought their livelihoods ashore, and there was much coming and going. Three towns on the Main played a particularly important part in the Darlings' lives, and without the links established with them it is difficult to see how Grace's fame could have spread.

Bamburgh was the nearest, Mrs Darling's home town, and the place where her children were born. In St Aidan's churchyard the Darlings are buried. Grace was born and died in Bamburgh. The town is dominated by its castle, standing on a massive rock, overlooking the sea in one direction and the town in the other. Bamburgh is indeed shielded from the sea by the castle, its business more the servicing of the surrounding agriculture than a direct engagement with the sea. In a small town like Bamburgh, its population in the 1830s under five hundred, the Castle and the Crewe Trustees were dominant. Always resident, and inevitably the man with most power in Bamburgh, was the trustees' agent, in the 1830s Robert Smeddle.

Alnwick was the second town to play a part in the life of the Darlings, primarily through its most important residents, the Duke and Duchess of Northumberland at Alnwick Castle. Both Duke and Duchess play a large part in our story. At Bamburgh the castle stood at a little distance from the town; in Alnwick the town nestled alongside the vast castle. 'A visit to Alnwick', wrote William Howitt, 'is like going back into the old feudal times. The town still retains the moderate dimensions and the quiet air of one that has grown up under the protection of the castle, and of the great family of the castle.'[42] The Northumberlands were immensely rich aristocrats, with coal in the north east and land in many counties. They spent £15,000 to £20,000 annually in London, and dominated Northumberland society from Alnwick. At national level few had much respect for the 3rd Duke. When the Duke of Wellington appointed him Lord Lieutenant of Ireland in 1829, the diarist Charles Greville thought 'it surprising that he should have consented to go, but he probably likes to do something and display his magnificence. He is a very good sort of man, with a very narrow understanding, an eternal talker, and prodigious bore. The Duchess is a more sensible woman and amiable and good-humoured. He is supposed to be ruled in all things by her advice.' As Lord Lieutenant, 'he possessed neither the talent nor the energy to make himself thoroughly hated', a backhanded commendation. When the Duke died in 1847 *The Times* described him as 'a man whose intellect and attainments procured for him a very moderate degree of respect, and nothing could be more obvious than that if he had not been "born great" he was not very likely to have "achieved greatness" ... of the House of Lords, he was by no means a distinguished member'.[43] If at national level he failed to shine, however, this 'very good sort of man' made a mark locally. He and his predecessors had long taken an interest in the prevention of shipwrecks on the north-east coast and in rescues when they occurred. He had visited the Longstone Lighthouse when it was being built in 1825, and had then met William Darling.[44]

Newcastle, an infinitely more important centre of power and influence than Bamburgh or Alnwick, was the third town with which the Darlings had connections. In the 1830s it was being transformed, becoming one of the wonders of the age. In population terms, with 70,000 inhabitants in 1841, it was in the second rank, behind the eight provincial cities, headed by Liverpool with 286,000, which had populations over 100,000. Newcastle was on a par with other port cities such as Belfast, Hull and Plymouth. But its coal trade, cultural institutions and the changes that were being wrought in it, made it more important than size alone warranted. Thomas Dibdin, in his account of Newcastle in 1836, could not restrain his praise of 'the varied wonders and rising glories of this most remarkable town' where 'the spirit of enterprize, liberality, and sound sense, may be said equally to prevail'.[45] William Howitt in 1840 echoed these sentiments. Newcastle, he said, 'is one of the most remarkable towns of the British empire'. It had history. It had coal; on either side of the Tyne, stretching for miles up and down river, there were 'coal-mines and railways and steam-engines, and a hundred thousand grimy buildings and creatures, smokes and fumes, noises and commotions', black the dominant colour. Newcastle also had 'improvements'. 'You walk into what has long been termed the Coal Hole of the North, and find yourself at once in a city of palaces; a fairyland of newness, brightness, and modern elegance.' Away from the Tyne, the architect Richard Grainger was demolishing old narrow streets and replacing them with wide avenues and classical facades, the centrepiece being the column built to commemorate Earl Grey, the Prime Minister who had pushed the Great Reform Act of 1832 through Parliament. Was Newcastle, people wondered, going to provide a townscape and facilities superior to Edinburgh's New Town? Were the new streets on a par with or even superior to London's Regent Street? It was, thought Howitt, 'Beautiful to see the most extraordinary metamorphosis that any town in modern time has undergone'.[46]

A multiplicity of cultural institutions was testimony that there was more to Newcastle than coal. The Literary and Philosophical Society dated back to 1793, and itself spawned the Antiquarian Society (1813), the Natural History Society (1829) and the Fine Arts Society (1836). Newcastle boasted three established newspapers. The *Newcastle Courant*, mildly Tory and under the proprietorship of John Blackwell since 1832, sold 4,000 copies a week. Thomas and John Hodgson, who owned the *Newcastle Chronicle*, 'the leading political organ between York and Edinburgh', were progressive Whigs, whose paper sold nearly 3,000 copies a week. William Mitchell's *Tyne Mercury* had a smaller circulation but added a distinctive radical voice. All three proprietors were well-known local figures; they were members of the town council, and both John Hodgson and John Blackwell served as mayor. 'No town in the kingdom', claimed Howitt, 'can boast of a finer body of men of all classes, breathing a more liberal and active spirit, and desirous of distinguishing their native town by its love of literature and science.'[47]

Newcastle's new found fame was dramatically on display only a matter of days before the wreck of the *Forfarshire*. On 20 August 1838 the British Association for the Advancement of Science opened its annual meeting in Newcastle, the outcome of intense lobbying over many years and a triumph over other bidders for the honour, including Manchester and Birmingham. For a week the town was in celebratory mood, welcoming the eminent visiting scientists with a hospitality which, while it left behind a sizeable debt, could not have failed to impress. Heading the welcome, as President of the British Association, was the Duke of Northumberland, his moderate Toryism infinitely preferable to the radicalism of the other candidate, Lord Durham.[48]

The Darlings were in contact with some of the leaders of the regeneration of Newcastle. Take the Natural History Society. William Darling on the Farne Isles was himself no mean naturalist, and was in a perfect position to collect specimens, and to act as a guide to visitors. On 6 April 1830 he noted in his journal, 'I shot three Egyptian geese, and sent a pair to Newcastle Museum: the other to Mr Selby, Twizle House.' P. J. Selby, a Vice-President of the Natural History Society, was a noted ornithologist.[49] Other prominent young naturalists in Newcastle knew the Darlings well. They included Albany Hancock, Curator of Ornithology, his brother John, and William Hewitson, Curator of Entomology.

Hewitson's uncle, Henry Hewitson, had known the Darlings since the 1820s. He helped to get a new boat for the lighthouse, kept a watchful eye on Darling's sons in Newcastle, visited the lighthouse, and maintained a correspondence and exchange of gifts with the Darlings.[50] In March 1833 he was wondering whether Darling had received the Bible and commentaries he had sent, reporting that he had received a sovereign for Darling from John Brandling, Mayor of Newcastle in that year, in return for the eider duck eggs Darling had sent. A year later, in May 1834, writing to 'My dear Friend', Hewitson thanked Darling for 'your last kind present of ducks and down', enquired after the Darling children, hoped that Mrs Hewitson and his nephew may come to Longstone in the summer, and passed on Mrs Hewitson's gratitude to Mrs Darling for the 'comfort and warmth of her eiderdown'.[51] In 1837 Hewitson was in touch with Dr Headlam, a prominent doctor and Mayor of Newcastle, to make arrangements for Darling's son, George, to receive treatment in the Infirmary where Hewitson was a Governor – but the ungrateful George refused.[52] In sum, in the 1830s the Darlings were known to and in touch with Newcastle's civic leaders, and there were therefore easy means of introducing to the Darling family those in Newcastle keen to disseminate the story of the rescue. The Hancock brothers, for example, wrote letters to William Darling introducing their friend, the painter Henry Parker.[53] For amongst its other attributes, Newcastle was a centre of printing and art, the latter headed by William Richardson and his son, and including also the well-established J. W. Carmichael and Henry Parker: all were in *Pigot's Directory* of 1834, all carrying on their businesses in Blackett Street.

A report by two engineers appointed by the government succinctly explained the reasons behind the loss of the *Forfarshire*. 'The primary cause of this shipwreck was the defective state of one of the boilers; that its condition was well-known to the owners and commander when she left Hull on her last voyage, and that its repair had been delayed. Further, that in her greatest peril, she might possibly, and very probably, have been saved by her anchors – her hull being sound and good – but that the cables were foul, so that the anchors could not be let go.' In short, on two grounds, the state of her boilers and of her anchors, the *Forfarshire* was unseaworthy. There was no regular system of inspection of the boilers. The *Forfarshire* was by no means unusual in her lack of seaworthiness. The engineers described ships whose boilers were paper thin, ready to leak. But this known weakness of the boilers in the early steamships should have induced caution in Captain Humble. When the danger became apparent off Flamborough Head, the report concluded, the captain should have put into port and saved his ship, the passengers and the crew – and of course also saved Grace Darling from becoming a heroine.[54]

Shortly before the *Forfarshire* struck the Big Harcar, Humble gave orders to

James Duncan, the mate, for the anchors to be slipped, and three of the men were doing so, when Duncan, followed by crew members, ran off to launch the starboard quarter boat, perhaps having failed to release the anchors.[55] Eight members of the crew, including the mate, and one cabin passenger, Mr Ritchie, got on board the quarter boat. Ritchie, on his own account, rushed up from his bunk, clutching his trousers, and leapt into the boat after it was launched. Others disputed this: 'His assertion of leaping into the boat when she was five yards from the steamer ... is flatly contradicted by the whole of his companions who were saved in the same boat – they affirming that Mr Ritchie was the third who got into the boat, and that was previous to her being lowered from the davits.'[56] Ritchie left his aunt and uncle on board, and they drowned, so he may well have wished to present his survival in the most heroic light possible. So also may the members of the crew, who claimed that they were hoping to pick up survivors. As it happened, the boat was swept away from the wreck through Piper Gut and was quite unable to help. The lucky survivors were later picked up by a sloop from Montrose and taken to Tynemouth.

Captain Humble, his wife and most of the passengers drowned immediately. The survivors, hanging on to the bow stranded on the Big Harcar, numbered twelve. There were five crew members, John Tulloch, carpenter, Jonathan Tickett, cook, John Kidd and John Nicholson, both firemen, and John McQueen, trimmer. The surviving passengers were Mrs Dawson and her two children, the Reverend John Robb, James Kelly, a weaver, Thomas Buchanan, a baker, and Daniel Donovan, a passenger with some seafaring experience who had helped man the pumps and who became the most notorious narrator of the circumstances leading to the wreck.[57] The two Dawson children died from exposure, as did the Reverend John Robb, leaving nine alive. They sought a degree of shelter and safety by clambering onto a rock that, sloping south, offered some lee while the wind remained in the north.

At the Longstone Lighthouse, William Darling, his wife Thomasin and Grace had prepared for the storm. Grace's brother, William Brooks, had gone ashore to help with the herring fishing, so there were just the three of them. Shortly after midnight William Darling woke Grace, and together, knowing that the dangerous high tide would be at 4.13 a.m., they secured the coble. At 4.45 a.m. on Friday 8 September, Grace, either on watch in the lantern, or possibly from her bedroom, saw the wreck on the Big Harcar. She woke her parents.[58] According to William Darling, 'owing to the Darkness and sprey going over her could not observe any person on the Wreck although the Glass was incessantly applied, untill near 7 o'clock, when the tide being fallen we observed three or four Men upon the rock ...'[59]

There followed the most dramatic moment in the story of Grace's heroism, the decision to row out to the rescue. Only three people had any knowledge of exactly what happened: William Darling, his wife Thomasin and Grace. William and Grace both wrote near contemporary accounts of what happened. William's fullest account is contained in a letter he wrote to Trinity House on 6 October (a month after the wreck), in response to a request for details of the rescue:

> We agreed that if we could get to them some of them would be able to assist us back, without which we could not return; and having no Idea of a Posibility of a Boat coming from North Sunderland, we amediately launched our Boat, and was Enabled to gain the rock where we found 8 men and 1 women, which I judged rather too many to take at once in the state of Weather; therefore took the Women and four Men to the Longstone; two of them returned with me and succeeded in bringing the remainder, In all 9 persons, safely to the Longstone about 9 o'clock.

In his journal, even more succinctly, Darling had described the wreck, and then written, '9 held on by the Wreck and was rescued by the Darlings'.[60]

Grace's account is given in a draft of a letter, probably written in March 1839, to a Mr Smith in Alnwick, in which she points out errors in a song about the rescue written by P. M. Stewart:

> I was the first that saw the Distressing affair and amediately acquainted my Father. The Distance was near the same as mentioned but no cries could be heard half the Distance in a gale of wind and raging sea; it was sufficient to affect the strongest nerve to view the Wreck. I was very anxious and did render every assistance that lay in my Power but my Father was equally so and needed not to be urged by me he being Experienced in such things and best knowing what could be done.[61]

These are the only three accounts that have any claim to be primary sources. No one can dispute the accuracy of the journal entry, but it conceals as much as it reveals. The letter to Trinity House and Grace's letter were written after there had been considerable discussion of the rescue and of Grace's role in it, and must be read in that light. What is striking is that William Darling starts off 'We agreed ...', not 'I decided ...'. This was a family decision, or possibly a decision made by William and Grace. Grace's account is consistent with this: she helped, but her father did not need 'to be urged by me'. Later, at the rock, it was William Darling in command: 'I judged' that carrying nine passengers would be too many. There was a high risk involved, not only in launching the coble and rowing there – normally three men would man it in bad conditions, as happened on the second trip, or four as in the rescue of James Logan in 1834 – but, even more, in making the return when wind and tide conditions would be against them. Without the help of those they hoped to rescue, starkly, 'we could not return'; the difficult point would be crossing Craford's Gut with the wind against them.[62] Later accounts, as we shall see, depict Grace as the instigator of the rescue, persuading a reluctant father and even more reluctant mother that they must try to save the lives of those they could see on the rock. William Darling, it must be said, was unlikely to admit in what was an official account that he had allowed his judgement to be overruled by his daughter. The 'We agreed' may be read as at least some kind of admission that Grace was party to the decision to row out and to the thinking, and what we would now call risk assessment, that lay behind it. A crucial point, and one that reverberated far into the future, was the claim that the Darlings assumed that no boat would put out from North Sunderland to try to effect a rescue. In fact, as we shall see, the North Sunderland boat did get to the wreck, but only after the Darlings had rescued the living.

The Darling family narrative remained broadly true to this first account. According to Thomasin, Grace's sister, Mrs Darling had argued against the rescue but was overruled. She then 'helped her one remaining child and her husband to launch their boat, then ascended the light-house to watch their progress', and swooned. Thomasin felt for her mother: 'I think I could have gone in the boat, but even yet I do not think I could have stayed behind.' But it was her father whose role she was keenest to defend. 'The romanticists who, in the affair of the *Forfarshire*, made the entreaties of his daughter overrule his judgement, did not know about whom they wrote. It is very likely', Thomasin admitted, 'that the proposal to aid her father in the boat first came from Grace; but had he not himself thought the attempt practicable, he was not the man to endanger her life and his own in weak concession to girlish importunity.'[63] These recollections came in the late 1870s and 1880s, towards the end of Thomasin's life, when she had become the guardian of the family's reputation.

Grace and her father had about a mile to row to reach the wreck. To have gone as the crow flies would have been suicidal for they would have been exposed to the full fury of the storm. They needed to slip through Craford's Gut, the channel separating the Longstone from Blue Caps, and then take advantage of the lee provided by Blue Caps, Little Harcar and Big Harcar. The coble was a long rowing boat, measuring 21 foot 6 inches. With an oar each, the Darlings reached the rock, where there was the second critical moment in the rescue. William sprang onto the rock, leaving Grace to control the coble in a high sea and with the danger of being smashed against the rock. Possibly, as surely would have been sensible, William held fast to a rope attached to the coble, but there is no contemporary evidence of this.[64] A later writer, a man who knew the sea, described her achievement thus:

> In that day and age it would have been a considerable feat for a girl of her build to manage such a craft on a park lake on a fine summer afternoon. She did it in tidal waves on a treacherous reef under a lowering sky with a northerly gale screaming over her head, with the creeping cold numbing her fingers and eating into her bones through her wet clothes; and with ten lives, including her own father's, for a few minutes at least, precariously held in the hollow of her hand.[65]

She managed this, and five survivors were helped into the boat.

Grace's rowing was now over. William Darling later described the return journey for an artist: 'five seats, one of them astern. Grace sat on the midships, the woman sat upon flooring forward with her head lying against the side as she was not fit to sit on the seats and one of the men was lying aft in the same manner with a blanket round each. The children were both left at the wreck, dead. Four oars used in pulling back, no rudder shipped. The steamer's head lay due E., our house bearing ENE, distant three-quarters of a mile and 1 mile the way we had to go.'[66] Back at the lighthouse, Grace was fully occupied in making provision for the survivors, while her father and two others went off to collect the remaining four men on the rock. The whole operation was over in two hours from the first sighting of the men on the rock. Grace's own exposure to danger was probably no more than one hour.

The Darlings had assumed, reasonably enough, that no rescue could be attempted from shore. They reckoned without the determination of the North Sunderland fishermen. The wreck of the *Forfarshire* was spotted at Bamburgh Castle, and the system set up by the Crewe Trustees went into operation. Robert Smeddle, the trustees' agent, ordered their flag to be hoisted half-mast and a thirty-two pounder gun fired to notify any survivors that the wreck had been seen. Then he rode the three miles to North Sunderland where the fishermen were counting the cost of the storm. They were reluctant to go out in the lifeboat but agreed to take an ordinary fishing coble. Six oarsmen were needed and someone to man the tiller. The volunteers were William, James and Michael Robson, Thomas Cuthbertson, Robert Knox, William Swan, who was boatman to the lighthouses, and Grace's brother, William Brooks Darling. Setting out at about 7.30 a.m., they had five miles to cover. The Farne Isles themselves offered some protection, but it was an arduous and dangerous journey. When they reached the Big Harcar at 10 a.m., they found the dead bodies of the two children and of the Reverend John Robb, and moved them to the high part of the rock.

They must have thought of rowing back to North Sunderland, but the tide would have been against them, so they decided instead to head for the Longstone Lighthouse. They had 'great difficulty' in reaching the Longstone, and had to land in a narrow inlet on the lee side. Arriving at the Longstone, they learned for the first time that there were survivors from the wreck – and that the survivors had first claim on the accommodation at the lighthouse. The fishermen had to make do in the barracks that had been erected in 1825 for the men building the lighthouse. They were there for two nights, the sea being still too stormy to allow them to return to the mainland. When they did row back, on the Sunday, they took William Darling with them so that he could make arrangements with the Crewe Trustees for the care of the survivors. They stopped to collect the three dead bodies at the wreck, but found it impossible to land at North Sunderland, going on to Beadnell, further south, 'so heavy did the swell continue'.[67]

How severe was the storm on the night the *Forfarshire* was wrecked? Crucial to any conclusion about the degree of courage displayed by those who ventured out to the wreck, it became a matter of considerable dispute. When William Howitt visited the Farne Isles in 1840, the harbour master at North Sunderland told him that 'the people saved themselves. They walked across from the vessel at low water to the next island, and the Darlings fetched them off when the water was smooth, and when there was scarcely any water at all. I wonder they took any boat. I wonder they didn't walk over'.[68] This was an extreme form of a version of events that retained considerable purchase in North Sunderland right through the nineteenth century. Some support for the view that the danger was minimal comes from the apparent ease with which the survivors managed to clamber on to the coble, and from the way in which Grace, however able an oarswoman, was able to steady the coble when her father had leapt onto the rock. On the other side, there seems to be overwhelming evidence that conditions at sea were extremely dangerous. Consider first the rescue boat from North Sunderland. The option of rowing back ashore was ruled out. They even had difficulty getting to the Longstone, having to take their coble round to a lee to the south and then carry it over to the lighthouse. And they surely would not have stayed in uncomfortable conditions on the Longstone for two further nights if they could have rowed back later that day or the next day. And then there is evidence in William Darling's journal that on the morning of the wreck there was another boat at the scene of the wreck. At about the same time as the North Sunderland boat got there, 10 a.m., 'the fishing smack's boat got to the wreck, and after carrying a quantity of things to the water's edge, two boxes of soap included, owing to the surf could not take them on board; and after being nearly capsized, returned to the vessel, with two light hair mattresses. This I had from T. Smith, he being on board.' The fishing smack was the *Union* from Blackwell in London, its haul eventually recovered by the Lloyd's agent.[69] Thomas Smith was the keeper on the Inner Farne Light. The evidence of the strength of the surf and the danger of capsizing suggests that this was at the very least a turbulent sea. Finally, there is the report in the *Berwick and Kelso Warder* for 15 September 1838, written by a reporter, a Mr Kennedy, who spoke to as many survivors and participants as possible. At North Sunderland, he says, 'the sea raged with a degree of violence that has not been exceeded on any occasion within the recollection of the oldest fishermen belonging to North Sunderland'. One hundred barrels of salt on the quay were swept into the sea. Everything suggests that the storm on the night of 7 September would have been remembered even if the *Forfarshire* had not been wrecked.

In October 1838, only a month after the wreck of the *Forfarshire*, Trinity House drafted new regulations. They had been for some time in the pipeline, so were not prompted by the loss of the *Forfarshire*. Under these regulations, every lighthouse was to have both a principal and an assistant light keeper, and in November 1838 William Brooks Darling, Grace's younger brother, was appointed assistant at the Longstone with the requirement, in return for a salary of £45, that he would have 'to give his whole time and attention to the Duties thereof'.[70] Had these regulations and this appointment been in place a few months earlier, William Brooks would not have been ashore helping with the herring catch. He would have been at the Longstone on the night of the wreck of the *Forfarshire*, and we would never have heard of Grace Darling.

But without her brother there, the onus fell on Grace. She and her father risked their lives in going to the rescue of the survivors of the *Forfarshire*. That was the measure of their courage and heroism. They had every reason to suppose that the survivors would have perished if they had not gone to the rescue, and they had the experience to weigh up the dangers they were likely to encounter. With luck, skill, and on the balance of probabilities (for William Darling was not a man to embark on a suicide mission), they would succeed, but the danger of failure must have been always present to them. For them, it was all part of the business of running a lighthouse, and they would not have imagined that what they had done would create a great stir. Rowing out to the *Forfarshire* was less dangerous than the rescue of James Logan at Christmas 1834 when William Darling and three of his sons came near to death. The world was to take a different view.

3

In the Spotlight of the Media

Within days of performing her deed, Grace was being hailed as a heroine. From the outset contemporaries assumed that her fame would endure to the end of time. So began the acts of remembrance. Journalists, playwrights, novelists, sculptors, painters, and potters set out for their contemporaries and posterity their versions of Grace's deed. The media interest was intense, the commercial opportunities manifest. Grace and her deed were placed under the spotlight.

The local press took the lead. From Hull to Dundee newspapers vied with one another to be first with news, initially of the wreck and then of the rescue, with the story of the Darlings increasingly prominent. Most of the newspapers in the north east were weekly, and their favoured day for publication was Friday. It was on a Friday, 7th September, that the *Forfarshire* was wrecked, so it was a week before most papers could get news of any kind to their readers. This gave an advantage to the papers that appeared on other days, notably the *Gateshead Observer* (Saturday), and the *Tyne Mercury* (Tuesday). A fishing smack, it will be remembered, had brought the members of the crew and Mr Ritchie, rescued from the *Forfarshire's* lifeboat, to Tynemouth. From there they made their way to Newcastle, where reporters quickly picked up news of the wreck. The first report, in the *Gateshead Observer* on the Saturday afternoon, was thus able to give an account of events leading up to the wreck, hope that there were still survivors, but of course it carried no details of the Darlings' rescue mission – firm news of which did not get beyond the Longstone until Sunday 9 September.[1]

The story of the wreck quickly broke out of the north east. In 1838 there were no rail links between Newcastle and London. But coaches could travel fast, and with them went news. On Tuesday 11 September *The Times* carried the *Gateshead Observer's* report, 'obligingly forwarded to us by express'. This set the pattern for the national reporting of the news. Newspapers did not send their own reporters to the scene, they simply reproduced accounts culled from local newspapers. Even north-eastern papers copied each other. Thus the *Tyne Mercury* on 11 September reproduced the report of the wreck given a few days earlier in the *Gateshead Observer* – though it appended more up-to-date news. The *Tyne Mercury* report itself was in the *Scotsman* in Edinburgh a day after publication in Newcastle, and in *The Times* on the following day.

There was intense interest in the wreck along the east coast, and reporters had a chance to pick up scraps of information from the crew members and Ritchie as they made their way north from Newcastle to Dundee. The *Berwick and Kelso Warder* reporter had seen Ritchie as he passed through Berwick on Monday 10 September.[2] In Dundee itself the night mail on Sunday arrived at 11 p.m. Rumours of the wreck were already spreading, and 'a dense crowd' was there to hear if there was any news. Sadly there was. Letters from Ritchie, Smeddle and James Duncan, the mate of the *Forfarshire*, confirmed the wreck and the loss of some thirty-five lives. Duncan himself, and other members of the crew, arrived in Dundee on the Tuesday, having travelled by steamer from Leith.[3]

In the first reports the emphasis was on the cause of the wreck and on listing of the names of those who had survived and those who had not. The *Tyne Mercury* on Tuesday 11 September told how since the first reports in Newcastle on Saturday afternoon, 'the most contradictory statements have been made respecting the loss the *Forfarshire*'. Its own assessment was that between thirty-five and forty people had drowned, and it reported that nine people were said to be alive on the outer island, though it gave no details of how they had got there. By then William Darling and the North Sunderland fishermen were ashore, so the news must have come from them.

On Tuesday 11 September there was another event to capture the attention of reporters and readers who were following the story. An inquest on the bodies found on the rock was convened. Rumours of the poor state of the *Forfarshire*'s boilers were running wild. Ritchie, passing through Bamburgh, had said that Captain Humble had told him that the boilers were defective from the outset. Daniel Donovan, first at the Longstone, and then to anyone ashore who would listen to him, was constructing a convoluted story of carelessness. He claimed to have been travelling as fireman on the *Forfarshire*, said that the boiler was leaking badly before they left the Humber, and that they should have returned to Hull. The Lloyd's agent in Bamburgh, Bartholomew Younghusband, was ill, so a sub-agent from Berwick, James Sinclair, went out to the wreck and made erroneous conclusions from an examination of a fragment of boiler-plate. The owners of the *Forfarshire* were on the rack. The jurors concluded that the victims had died because of 'the imperfections of the boilers, and the culpable negligence of the captain in not putting back to port'. A deodand of £100 (effectively a fine) was placed upon the vessel. Shortly before the verdict was given, William Just, the manager of the Dundee and Hull Steam Packet Company, together with Mr Boyd, a director, had arrived in Bamburgh. On hearing of the wreck, they had posted down from Dundee on the Monday, and had been out to see the wreck on the Tuesday morning, but were now given no opportunity to present their evidence.[4]

The fall-out from the verdict was considerable. The coroner, Stephen Reed, wrote to Lord John Russell at the Home Office calling for 'the interference of the Legislature'. This demand was reinforced by a public meeting in Newcastle, and by editorial comment in nearly all the newspapers. Russell handed over the issue to the Board of Trade, which set up an enquiry, first, into the loss of the *Forfarshire*, and then more broadly into steam vessel accidents over the previous ten years.[5] In due course Just was able to secure affidavits from many of the crew members and from engineers who had installed and inspected the boilers to contradict Donovan's account. An inquest in October on another body was much less censorious, concluding that the *Forfarshire* 'was wrecked in consequence of tempestuous weather'. Nevertheless, the government's inspectors found some of the principal engineer's evidence 'a little equivocal', and by no means gave a clean bill of health to the *Forfarshire* and its owners.[6]

All of this diverted attention from what was to become the lasting memory from the wreck of the *Forfarshire*. A week after the wreck, however, on Friday 14th and Saturday 15th, the Darlings' rescue of the survivors began to receive attention. The *Newcastle Courant* reported it on 14 September, the *Newcastle Chronicle* and the *Berwick and Kelso Warder* on 15 September. The most enterprising of the reporters was David Kennedy of the *Berwick and Kelso Warder*. He had visited the wreck and included a dramatic sketch of the forepart of the *Forfarshire* stuck on the rock. He had also had 'personal communication with many of the survivors', for example John Tulloch the carpenter, who told how the survivors had seized hold of the windlass, an action that had saved their lives. He had met Sarah Dawson, the woman whose children, a boy aged seven and a girl of five, had died. And he was able to describe the rescue by the Darlings, though he had not yet met them. Their heroism, however, he was in no doubt, ranked 'amongst the noblest instances of purely disinterested and philanthropic exertion in behalf of suffering individuals that ever reflected honour upon humanity'. He hoped that their conduct would be 'appreciated in the proper quarters'. Grace it was, he said, who persuaded her father to go out. He described one of the survivors weeping as he told Kennedy of his astonishment that one of the rescuers was a woman. Kennedy sent off a copy of his report to William Darling, requesting more information about the wreck.[7]

The two most influential reports were in the *Newcastle Chronicle* and *The Times*. The former had sent a 'special reporter' to the scene. He focused on the moment when William Darling jumped onto the rock, and

the frail coble, to preserve it from being dashed to pieces, was rapidly rowed back among the awful abyss of waters, and kept afloat by the skilfulness and dexterity of this noble-minded young woman … This perilous achievement stands unexampled in the feats of female fortitude. From her isolated abode, where there was no solicitation or prospect of reward to stimulate, impelled alone by the pure promptings of humanity, she made her way through desolation and impending destruction, appalling to the stoutest hearts, to save the lives of her fellow-beings.[8]

The Times on 19 September carried a long report from a correspondent, M. S., writing from Morpeth on 15 September. Much of it was an account of the inquest, but M. S. ended with the Darlings: 'Connected with this, the most calamitous case of ship-wreck perhaps that has occurred since the loss of the *Rothesay Castle* off the Isle of Anglesea [in 1831], is an instance of heroism and intrepidity on the part of a female unequalled perhaps, certainly not surpassed, by any on record. I allude to the heroic conduct of Miss Grace Horsley Darling.' Grace, according to M. S., heard the 'cries of the sufferers' at the scene of the wreck and woke her father. As they rowed out to the rescue,

> On every hand danger presented itself in a thousand terrific forms. The ocean, lashed by the tempest into the most tumultuous commotion, presented a barrier which would have seemed to all but those two intrepid persons wholly insurmountable by human energy. Again, on the other hand, there was no hope of reward – no encouraging plaudit, to stimulate so brave exertions, or to awaken emulation. Nothing but the pure and ardent wish to save the sufferers from impending destruction could have induced these two individuals to enter upon so perilous an expedition fraught as it was with the imminent hazard of their own lives. Surely, imagination in its loftiest creations never invested the female character with such a degree of fortitude as has been evinced by Miss Grace Horsley Darling on this occasion. Is there in the whole field of history, or of fiction even, one instance of female heroism to compare for one moment with this?

Like the reporter for the *Berwick and Kelso Warder*, both the *Newcastle Chronicle* and M. S. hoped that 'such unexampled heroism will not go unrewarded'.

These two reports in the pre-eminent local and national newspapers provided a template for all subsequent attempts to evoke the magnitude of Grace's heroism. Many simply plagiarized it, words and phrases echoing down the years. We may take from it two things. First, the language was overwrought. Danger presents itself 'in a thousand terrific forms', Grace is alone amidst 'the awful abyss of waters', the 'ocean [is] lashed by the tempest into the most tumultuous commotion'. We are, and this is how it must have seemed to many contemporaries, in one of J. M. W. Turner's sea storms. Second, there is the astonishment that a female could have done what Grace did. History lends no precedent. The facts are more amazing than anything in fiction. 'Imagination' itself could not rise to the heights that Grace had attained.

In this early response to Grace's deed there is a pervasive sense that the rescue was not a seven days' wonder: what had happened would be remembered. It was, in both the *Newcastle Chronicle* and *The Times*, immediately placed in history, and found to be without parallel, in the former's much-repeated alliteration 'unexampled in the feats of female fortitude'. Private individuals thought the same: it was, for John Young of Coupar, Fife, 'that ever memorable event which will be Remembered so long as time can last'. 'Your name and praise shall stand for Centuries to come', enthused Christiane Darling, admittedly in a begging letter, one of two Darlings who hoped to cash in on the shared name.[9] On seeing a portrait of Grace, a poet in the *Gateshead Observer* delighted that

> Her gallant deed shall live in fame,
> Through England's latest days.[10]

The astonishment that a woman could do what Grace did, and the subsequent celebration of her deed, begins to make sense if we familiarize ourselves with two features of the minds of those likely to be reading *The Times* or other writing addressed to the well-to-do. The first dates back to the distinction between the sublime and the beautiful made by Edmund Burke in his *A Philosophical Enquiry into the Origin of our Ideas of the Sublime and the Beautiful* (1757). For Burke a sense of sublimity was aroused by contemplation of those aspects of nature which impressed the mind with ideas of infinity, for example landscapes that were vast, threatening and awesome, and sea storms. The sublime in nature was the cause of astonishment, horror and terror. Most germane to our purposes, 'the ocean', wrote Burke, 'is an object of no small terror'. Beauty, on the other hand, resided in the small and perfectly-formed. 'The sublime ... always dwells on great objects, and terrible; [beauty] on small ones and pleasing.' Strength, one of the qualities of the sublime, was 'very prejudicial to beauty. An appearance of *delicacy*, and even of fragility, is almost essential to it.' It followed from this that the sublime, and the capacity to respond to it, was fundamentally male. Beauty was female, and both belonged and appealed especially to women. Indeed, 'The beauty of women is considerably owing to their weakness, or delicacy, and is even enhanced by their timidity ...'[11] The 'separate spheres' of men and women had their root (and justification) in this gendered distinction in responses to the sublime and the beautiful. To the early Victorians in the 1830s, some eighty years after Burke had first drawn out the distinction between the sublime and the beautiful, it seemed to contemporaries to be entirely natural. Grace Darling challenged this fundamental assumption. Her response to the terror and horror of the sublime – and nothing was more sublime than a sea storm and a wreck – was, in the way contemporaries saw things, entirely masculine. So entrenched had become the distinction between sublime/male and beautiful/female that contemporaries could not begin to imagine how a woman whose sphere was beauty could respond to the sublime in a manner that no man could have bettered. Grace, it was thought, must therefore be an Amazon or have dominantly male features. But, as the early reporters and painters showed, she was feminine in appearance and behaviour. How could her heroic deed be explained? Did it perhaps cast some doubt on Burke's distinctions?

If Edmund Burke was one source for contemporaries' response to Grace, Sir Walter Scott was the other. Scott was firmly committed to the Union of Scotland

and England and to the Hanoverian monarchy, but his novels had nevertheless cast the more colourful aspects of the history of both countries in a Romantic light. His Romanticism was very different from that of an earlier generation of writers who had gloried in the outbreak of the French Revolution and preached radicalism. Scott's Romanticism was thoroughly conservative. He believed in a society that was hierarchical and ranked, but – and herein lay his Romanticism – he could find nobility of character and behaviour in the lives of the common people, just as he could champion a writer like James Hogg, the 'Ettrick Shepherd'. In his historical novels Scott brought home to readers the ways in which ordinary people could become caught up in historical events, and play a part in them. Of all Scott's heroes and heroines, Jeannie Deans, daughter of a cow-keeper, and heroine of *The Heart of Midlothian*, would have been most in people's minds when they read of Grace's deed. Jeannie's heroism, based on a true story of the early eighteenth century, lay in her refusal to utter a white lie that would have saved her sister from the gallows for the crime of infanticide. Instead she journeyed all the way to London to plead for mercy for her sister at Court, winning an interview with the Queen which saved her sister from death. Jeannie 'was a plain, true-hearted, honest girl', to whom 'nature, and the circumstances of a solitary life had given a depth of thought and force of character superior to the frivolous part of her sex, whether in high or low degree'. In appearance, 'She was short, and rather too stoutly made for her size, had grey eyes, light-coloured hair, a round good-humoured face, much tanned with the sun, and her only peculiar charm was an air of inexpressible serenity, which a good conscience, kind feelings, contented temper, and the regular discharge of all her duties, spread over her features.'[12] In background, appearance and character she was as near as could be to a fictional Grace Darling. People's response to Grace was mediated through fiction, through Jeannie Deans, 'our heroine' as Scott called her. First published in 1818, the book really took off on republication in 1830. Scott died in 1832, but his name was very much before the public in the later 1830s. Edinburgh's Princes Street saw the building of the imposing and Romantic Scott Monument in 1836, and J. C. Lockhart's famous *Memoirs of the Life of Sir Walter Scott* was published in 1837–8. Grace Darling was a Scott heroine, waiting to be discovered.

Grace Darling was thus an intriguing mix: a challenge to Burke's by now conventional distinction between the sexes and a reinforcement of Scott's discovery of the nobility of ordinary people. The challenge she posed to Burke provides the explanation for the astonishment at Grace's deed, and for the sense that it was and would remain unique in history. But it did not in itself lead to a reassessment of Burke's claims. Grace Darling was in some ways seen as a freak, a oneoff, unprecedented and never to be repeated. Neither history, nor even fiction, had any record of such a deed. So, although Grace had momentarily broken through the conventional distinctions between the sexes, she was not, in this respect, held up as a model for others to follow. Rather, the focus after the deed, in literature and in painting, was on her distinctively feminine characteristics. This helped to make Sir Walter Scott the dominant influence in the way people responded to Grace. Like Jeannie Deans, heroic as she was, she knew her place. Perhaps the Duke of Northumberland modelled himself on Scott's Duke of Argyll, who had taken Jeannie under his wing. In the 1830s conservative Romanticism provides the key to unlocking the strangeness of the response to Grace's deed.

We can see the twin influences of Burke and Scott at work in the way that journalists constructed their stories. They embellished with fiction a story that might have seemed able to stand on its own feet. Two consistent features in their reports added to the drama of events. First, they were insistent that Grace was alerted to the existence of the survivors by hearing their cries for help. And secondly, and linked to the first, they wrote that it was Grace who had to persuade her aged and reluctant father to put out in the coble.[13] A cry heard from a distance was a much more powerful motive for action than sight alone. The cries would strike through to Grace's receptive heart, and bring forth the courage and nobility of her character. The Darlings themselves made it clear that there was no truth in either of these embellishments. They insisted that no human voice could have carried half a mile in the midst of a storm, and they denied that William Darling would have allowed his judgement to be overruled by his daughter. Their denials floated away in the wind.

Journalists also tried to convey the mixture in Grace of masculine qualities of determination and courage, exemplified in the rescue, and femininity. On the one hand, they wanted to celebrate the fact that Grace had shown, as a speaker at a public meeting in Newcastle put it, that 'they must now allow a female character to be no way inferior for that woman had exhibited a firmness of mind, a duty to her father, a duty as a christian, equal to any man in the country'.[14] But, on the other, if Grace was going to survive and flourish as a heroine she had to be recognizably a woman – and it was the woman that most observers searched for, and happily found. 'Many have been to see this heroine', reported the *Shipping and Mercantile Gazette* as early as 20 September, 'and all have been agreeably disappointed in her appearance. She is not the amazon that many would suppose her to be, but as modest and unassuming a young woman as you can imagine … her features, though not what can be called absolutely pretty, are regular, and their expression is remarkably pleasing.'[15] David Kennedy, for the *Berwick and Kelso Warder*, confirmed the apparent contradiction between the manner of the deed and the character and appearance of the person. He had engineered a second visit out to the Longstone, and had this time secured an interview with the Darlings. Grace, he reported, 'is nothing masculine in her appearance, although she has so stout a heart. In person, she is about the middle size – of a comely countenance – rather fair for an islander – and with an expression of benevolence and softness most truly *feminine* in every point of view'. When Kennedy praised her conduct, Grace blushed, 'smiled at our praise, but said nothing in reply – though her look the while indicated forcibly, that the consciousness of having done so good and generous an action had not failed to excite a thrill of pleasure in her bosom, which was itself no mean reward'.[16]

If the press were first on the scene at the Longstone, painters and sculptors were not far behind. The Gateshead poet had rightly seen that a visual record of Grace and her deed was essential if her name was going to last. Others were of like mind. Many ladies and gentlemen, it was reported from Wooler in Northumberland, wanted to have her portrait done 'to perpetuate the likeness of one so heroic to future ages'.[17] Artists were not slow to rise to the challenge. In the months after the rescue twelve painters and one sculptor made their way to the Longstone Lighthouse; others had to be turned away. With one exception, Miss Laidler from Edinburgh, these were all men. So were the writers who tried to paint in words a likeness of the heroine. Few young women in the early nineteenth century can have been so publicly subjected to the male gaze, Grace's chief rival in this respect being the young Queen Victoria.

Mr Andrews of Edinburgh may have been first on the scene. Engravings of his painting of the wreck with the Darlings carrying out the rescue were being advertised from 4 October.[18] David Dunbar, a sculptor, was not far behind him. By 25 October he was advertising finished casts at one guinea each. Edward Maltby, the Bishop of Durham, purchased one version of the marble bust – and bequeathed it in 1859 to the National Gallery. It is now in the National Portrait Gallery's display of nineteenth-century work at Bodelwyddan Castle in north Wales – and there Grace is not in the drawing room devoted to other great Victorian women, but in the male world of explorers and imperialists.[19] Dunbar had his studio in Newcastle, a flourishing artistic and printing centre, and he had soon introduced his artist friends, John Carmichael, Henry Parker, John Reay and Robert Watson. Some were experts at portraiture, others at shipwrecks. All of them established good and lasting relations with the Darlings. Parker named his baby daughter Grace, and Grace Darling sent her namesake presents.[20] Dunbar travelled from Edinburgh in the 1860s specifically to see William Darling again.[21] Many of them sent William Darling presents of books.[22] But alongside the friendship was a professional concern to make the most of the opportunity that had come their way.

Nowhere is this clearer than in the case of Henry Parker. Parker describes in his autobiography an early lesson he had learned as a portrait painter. He did an exact likeness of a purser in the navy who had had a paralytic attack that had injured an eye. The purser's wife was very angry, providing Parker with a valuable lesson 'in seasoning him for the continued perplexities of this nature attending the profession of a Portrait Painter'. Parker's autobiography records a struggle between 'the seed of independence that had been sown by nature in his composition' and his need for aristocratic or rich patrons. He had moved from his native Plymouth to the north east on the strength of a family connection that proved a disaster. Despite this setback, he established connections in Newcastle with the artistic community, including Thomas Bewick and T. M. Richardson, and received patronage and support from both Charles John Brandling MP and Henry Hewitson, both of them, as we have seen, from important families in linking Newcastle with the Darlings. But in 1838 Parker seems to have been down on his luck, beset by enemies and without patrons, until 'an event took place that afforded him an opportunity to command publicity' – that event being the loss of the *Forfarshire*.

In early November Parker and Carmichael paid some fishermen to row them out to the Longstone Lighthouse where they received a mixed welcome. William Darling told them that 'You have heard a great deal of nonsense about what I think nothing at all off [sic]'. Mrs Darling called Grace down from upstairs telling her, 'dinna be sa full of sic bashful nonsense'. 'Grace then came down stairs, and a more retiring modest and simple creature could not be seen.' William Darling was 'not without some degree of hesitation' about the proposed portraits: 'It was making a vast of fash about noute [nought]', but eventually agreed. While Carmichael rowed about making sketches of the wreck, Parker made studies for his portraits. Then a storm blew up, and Parker found himself a guest of the Darlings for a week. It was, he recalled, 'a rich treat to mix amongst these true children of nature and be considered one of themselves, and he therefore got so familiar with them after a couple of days that they looked upon him as indeed one of themselves'. When he left, all shed tears. But Parker had more cause for rejoicing than tears. Returning to Newcastle 'with a large stock of sketches', he lent them to Mr Penley, the manager of the theatre, who produced on stage tableaux and scenes 'which was a great means of bringing the Artist's abilities again before the public'.[23] Parker's paintings of Grace were 'exceedingly popular'; so much so, it was said, that 'nearly everybody must have seen at some time or another a print of his picture of Grace Darling'.[24] Parker was not the only artist to receive a welcome shot in the arm from the loss of the *Forfarshire*. Thomas Musgrave Joy's portraits of Grace and her father and his 'Wreck of the *Forfarshire*', commissioned by Lord Panmure, brought in sufficient funds to enable him to marry after a seven-year engagement.[25]

Grace's face and figure puzzled those who tried to describe or portray her. It is quite possible to look at different portraits of her in her own lifetime and wonder whether they are of the same woman. A correspondent of the *Sunderland Herald* had reported that the heroine's 'features are admirably adapted for the skill of the painter, and equally so for the chisel of the sculptor',[26] but professionals on the spot confronted some challenges to their skill. William Howitt claimed that 'She is not like any of the portraits of her'. In what he went on to say he perhaps touched on the difficulties that faced the portrait painters: 'She is a little, simple, modest young woman ... She is neither tall nor handsome; but she has the most gentle, quiet, amiable look, and the sweetest smile that I ever saw in a person of her station and appearance.'[27] Portrait painters were not accustomed to confront sitters of Grace's 'station and appearance'. There were no obvious conventions they could fall back on. People of Grace's 'station' might feature in genre paintings of rural and seaside scenes, but not close up; that was reserved for ladies. And while the sweetness of the smile might redeem much in face-to-face encounters, portrait sitters did not smile, their mouths were closed. But Grace was a 'heroine', and somehow the portraits of her had to hint at, if not proclaim, the sources of that heroism. She had to be both ordinary, of the people, and extraordinary, the heroine of the Farne Isles.

As Parker and the other artists gazed at Grace, trying to tease out some feature of her face or posture that might mark her out, they noted some peculiarities, but they were peculiarities which made their task more rather than less difficult. Grace's ears were set exceptionally high on her head; that could be dealt with by suitable disposition of hair or hat. The mouth and chin, however, could not be concealed. Parker gave the fullest description of this in a letter to David Lucas who was making engravings from his portrait – he was also John Constable's engraver. Some crucial words from Parker's letter have been torn off. We read,

> There is a compressed expression of the mouth which is very peculiar to Grace Darling, almost to what is commonly called a [torn off] gives a firmness of character which is [torn off] ... There is also a peculiar character about the lower part of the face & chin ... It is somewhat of Bonaparte's character, the little shadow immediately below the underlip going so far in gives a little projection to the lower part of the chin.[28]

There has been speculation that the first words torn off, in the penultimate line of the page, were 'hare lip that': was the heroine, like her sister Thomasin, facially disfigured?[29] Certainly the 'compressed expression of the mouth' gave little scope for even hinting at Howitt's 'sweetest smile'. And was it entirely appropriate that an English heroine should resemble Bonaparte in the cast of her chin? A resemblance to Bonaparte is also evident in Dunbar's bust, but perhaps that was Dunbar's style: the young Elizabeth Gaskell, for whom Dunbar also did a bust, was teased that people thought she looked 'so very like Napoleon'.[30] In correcting the proof sent him by Lucas, Parker 'put a little more shadow on the cheek to give it more plumpness and also the shadow about the eye gives a better effect to the face'. 'These little trifles', he concluded, 'will most astonishingly improve the face.'[31] 'Improve', we may ask, in what sense? Make it more like Grace, or more acceptable as a portrait of a heroine about to be sold to a mass market?

Out of Parker's 'large stock of sketches', four portraits of Grace seem to have survived, two of them in the National Portrait Gallery, two in the Grace Darling Museum – and there are also there Parker's portraits of Grace's mother and father. One of the portraits of Grace, in the Museum, dated 10 November 1838, is inscribed, 'The original sketch of Grace Horsley Darling, for which she sat for the likeness'; there is a similar drawing, with the same date, in the National Portrait Gallery, inscribed 'This sketch I began from Grace Darling, and thought it so like that I would not finish it', a rather curious admission. The other two portraits, one dated 13 November, also bear a similarity, though Grace is wearing different clothes. For one of the sketches, Grace was wearing the cape she had worn when she performed her deed. In the 10 November sketches Grace is in half-profile in a pose which brings out the prominence of the chin, suggests determination, but gives little hint of the compressed mouth; that is much more evident in the other two.[32] A compression of the mouth is even more evident in Thomas Joy's portrait. Quite different are the portraits by John Reay, of which one survives. Here the face is much more rounded and less angular. Grace's brother was reported to have said of Reay's portraits that 'it would be a difficult matter to have more striking likenesses'. He was much less impressed with that by Edward Hastings who had engravings taken, but overpriced them and then sent a batch to the Darlings, hoping that they might sell them and take half the profits: in these, Grace is, as Constance Smedley put it, 'simpering like a frontispiece to a Book of Beauty, except that few Books of Beauty would have published a picture so badly drawn'.[33] Quite different again is the portrait in oils done by Horatio McCulloch. It has Grace looking over her right shoulder as though seeing the shipwrecked sailors, and looking suitably determined and heroic. All these and others were reproduced, mostly as lithographs, a method of reproduction invented in the late eighteenth century, and having the advantage over engravings that there was almost no limit to the number of prints that could be taken.

Inspired by the Dutch in the late seventeenth and early eighteenth centuries, marine painters had an established market for their products by the early nineteenth century. Paintings of shipwrecks were a sub-speciality, 'part of the stock-in-trade of Romantic art'. Their appeal lay in the rendering of humans at their most vulnerable in battle with nature at its most tempestuous; they inspired awe, and were the epitome of the sublime.[34] There were two ways of painting a wreck. One was to focus on survivors in small boats or clinging to rocks, as, for example, in James Gillray's 'The Wreck of the *Nancy Packet*' (1784), or Robert Smirke's 'Wreck of the *Halsewell*, 1786', or, most famously of all, in Théodore Géricault's 'Scene of Shipwreck', better known as 'The Raft of the Medusa'. Géricault's vast painting was on display in London in 1820 and attracted 40,000 visitors. It depicted the survivors of the wreck of the *Medusa* on a raft, some of them catching sight of a ship coming to their rescue, others of them dead, the viewers aware from the enormous publicity generated by the wreck that there had been resort to cannibalism. Géricault's canvas, exhibited in London at ground level, diminished the sense of distance between painting and viewer, facilitating an empathy with the victims. It became the picture against which all future paintings of survivors were measured.[35]

J. M. W. Turner was the dominant figure in the second tradition of painting shipwreck. Here the sea itself was central, humans and ships being tossed around at its mercy. Turner established his reputation as a painter of shipwrecks with *Shipwreck* in 1805. Since then he had painted both the Eddystone and Bell Rock lighthouses, and had linked up with George Manby, an inventor of apparatus for saving life at sea. Turner's painting of one of Manby's mortar ropes being fired off in the direction of a stranded ship put art at the service of life saving. Turner had also had himself lashed to the mast of a ship so that he could visualize a storm, and had most recently turned this experience into oil in 'A Disaster at Sea' in the mid-1830s. It depicts the break-up of the *Amphitrite* off Boulogne, with over a hundred deaths, mostly of female convicts bound for Australia.[36]

John Carmichael, a native of Newcastle, was a marine painter with an established reputation. His first renderings of the rescue were done for a fund-raising venture for the Darlings operating from Leeds before he had visited the Farne Isles, and are a product of his imagination. We see Grace and her father rowing to the rescue, and then returning with all nine survivors on board. The *Forfarshire* itself is still intact. After visiting the Farne Isles, Carmichael and Parker produced a more accurate version, with the eye again drawn to Grace and her father rowing out to the rescue in a rough sea.[37] The focus and light in both paintings is on the Darling's coble, and the sea and sky are portrayed in ways influenced by Turner. The second major painting of the rescue was by Thomas Musgrave Joy, commissioned by Lord Panmure. Here, as in Géricault, the focus is on the survivors, and in particular the woman with her two dead children, awaiting rescue as the Darlings draw near.

Sculpture and painting were not the only ways of picturing Grace. You could also see her on pottery. Not surprisingly, given their geographical position, the potters of Sunderland produced a version of the rescue in the medium they became best known for, pink or purple lustreware. From a design engraved on a copper plate any number of impressions could be taken on moistened paper, which was then pressed and rubbed on the surface of the pot. It was accompanied by one of the over three hundred standard rhymes or mottoes which were associated with Sunderland ware;[38] thus the pot on display in Bamburgh Castle has Grace and her father in the coble approaching the *Forfarshire*, and on the other side:

Freely take this gift of mine
The gift and giver I hope are thine
And tho' the value is but small
A loving heart is worth it all.

Grace was also commemorated in Staffordshire figures. These were quickly and cheaply produced and sold at fairs and street stalls, and by itinerant traders. They made little attempt to be accurate, old models being frequently reused. The first Staffordshire Queen Victoria was taken from an earlier figure of an opera singer, and it was said that the same mould was used for the Duke of Wellington's nose as for the teats on cow milk jugs. Now highly valued, Staffordshire figures were initially mantelpiece ornaments for the masses. In two of the extant Staffordshire figures of Grace, she is pictured with her father in the coble with the lighthouse as background. In another Grace stands alone, wearing heavy long boots, or pantaloons, and a knee-length skirt, with her arms crossed. The femininity so prized in many reports is signally absent. Grace looks tough and determined, ready for anything. It is impossible even to guess at how well such figures of Grace sold, but we do know that in the twentieth century there was a lucrative trade in forgeries of them.[39]

Further commercial opportunities lay in panoramas, huge cylinders that surrounded the audience with views of the rescue or other appropriate scenes. Henry Parker's sketches, as we have seen, formed the basis for a view of the interior of the Longstone Lighthouse that was on display at the Theatre Royal, Newcastle in December 1838. A more ambitious panorama, painted by Robert Watson, opened at the Sunderland Theatre on Boxing Day, and proceeded in mid-January to Hull. It was, apparently, 'very unsuccessful in Hull … but in Sunderland did well'.[40] Then at the Egyptian Hall in London, at the end of January, Captain George Manby and John Dennett, who had pioneered life-saving inventions, displayed panoramas which capitalized on the Darlings' rescue – it was the first but not the last initiative to link the name of Grace Darling with the wider cause of saving lives at sea.[41]

The story of Grace Darling's heroism might seem to be sufficiently dramatic that the facts could be allowed to speak for themselves. Yet one of the most extraordinary features of the contemporary response was the addition to it of one, or often multiple, layers of fiction. Journalists tampered with what had happened only at the margins. Other writers engaged in wholesale fictions. The first four books with 'Grace Darling' in the title were all fiction. Writers may have been the first, but were not the last, to discover that her name could sell things.

In November 1838 the well-known London theatre manager, Frederick Yates, tried to get Grace on stage. Writing from the Adelphi Theatre, he offered Grace travelling expenses for herself and one companion, board and lodging, and £10 per week for five weeks, perhaps extended to ten or more, if she would appear every evening for about quarter of an hour in his production of Edward Stirling's *Grace Darling; or, The Wreck at Sea*, first performed on 3 December 1838. If Grace had agreed to this offer she would have been surprised at the plot. In the play Grace's mother has died when she was an infant, her father is anxious to marry her to an elderly retired naval officer, and despatches her real lover, Harry Stannion, off for a year. After his year's exile Harry is returning in the *Forfarshire*, whose captain is Grace's brother. Thanks to Grace's heroism, everyone on the *Forfarshire* is saved – and Grace faints in Harry's arms. All this and some farcical sub-plots. It was the first indication of how fiction, way beyond the limits within which the journalists had confined themselves, could weave its way round Grace's life. The *Spectator* was highly critical: the play was 'a melodrama, as monstrous as ever was brought out', and 'to bring that maiden on the stage at all is a gross impropriety, and a profanation of a noble action'.[42]

Another London publication, in 1839, was *Grace Darling; or, the Heroine of the Fern Islands. A Tale*. The author was the young G. W. M. Reynolds, later to acquire fame as a radical and founder of *Reynolds's Newspaper*. The book is dedicated to Grace, and starts with a Preface that must stand as an early assertion of women's rights. There have been, writes Reynolds, 'but few instances of female heroism in England; whereas France, and some other continental nations, have produced from time to time many illustrious examples of women's magnanimity'. Reynolds ascribed this difference to the fact that in France women engaged in politics and business and acquired thereby 'masculine powers of thought'. Reynolds did 'not believe that the mind of woman is constitutionally weaker than that of man', and concluded that 'Next to the demoralizing idea that white men have a right to enslave the blacks, the belief which the English entertain relative to the necessity of the un-importance of woman is the most unjust and unfounded'. Grace, who had of course engaged neither in politics nor business, and therefore presumably had few opportunities to acquire 'masculine powers of thought', was here being hijacked to serve Reynolds's admirable agenda. After the Preface the book is something of a surprise: 158 pages long, Grace does not make an appearance until page 46, when, conveniently in London with her father in 1833, she tends to the hero after he has been assaulted in the street. The plot revolves around staples of London-life fiction: indebtedness, incarceration in the King's Bench prison, a woman locked up and ill-treated in a madhouse, a titled villain masquerading under a false name, a hero resolute for justice. When the Darlings make their cameo appearances patriotism is to the fore: William Darling has served in the Napoleonic Wars. When Grace, 'the dutiful daughter', gets up in the morning and prepares breakfast, she 'warbled one of those patriotic songs which her venerable sire loved so much to hear – "The Red-Cross of Albion"'. With fifteen pages to go, 'the narrative takes a leap over several years' and comes to the wreck of the

Forfarshire: needless to say all the dramatis personae are present in one form or another, Grace's 'delicate hands plied the rude oar with skill and vigour', the hero and villain are saved – but then kill each other in a duel. It is difficult to avoid the conclusion that Reynolds, having all but finished his book, inserted the story of the Darlings at a late stage to give it topicality.

Grace Darling, The Maid of the Isles, written by Jerold Vernon, printed and published by W. and T. Fordyce of Newcastle, 480 pages long, and published initially in thirty-six weekly numbers at 6d. each, or in six parts at 2s. each, was to have much more impact than Reynolds's book. 'Jerold Vernon' is almost certainly a pseudonym. Perhaps he was one of the Fordyces. In the mid-1840s William Fordyce was proprietor of the *Tyne Mercury*, but thereafter he seems to have faded from prominence, his death in 1865 scarcely noted. If 'Jerold Vernon' himself, both at the time and subsequently, is irrecoverable, the embellishment of the book with the name of a Newcastle publisher must have given it an air of verisimilitude – someone so geographically close to the scene must surely know what had happened. And there are indeed sections of the book which quote from contemporary newspapers and draw on such sources as William Darling's journal. But no one could fill 480 pages with such material. Much of the book is set in London and Spain, a complicated tale of aristocratic romance and adventure, with characters whose names alone might make even the most naive of readers wonder whether this was fact: a Polish Count Werner, Reginald St Clair, Shafto Fitzroy, Sebastian, Marquis of Santalina. Most readers doubtless put all this down as fiction. Vernon himself, sending the first ten numbers to Grace, did not pretend otherwise: 'you will find there are various scenes and characters of an imaginary nature introduced, this I trust you will easily excuse as from the miscellaneous nature of your reading you will often have discovered the reins given to Fancy and that fiction is frequently mingled with the gravest truths for the purpose of adorning a moral and giving point to a tale'.[43] But where did Vernon draw the line between fact and fiction? He was skilful enough to interweave into the fiction material that gave what must have seemed a plausible account of Grace's childhood and adolescence. Many later writers drew on it unashamedly.

Vernon describes in vivid detail how in September 1832 William Darling went out to rescue a yacht caught in a storm, aboard which were Charles and Caroline Dudley, brother and sister, both key characters in the novel. Recovering at the Longstone Lighthouse, Caroline strikes up a friendship with Grace despite their vast difference in social rank. Grace fascinates Caroline in her recital of 'many legendary tales' of the Northumberland coast. Part of the attraction of Grace, wrote Vernon, was that her education, at the hand of her father, 'whilst it developed her excellent understanding, had not destroyed that child like simplicity and freedom from all guile, which formed so amiable part of her character'. In short, Grace is, in Vernon's words, 'a child of nature', an irresistible

counterfoil to Caroline who is about to plunge into aristocratic Society. All too
soon, Caroline, Charles and their widowed father are summoned back to London
to meet their Spanish mother's brother, the Marquis of Santalina, on a mission
from the court of Madrid. Caroline seals the friendship by sending Grace a locket
of her hair, and thereafter it is sustained, though intermittently, by Caroline's
letters, the contrast between the two girls' lives being constantly driven home:
'The gay and brilliant life which Caroline described herself as enjoying, would
oftentimes excite amazement in the mind of the simple child of nature.'[44]

The life of the child of nature is indeed a simple and enviable one in contrast
to the performance required by Caroline and her friends. Caroline is drawn to
the Romantic figure of Count Werner, a Pole brought up by the patriot hero
Kosciusko, and dedicated to fighting in his country's cause, not least because
the Russians have (apparently) slaughtered Constance, the love of his life.
Lord Delmore, a much more suitable Englishman, presses his suit without any
response from Caroline. Before these developments reach any fruition, the
Dudleys set off for Spain and become actively involved in the Spanish civil war,
Charles risking life in fighting for the losing cause of Don Carlos, but managing
to fall in love with Camilla, who is incarcerated in a convent. In the dénouement,
Werner discovers that Constance in fact escaped the massacring Russians. They
marry, and then are making their way to Scotland to take possession of an estate
bequeathed to Constance by a Scottish paternal grandfather. They get to Hull
and board the *Forfarshire*. Caroline meanwhile has fallen for her previously
unsuccessful suitor Lord Delmore, now the Earl of Clanranald, and also engaged
in the Spanish civil war, though on the opposite side to Charles, who escapes
from prison, rescues Camilla and marries her. Werner and Constance drown with
the *Forfarshire*, but in the summer following (at a date after the publication of
the book in February 1839), the Earl and Lady Clanranald, Charles and Camilla
Dudley, and the ageing Major Dudley visit the Longstone.

There are other slightly more plausible sub-plots. The Darlings are friends
with the Herberts, the head of whom is 'a farmer of considerable wealth' near
Bamburgh. Grace goes to stay for a week and the younger son falls in love with
her. Grace, though not unattracted, gives him no encouragement, thus sparing
him the pain of refusal. The elder Herbert boy meets up with a former student
friend from Durham, Reginald St Clair, once an outgoing and exuberant young
man, but now sunk in melancholy, understandably, since another close friend
has died, and the friend's sister whom he was about to marry collapsed before
the altar, and 'died a victim to the intensity of her feelings'. St Clair, however,
like Caroline before him, is taken by Grace's knowledge of local legend, and her
lengthy recital of 'The Wandering Knight of Dunstanbrough Castle'.[45]

If there is a moral in all of this, it is that neither wealth, status and 'the artificial
luxuries of society', nor the more noble pursuit of glory for a just cause, are any

guarantee of happiness or fulfilment. Love, too, is a field of danger. Grace has a number of suitors in the book, to some of whom she is attracted, but she gives higher value to her life with her parents and resists them all. 'And is not the island maiden happy in her rocky home? As much so as the princess in her gorgeous palace! There she continues to gladden her parents with her presence.'[46]

Grace had replied noncommittally when she received the first ten numbers from Vernon. 'Being sensible of your good intentions', she wrote, 'I wish you every success in the world. P.S. Although I have no wish for anything of the kind, permit me to say that a little book after the manner of the *Kent Indiaman*, or the *Rothesay Castle*, would have been much preferred by your Much obliged humble servant, G. H. Darling.' In December 1841 B. R. Gooch from Norwich, who had bought the book, wrote to ask about 'the various characters and all their combined and most extraordinary circumstances'. Were these 'historical memorial facts' or 'mere novelty'? Grace replied that 'although most of the things concerning the *Forfarshire* are facts, yet as I am quite unacquainted with the persons mentioned it certainly gives the appearance of Romance altogether'. Before replying Grace had written to her sister Thomasin, asking her to send back 'my book'.[47] And Grace herself may have played some part in the book's composition, and one of its more extraordinary features: the adventures in Spain are suddenly interrupted with a full list of the subscribers to the Newcastle fund for Grace. There exists a draft letter from William Darling in which he says that in accordance with Grace's wish to see the names of subscribers he would like them all in writing and 'afterward printed in the Maid of the Isles', which suggests that the Darlings were following its progress more closely than might be imagined.[48]

The final contemporary 'Grace Darling' work of fiction, *Grace Darling; or the Loss of the 'Forfarshire'. A Tale by a Young Lady* was published by William Collins in Glasgow in 1840. The 'Young Lady' is, she tells us, a mere sixteen, and had not intended this 'juvenile production of a young person' for publication; but she was prevailed upon. Precociously well-educated, the author litters her text with phrases in French and Italian, inserts random discussions of literature (Walter Scott, Hannah More, and many others), includes a superfluous tour of England by one of the heroines, and never misses a chance to point an evangelical moral. A particular concern is for the conversion of India to Christianity. 'Oh! That Hindostan, dear Hindostan, were a Christian country', sighs a colonel. Like the other three fictions, the plot is designed to reach its climax with the arrival in Hull in September 1838 of all the characters who have previously been spread around the globe, often unaware of each other's existence. In a book of 316 pages, Grace makes her first appearance on page 278. She is in some ways outshone by another real-life character, the Reverend John Robb of Dunkeld, whose piety and courage are highly praised, and who met his death on the *Forfarshire* 'with placid serenity'.[49]

Grace, 'the bravest of England's daughters', nevertheless has her moment in the book. She tries to persuade her father to let her go out to the rescue, but he, 'tottering on the brink of the grave', adamantly refuses. Grace turns to her mother, claiming that God will protect her, and is successful. Mother and daughter launch the boat, father at last stirs himself to join Grace, and they set off on their perilous journey. Those waiting to be rescued are of course all the characters whose fortunes and misfortunes have sustained the narrative. The Colonel so anxious for the conversion of Hindostan once again excels himself when, clinging to the rock, he sees a female rowing to the rescue: '"O! wondrous land", said the Colonel, "O! justly renowned Great Britain! who possesses a daughter of such unparalleled bravery. Brave are your sons is the general cry, but braver are your daughters may I add, who thus dare the ocean's fury for to save"'. The authorial voice comes to the fore when Grace holds the coble while William Darling leaps onto the rock. 'Think not lightly of this action, reader: at that moment Grace Darling performed an exploit that would have appalled the heart of the most heroic British tar.' For 'though possessed of a mind adorned with every feminine virtue', Grace has 'a heroic, courageous heart'. Her name 'should be written in letters of burnished gold – more illustrious because more humane than any heroine of old'. 'Her country', reflects another character, 'may feel proud of this humane and heroic deed.' But if Grace belongs to England or Great Britain, she is also something else, and in some ways more potent. Like Vernon, 'a Young Lady' sees Grace as a child of nature. 'She was nature's own fair and lovely daughter, and her soul was as pure and untainted as the clear mirror of truth.'[50]

A similar picture of Grace shines through the songs or ballads composed to celebrate and commemorate the deed. In all of them Grace is preternaturally alert to the dangers of the storm. She alone hears the cries of the shipwrecked, and she persuades her father to row out to the rescue. In W. H. Ollivier's *Grace Darling*, father urges Grace to sleep, but

> 'Oh! Father', said the startled maid
> 'I slept – but such a cry
> Of horror woke me, I'm afraid
> There's death or danger nigh.
> And hark! again Oh! let us haste
> 'Tis some bewildered crew
> Upon the reckless waters waste
> Oh! fly in pity do.'

In Christopher Thomson's version, Grace is similarly restless:

> 'No! father, no! I cannot sleep,
>   My fears are past control;

There's some distress upon the deep,
It haunts my very soul.'

And in George Linley's *Ballad*, once again urged to go back to sleep, Grace responds,

'I cannot sleep, their shrieks appal me,
Oh! Father, hear that piercing cry?
Arise ye, hasten, the day is breaking,
Look out, look out, a wreck I spy!'

At the centrepiece of each of the three ballads are the two elements in the story that the Darlings denied: that Grace heard the cries of the shipwrecked, and that she persuaded her father to go out. And it was through these ballads that many members of the public absorbed their version of what Grace had done – and perhaps, too, of what she looked like. Linley's ballad was accompanied by a picture of Grace in an evening dress and wearing the daintiest of shoes, hair loose in the wind, her oar a mere fashion accessory.[51]

There was one further important ingredient in establishing Grace Darling's fame: her name. 'Were two such words ever before combined to form a name?' wondered the *Monthly Chronicle*, 'The one expressing the natural quality of the bearer of it, and the other defining what her deeds have made her in the regard of others'.[52] 'Euphonious is thy Darling name' was the contribution from an acrostic in the *Leeds Mercury*. 'Grace Darling', wrote the *Scotsman*, '… is a name to take one's heart and one's memory … Had Grace Darling been a married woman, dwelling in some poor alley in an ordinary town, and with no rarer or prettier an appellation than Smith, Brown, McTavish, or Higginbottom, a greater deed would, perhaps, have won her less favour.'[53] The *Spectator* marvelled that a heroine 'of real life' should have 'a name at once euphonious and cherishable. Grace Darling! – Poet or novelist need not desire one better fitted to bestow on a paragon of womankind … it will "live in our land's language"'. The *Spectator* gallantly claimed that she would 'have been loved and admired as heartily had she been Dorothy Dobbs, with a wide mouth, snub nose, and a squint', but we may doubt it.[54] The words 'Grace Darling' came to have a potency that stretched far beyond the bearer of the name. 'Grace Darling! How vivid, how graphic, a picture rises before us at the very sound of that singularly expressive name!'[55] What made up the picture? Doubtless by 1861, when this was written, a picture of Grace herself, and of the rescue, but, one may speculate, by association beyond that.

'Grace' has some fourteen different meanings in dictionaries, all of them positive: at a secular level 'attractive', 'charming', 'becoming', 'unconstrained goodwill', 'beautiful' as in the three Graces, the Greek goddess sisters who bestowed beauty and charm. At a theological level, and this was at least equally important, grace was an unmerited gift from God, a strengthening and inspiring influence, under whose influence you might attain 'a state of grace'. When Victorians sang John Newton's eighteenth-century hymn, 'Amazing Grace', did their thoughts extend to Grace Darling? It would have been natural to do so:

> Through many dangers, toils and snares
> We have already come;
> 'Tis grace has brought us safe thus far,
> And grace will lead us home.

The verse seems to speak directly to those who had been rescued from the *Forfarshire*. Grace had indeed brought them safe and led them home.

Men could be gracious, but the qualities associated with grace were essentially and positively feminine. Men could and did fantasize about 'Grace Darling' – a Grace who was a 'darling'. Women could set her up as a role model, with a potent combination of traditional feminine attributes and masculine courage.

Within months of performing her deed, Grace Darling had been established as a national heroine. The words and the images that would inform all future accounts were in place. No one could now doubt that Grace Darling would be remembered. But what would be remembered was, to an astonishing extent, fiction. There were the minor fictions of the journalists and songwriters, the adjustments of Grace's face and figure by the artists, and there were the wholesale fictions of the novelists and dramatists. The media created the Grace they and their audiences wanted. The 'Grace Darling' of the 1830s and 1840s was the product of a society that could respond to her deed only through the distorting lens of conservative Romanticism.

4

The Life and Death of a Heroine

Once her name and deed had achieved national coverage, a struggle for ownership of Grace ensued. Some wanted to exhibit her, to make money out of and perhaps for her. Grace might in this way become a heroine of the people, accessible to the people, and a celebrity. Others wanted to protect her from such exposure, urging her to shun publicity and seek refuge under the protection of powerful figures in the upper classes. Either way, she had to work out how to comport herself in this new and quite unforeseen role as heroine. As it happened, it was a short-lived role, for Grace died only four years after her deed, at the age of twenty-six. Some thought it was the pressures of being a heroine and celebrity that killed her.

On 27 November 1838 Stephen Wright, of 35 Strand, London, wrote to William Darling advising him that if Grace 'were brought out in proper style in London as an exhibition … much would be done for her good'. He himself had 'an excellent situation and good apartments for the purpose', and had it in his 'power to introduce her to some of the first connections in England'.[1] The exact nature of the 'exhibition' proposed was never clarified, but Wright was simply more explicit than others in recognizing that people wanted to see the heroine and to imagine for themselves the dangers of the rescue; and also more explicit in recognizing the commercial opportunities available both to entrepreneurs and to the Darlings themselves. Seven weeks after the rescue Grace was sufficiently well-established as a heroine for the enterprising, like Wright and Frederick Yates, the London theatrical entrepreneur, to begin to think of cashing in on her fame. She was becoming a celebrity, someone whose presence, image, or even name alone could add value to anything to which they became attached. The ideal was that Grace herself would be exhibited, either in her natural habitat on the Farne Isles or in some public arena on the mainland; for there was as much curiosity about her as there was about exotic 'natives' from the South Seas or Africa, or poets who sprang from the people like Robert Burns or John Clare.

The Darlings were resigned to the prospect of visitors. In February 1839 William Darling reported that 'as soon as the weather will permit we are assured of numbers [of] people visiting this place to satisfy curiosity which we could wish to avoid, but that cannot be done after so much kindness shown to us by the Publick'.[2] By May a handbill was advertising a 5s. trip from Newcastle and North Shields to visit the 'Heroine Grace Darling, at the Longstone Lighthouse'.[3] In the summer of 1840, Grace reported to the Duke of Northumberland, there were no pleasure parties on steam vessels, but 'a good many visitors in small parties', including one couple who sent books of sermons. There is no doubt that the visitors were burdensome. When William Howitt visited the islands in 1840 he was told by Grace's father that 'she very much disliked meeting strangers that she thought came to stare at her'.[4] There were, alas, many keen to stare at her – not least, Howitt himself.

Those hoping for a public exhibition of Grace on the mainland were in the end disappointed. Unsuspecting, the entrepreneurs of popular culture entered into a battle for ownership of Grace with the upper classes. And it was the upper classes, in the person of the Duke of Northumberland, who emerged victorious.

The most serious attempt to lure Grace into a public exhibition of herself came from William Batty, who had a circus in Edinburgh. Batty had given the proceeds of his entertainment on 8 November 1838 to Grace, and sent the £20 raised via a Mr Sylvester direct to the lighthouse. Grace in reply thanked 'the people of Edinburgh; and it having been intimated to me that my presence in Edinburgh would greatly oblige those who have manifested so much anxiety for my welfare, I will take an opportunity shortly of visiting your arena in person'. Did she understand the full implications of the word 'arena'? Almost certainly not. As the *Edinburgh Courant*, rather clumsily, put it, 'It is clear that she has no conception of the nature of what she there proposes to do'. Armed with Grace's letter, Batty immediately had it published in the press, provoking an uproar.

Batty also expressed surprise that the £20 that Sylvester delivered was the first actual cash the Darlings had received, despite much publicity being given to fund-raising on their behalf. Why were the Darlings not receiving the proceeds?[5] There was already underway a fund-raising effort for Grace in Edinburgh, headed by Catherine Sinclair, daughter of Sir John Sinclair, the first President of the Board of Agriculture. Catherine Sinclair was a philanthropist and also a novelist, her children's book, *Holiday House* (1839), being described as 'certainly the best original children's book written up to that time, and one of the jolliest and most hilarious of any period'.[6] None of this humour was evident in the response to the prospect of Grace appearing in Batty's circus. Curiously that response was anonymous. Some 'Edinburgh Ladies' wrote to Grace deploring the fact that it appeared that she was going 'to visit the city for the purpose of exhibiting her *person*, in a *low circus* of Mountebanks'; if she were to do this, it 'would bring a stain upon those unfading laurels which she has so honourably gained: a *stain* which can never be effaced'.[7]

This was followed up a fortnight later by a letter addressed to William Darling, fearing that the first may not have reached the Farne Isles. Surely, the Ladies wrote, 'it cannot be her own wish to make a *fool* and a *laughing stock* of herself, as a female the more private she keeps herself so much the more will the world think of her virtues ... [we] assure you that *here* the best half and the most intelligent of the community treat the affair of her Exhibition in *such* a *place*, with *scorn* and *rediccule* [sic]'.[8] Equally condemnatory was another anonymous letter from Lindsay's Library in St Andrew's Street, Edinburgh, perhaps this time from Catherine Sinclair herself, saying that 'the greatest injury has been already done to the well-earned reputation of Grace Darling', and expressing 'the earnest hope of those who are now interesting themselves in collecting a permanent fund for the comfort of her future life, that she will refrain from an exhibition, which has already made a considerable change in the sentiments of those who were desirous to befriend her'. In face of this barrage, and letters from other well-wishers urging her not to put herself on display, Grace and her father rapidly abandoned any idea of going to Edinburgh, or anywhere else.[9]

We might be inclined to assume from this that Batty's 'Royal Circus' was indeed a place of low entertainment that no respectable person would come near. Circuses were to be found at all social levels, some doubtless meriting the opprobrium thrown on them by the Edinburgh Ladies. But in the 1820s and 1830s the royal family was patronizing Astley's, Andrew Ducrow was forging enduring links between circus and the legitimate stage, and Dickens was painting heart-warming pictures of circus performances and their audiences.[10] Batty was no mountebank. He himself was to rebuild Astley's after a disastrous fire in 1841 and take over the management. In Edinburgh between October and December 1838 the *Scotsman* carried numerous reports praising 'this popular place of amusement', Mr Batty sparing 'no pains or expense to render this place of amusement worthy of public support. He endeavours to meet every variety of taste. In addition to his singularly efficient company of equestrians, vaulters, tight-rope dancers, athletes, etc., and his admirable stud of horses, his establishment comprises an elephant, a zebra, a fox, and a monkey ...', with a lion in waiting. Special performances were provided for Colonel Carter and the officers of the Royals, for Colonel Clark and the officers of the 7th Dragoons, for the Masonic Lodges, and, most significantly of all, for the Lord Provost of Edinburgh on behalf of the Royal Infirmary, attended by the Lord Provost, Lady Forrest and family, Sir James Spittal, Sir William Newbigging, and other pillars of Edinburgh society.[11]

What irked the Edinburgh ladies were two things: that others might make money out of Grace, with Grace perhaps sharing in the profits; and that, as a female, she should exhibit herself in public. Grace, in their view, should be the grateful recipient of money raised on her behalf by the philanthropically inclined. Even the *Scotsman*, while noting that 'there was a good turn-out' for the benefit performance for Grace on 8 November, and while not 'disposed to underrate the heroic conduct of this young lady', began 'to fear lest she should be overwhelmed by the tide of public favour which has risen so rapidly around her ... The public having amply expressed their sense of her noble achievement, should now allow her to enjoy in quietness, the applauses of her own approving conscience.'[12]

There was a coda to Sylvester's visit to the Longstone, worthy of any Victorian fiction. The scene is a large London hospital, the year 1891. Under the pillow of a man who has died is found some folded and faded paper, 'all the worse for age, but, nevertheless, carefully preserved'. The dead man was a Mr Affleck; but, four months previously, Sylvester had died in the bed next to his. Presumably, as Sylvester approached death, he had entrusted the paper, his most valuable possession, to Affleck. In the paper Sylvester recounted his visit to the Farne Isles, and how he had been the first to give Grace any actual cash. 'I got her', he wrote, 'to write me a statement to this effect which she signed.' He went on to say that Grace had subsequently 'become acquainted with what was to her an unknown world', which she found unbearable. 'She sighed and died of a broken heart is the opinion of Thomas Sylvester, Ex Theatrical and Equestrian Manager.'[13] Sylvester was determined to leave a testimony, so that the world should know what he had done and seen at the Longstone, his one moment in history. Running through his account is his resentment at the treatment accorded to Grace by those who took responsibility for her welfare. She would have been better off, he seems to be saying, if she had thrown in her fortunes with Sylvester, Batty and the entrepreneurs of popular culture.

People wanted not only to stare at Grace, they wanted also to reward her. 'According to the fashion of Englishmen when their sympathies are aroused', wrote a commentator in the 1860s, 'admiration and approval soon began to take a substantial and a metallic form.'[14] Raising money for the heroine was, on the face of it, an odd response to an act of courage. It is true that there were other ways of recognizing Grace's achievement, but the cash, duly recorded in the newspapers, was the main one. Was this a peculiar national trait? Was this a society in which worth and courage could be measured only in cash terms?

The sum that was raised was certainly large. In total it came to at least £767 6s.8d., or in twenty-first century terms nearly £40,000, a huge capital sum for someone born in her position.[15] Most of it came from the well-to-do, headed by the Queen who gave £50. There were other large individual donors, for example Sir Francis and Miss Angela Burdett-Coutts, the latter at the outset of her career of philanthropy, who gave £30. Amongst the towns that sent subscriptions, Newcastle appropriately headed the list with £150, followed by Alnwick with £114, Glasgow with £100, the Edinburgh Ladies with £84, Dundee (the destination of the *Forfarshire*) with £50. Most donations came from the north east of England and southern Scotland, but there were exceptions: £50 from the London Exchange, £15 from Birmingham, a subscription list which made up in quality what it lacked in quantity: Joseph Sturge, G. F. Muntz and other present or future luminaries of Birmingham Liberalism made up the list.[16]

From Woodbridge in Suffolk came £1 16s.0d, the donor regretting that he had not started collection earlier as there had since been distress locally.[17] Grace was insistent on knowing wherever possible the names of all donors; as her father put it, 'she always thinks she sees a friend in a subscriber and means to have them all printed'.[18] Most donors seem to have subscribed a minimum of 5s. The £8 10s. from Perth had been raised 'by a few gentlemen'; it was 'the Ladies' of Edinburgh who subscribed. Many of the 225 Newcastle subscribers donated £2 2s.0d, none of them less than 5s. Only in one subscription list, that from Haswell Colliery, do we find donations as low as 1s. or 6d. – in all twenty people there subscribed £1 9s.0d.[19]

The upper classes had given – and then the upper classes in the person of the Duke of Northumberland retrieved the gift. The Duke set himself up as trustee for the sum raised, one of the oddest twists in the story of Grace Darling. He and his predecessors had long taken an interest in the prevention of shipwreck on the north-east coast and in rescue when it occurred. He had visited the Longstone Lighthouse when it was being built in the 1820s, and had then met William Darling. When he heard of the wreck of the *Forfarshire* and of the circumstances surrounding it he immediately began to pull the strings available to him.[20] He wanted proper recognition for what the Darlings and the North Sunderland boatmen had done, but he wanted also to protect the Darlings from those who were, in his perspective, trying to exploit the fame of the heroine in unworthy ways.

First, on 25 September, in his capacity as Vice-Admiral of the Coast of Northumberland, he wrote to the Duke of Wellington who was, amongst other things, Master of the Corporation of Trinity House, London, enclosing a certificate, signed by Robert Smeddle, John Tulloch, the carpenter, and Daniel Donovan, fireman, testifying to the Darlings' bravery.[21] As it happened, Trinity House on that very same day was stirring of its own accord. Hearing of the rescue, the weekly Board meeting ordered that 'Mr Blackett the Agent be requested to state for the Board's Information any circumstances connected therewith that may independent of any communication he may have had with Darling thereon have come within his Knowledge: Also that Darling be required to furnish a detailed Statement of the Facts for our Information'.[22] This perhaps suggests an unwillingness to take on trust newspaper reports, or indeed William Darling's own version of events. The requirement for Darling 'to furnish a detailed Statement of the Facts' prompted his famous letter of 6 October. The Court of Trinity House on 2 October had Northumberland's letter before them, but decided to defer action until they had received the reports they had asked for. A week later, when these were available, it was resolved unanimously to award £10 each to Grace and her father as a mark of the Court's approval 'of their meritorious Conduct upon that Occasion'.[23]

Trinity House, it is difficult to avoid feeling, was not going to be swept away by the wave of public sentiment that was announcing Grace to be the greatest heroine of all time. The Darlings' conduct was 'meritorious', not 'heroic'. And Trinity House may have had another concern. In December 1841 newspaper reports reached them of the rescue by the Darlings of the crew of the *Dart* and subsequently of the vessel itself. Blackett was once again asked to conduct an inquiry, and especially to find out more 'of the considerations which induced Mr Darling and his Son, and Mr Smith [keeper of the Inner Farne light] to quit their respective Light Houses ... and in whose Charge the maintenance of the respective Lights remained during the night the Keepers are stated to have been absent'. Blackett was able to give a clean bill of health. It was William Brooks Darling, the son, who had gone out; William Darling and Thomas Smith 'never left their Stations'.[24] Was there perhaps concern in 1838 that the Longstone Light had been left unattended at night, and might there have been 'considerations' (bonuses and salvage) to induce a rescue?

The Duke of Northumberland did not content himself with contacting Trinity House. As a member of the National Institution for the Preservation of Life from Shipwreck, he alerted the Newcastle branch of the institution to the events.[25] Finally, as President of the Royal Humane Society, founded in 1774 to encourage efforts to save life from drowning, he wrote to the London committee on 26 September, drawing attention to the Darlings' courage. The Glasgow, and Edinburgh and Leith Humane Societies were already about to award silver medals.[26] The London Committee in 1838 considered 191 cases, and gave honorary rewards or medals to thirty-seven claimants, pecuniary ones to 146. Basically a class system was in operation: honours for the well-to-do, cash for the rest. In the honorary category silver and bronze medals were available, gold having up to then been reserved for the unlikely figure of Tsar Alexander I, who in 1806 had assisted, or at least been present, at the saving of the life of a drowning peasant, the award of a gold medal being an indication of the society's eye for publicity.[27]

What would be appropriate for Grace and her father? In class terms, they were in the pecuniary rewards category. But 'The Committee in deliberating on the merits of the case, considered that to a young female who could fearlessly display such Heroism, an Honorary distinction would be more cherished by her, than a pecuniary reward.'[28] The Committee, at its monthly meeting on 17 October, proposed a gold medal for Grace, a silver medal for her father and £10 10s. for the lifeboatmen from North Sunderland – whose courage was specifically brought to their attention by the Duke. At a Special General Court held at the end of the month, on the prompting of the Duke, the silver medal proposed for William Darling was tactfully elevated to match the gold given to Grace. In agreeing to award gold medals, the Special General Court, meeting on 31 October, was persuaded that 'such extraordinary heroism never occurr'd before nor is likely to occur again'.[29] But it was also alive to the favourable publicity that might accrue to the society. A strong desire was unanimously expressed that the gold medals should be presented to the Darlings, hopefully by the Duke of Northumberland, at the ensuing Annual Festival. In the words of Benjamin Hawes, the treasurer, 'The universal impression made by the extraordinary conduct of Darling and his Daughter which, on the presentation of the very highest Honorary distinctions we can confer by Your Grace could not fail to bring our Society in so favourable a position prominently before the Public'. The Duke scotched this request both for his own presence, and more particularly for that of the Darlings, the society having to content itself with sending the medals to the Duke for him to present to the Darlings, while still hoping that 'every possible publicity be given to the award ... at the ensuing Festival'.[30]

The Duke's interest in the case of the *Forfarshire* was matched by that of the Duchess. She had been, from 1830–7, Governess to Princess Victoria, a role not involving teaching in the classroom but general supervision of the Princess's education and upbringing. It was perhaps natural that she should take an interest in another young woman who was suddenly catapulted to public attention. It appears to have been the Duchess who arranged for Grace and her father to make an appearance at Alnwick Castle in early December – the Duke refers to their 'accidental arrival'. The two gold medals were duly presented, being received in a 'very diffident but enthusiastic manner' that the Duke found 'truly gratifying'. The Duchess gave a Paisley shawl. The Darlings had the same day presented themselves at Sir Mathew Ridley's bank at Alnwick to receive the Queen's £50.[31] That might have been the end of the relationship between the Northumberlands and the Darlings but it was only the beginning. The Duke chose, and personally wrapped, Christmas presents for the Darlings, for Grace a silver-gilt watch with instructions written by the Duke, together with waterproof clothing, a prayer book and Bible notes, further waterproof clothing for her parents, a silver teapot for Mrs Darling, and more medals from the Shipwreck Society at Newcastle for Grace and her father.[32]

The next step taken by the Duke was to set up trustees for the money raised for Grace. The trustees were the Duke himself, the Venerable Dr Thorp, Archdeacon of Durham, the Reverend William Nicholas Darnell of Durham Cathedral, and the Reverend Thomas Singleton, Archdeacon of Northumberland, all of them trustees of the Crewe charity. Protracted negotiations led to a final agreement by the end of 1840. Grace effectively handed over most of the money raised for her to the trustees, retaining a right to some £5 of the interest every six months and, if she needed it, £200 of the capital sum. But the rest she could not touch: it was to be for her heirs. It is likely that one of the motives of the trustees was to protect Grace and her money from potential husbands – there was much talk at the time of offers of marriage pouring in on Grace. Grace herself does not seem to have foreseen any need for more than a small amount of interest, so the capital sum accumulated during her lifetime and afterwards. On her death, the interest went to her parents. On her father's death in 1865 the capital, now £780, was split among surviving relatives. Some of the trustees and the lawyers involved clearly wondered whether Grace should not have retained greater control over a larger portion of the sum, but, guided by the Duke, she declined to do so.[33]

Was this what the donors had intended? Only with the Ladies of Edinburgh do we get a clear sense of what they thought should happen: Catherine Sinclair wanted the money to provide Grace with an annuity: at least that way she would have used the money herself had she lived.[34] At a popular level, there are hints of suspicion about what was happening or might happen to the money. William Batty, as we have seen, made much of the fact that he had despatched Mr Sylvester to the Longstone with the £20 raised by his entertainment, and surprise was expressed that no other donations had yet reached the Darlings. There is, however, no evidence of misuse of any of the funds raised, rather of meticulous accounting by the Duke's staff, and of trust in the Duke on the part of the Darlings.

It was the Duke, not the Duchess, who corresponded with Grace as well as with her father. The Duke enquired how she was, whether she was going to get married, and whether the watch was still working. Grace replied in kind: the watch did not need cleaning, could he pass a message to 'my kind friend the Duchess', and she had not yet got married. Grace flowed abundantly: His Grace the Duke wrote to Grace and Grace wrote back to His Grace. In January 1840, addressing 'My Lord Duke by your Permission my Guardian', she reported how

> We had the pleasure of Drinking the Duke and Duchess healths both on Christmas and New Years Day in a Cup of Tea out of Mothers Teapot but like every thing in the world the first news we heard was Your Grace was very Ill. May it please God, this may find you in health, My Humble Duty to the Duchess & Misses Percies as I think I shall never forget there kind reception of me at Alnwick Castle.[35]

When she was ill in 1842 the Northumberlands provided accommodation and medical care in Alnwick, and the Duchess visited Grace. After her death, William Darling and the Duke continued to correspond, William Darling sending him game birds, the Duke responding with tea and sugar, his letters opening uncompromisingly, 'Darling'.[36] There is nothing to suggest any resentment on the part of the Darlings that the Duke and Duchess had made unwarranted interventions in their lives; quite the contrary. Whatever the donors may have wished, and however odd the concentration on provision for heirs may seem to us now, the Darlings seemed happy that Grace, in her early twenties, should accept a guardian.

The Duke's role as Grace's guardian does nevertheless drive home the point that her deed had captured the imagination of the upper classes from the very top downwards. The Queen evidently first heard of the deed from her Prime Minister, Lord Melbourne, and duly inscribed it in her journal for 28 September 1838, though she or Melbourne got the story wrong for, as the Queen tells it, Grace rowed out on her own – an early example of the marginalization of William Darling in the rescue.[37] Victoria then, as we have seen, subscribed £50 for Grace. Doubtless she was moved by Grace's heroism, but she was also under pressure from the intensity of interest in Grace. In early January 1839 she showed Melbourne what she described as 'an absurd letter of the Duchess of Somerset to Headfort, which made him laugh, about my hearing a song, composed for Grace Darling; Lord M. said: "it's a very troublesome, pushing thing; it'll put her out of humour if you don't do it; if you don't very much mind, perhaps you'd better do it, as there's so much said about this Grace Darling"'. So, on 14 January, 'at 4 I went into the drawing-room with all my ladies except Daisy, and heard Miss Birch sing this song about Grace Darling, accompanied by Sir George Smart; she really has a very fine sweet, pure, powerful voice, with fine high and low notes, but ought to open her mouth more. The words of the song are by Mr Patrick Stewart, the Duchess of Somerset's brother, and are very pretty; the air is a Scotch song called "Boatie row"; she sang it with great feeling, twice over'.[38] So the Queen did a favour for the Duchess of Somerset in the cause of advancing the career of the latter's brother, for of course news of the Queen hearing the song spread rapidly. But she was also, as Melbourne hinted to her, under pressure to assent, for a refusal would also have been noised abroad, and it would have done the young Queen no good to be deficient in enthusiasm for Grace's deed and everything associated with it. Doubtless she shared at least to some extent in that enthusiasm, and noted, as she sailed close to the Farne Isles on 31 August 1842, that she had seen 'Grace Darling's lighthouse'. Grace Darling herself, on the mainland, sadly 'lost the grand sight of the Queen passing; we would have liked very much to have seen it'.[39] And as further evidence of the Queen's commitment, or sense of what the public expected of her, in the spring of 1843 she and her mother subscribed to the fund for a monument to Grace.[40]

Below royalty, the members of the aristocracy were clearly touched by Grace's deed, and not only the Duke and Duchess of Northumberland. Lord and Lady Frederick Fitzclarence (he a son of William IV), on a visit to Bamburgh Castle, sent a small silver cup to Grace.[41] Lord Panmure gave generously to the fund, and, as we have seen, commissioned T. M. Joy to paint a portrait of Grace and pictures of the rescue, which were donated to Dundee. As the radically-inclined William Howitt put it, 'the titled have not failed to pay her the homage of their flatteries'.[42] And beyond an individual level, the institutions of the state and major philanthropic bodies had recognized the rescue, and accorded to Grace the highest honours available to them. All of this helped make her a national figure, highly valued by the state and those most closely associated with it.

Individuals in the middle classes were also moved by Grace's heroism. The poet and playwright Walter Savage Landor gave proceeds from two of his plays to the fund.[43] People wrote to Grace offering gifts, expressing their admiration, normally hoping for at least an acknowledgement. Anyone with any pretence of being a poet seems to have found it impossible to resist the urge to pen a few or many lines in honour of the heroine. Some of these poets were clearly smitten. 'For months past I have never had the thought of you out of my mind', wrote John Young from Coupar in Fife. Some correspondents had the excuse of a friend or relative drowned in the *Forfarshire*. One such was Miss Sarah Price of Nottingham. She sent books for Grace, and asked in return for some account of Grace's 'mode of life', clearly already having a fantasy version of it which Grace successfully knocked.[44]

However good or bad the poems, however useful or otherwise the gifts, however sincere the admiration, no one could be in any doubt that Grace was receiving letters from her social superiors. It was they, and not the mass of the population, who were most immediately moved by Grace. As the *Berwick and Kelso Warder* put it after her death,

> It was to
> 'The gentlemen of England
> Who lived at home at ease',
> and the ladies, nursed in the lap of luxury, whose cheeks 'the winds of heaven are not permitted to visit too roughly', and who had never known ought of a scene of tempest and shipwreck beyond what the boards of a theatre or the pages of a romance might have taught them – it was to them that the idea of a girl, under a humane impulse, voluntarily taking a boat's oar to drift through wind and tide amongst those jagged rocks, came home with electrifying effect.[45]

Other events could bring forth the workmen's pennies – at a national level, for example, in 1850 at the death of Sir Robert Peel.[46] In 1838 they might have paid to see Grace represented on stage, but they were not so touched that they felt it appropriate to reward her personally. The impulse to collect money for Grace, and to give her medals, came from the upper and middle classes. It was they who had taken up her cause, promoted it and responded to it. Any intervention from outside, from a Batty, was fiercely resisted. The gifts to Grace, whether of money or goods, were inextricably bound up with the image of her which was being created.

Amidst all the euphoria, there were some local doubt about Grace's achievement and heroism. At a public meeting in Newcastle on 24 September, 'Mr Straker somewhat surprised the meeting by inquiring what proofs they had of any danger which Miss Darling had incurred in going with her father on this occasion; the sea might have moderated from the time that the vessel went ashore'.[47] In late October the Reverend William Darnell reported that 'the risk they ran is considered very trifling indeed – at least this is Smeddle's version of the facts. I have no doubt it was formidable enough'.[48] Smeddle, the agent for the Crewe Trustees, had been responsible for sending out the North Sunderland fishermen on their wasted journey, and had perhaps adopted their view of what had happened. Bamburgh and North Sunderland had an uneasy relationship, one a picture postcard English village, with pretensions to grandeur, the other firmly facing out to sea, its livelihood dependent on it. By the time Howitt paid his visit, North Sunderland's doubts had solidified. 'The most characteristic thing is', he reported, 'that all the common people about, and particularly the sailors and fishermen, deny her all merit.' Howitt ascribed this to envy.[49] The *Berwick and Kelso Warder*, in its *Memoir of Grace Horsley Darling: The Heroine of the Farnes*, published in 1843, denied that it was envy, 'but rather conceive it to be the natural effect of those people's habitual situation', where husbands, fathers and brothers were daily exposed to danger.[50] Another possibility is that the people of North Sunderland were fully alert to the class-specific response to Grace's deed, and to the way the Darlings sheltered under the protective wing of the Duke of Northumberland, and on that account were moved to discount her heroism.

It is tempting to try to link this class-specific nature of Grace's appeal to politics. In the autumn and winter of 1838–9 the Chartists were for the first time putting their demands for democracy stridently and in massive public meetings before the British people. In the summer of 1839 ugly rifts within the social fabric in Newcastle were all too manifest in clashes between Chartists and their supporters and the forces of law and order.[51] The attainment of the six points would have amounted to a revolution in a country where the franchise was still restricted to some 20 per cent of the adult male population. Set against this alarming background, the story of a girl, from humble life, who did what Grace did and then, along with her father, accepted the advice and condescension of the upper and middle classes, might have seemed a beacon of hope and reassurance in a troubled world. Perhaps it was so, but I have seen no evidence that makes the link.

It is easy to depict Grace Darling in the years after her deed as at the mercy of commercial and other forces that ultimately, in some people's view, killed her. She herself, however, was not simply a victim. She played an active part in the creation of the type of heroine that she became.

Grace's conduct from the date of the rescue until her death four years later helped to preserve the mystique that quickly became associated with her name. One of her trustees, the Reverend William Darnell, reported reassuringly to Mrs Sharp. 'I am in hopes', he wrote in October 1838, 'from what I hear of the simplicity of character belonging to Grace Darling that she is not likely to have her head turned by the extraordinary notice she has attracted.' In July 1839, 'Grace Darling and her father paid me a visit a few days ago to make arrangements about their money. She talked of the Bible and box you gave her. Nothing can be more unchanged and consequently more pleasing than they both are.'[52]

Grace continued to live at the lighthouse, carrying out her duties, irritated at those who came to stare at her, and refusing to put herself on display on the mainland. She was kept very busy. As she put it to one correspondent, anxious to know how she spent her time, 'I have seven apartments in the house to keep in a state fit to be inspected every day by Gentlemen, so that my hands are kept very busy that I never think the time long, but often too short'.[53]

And there were of course new duties, amongst them coping with those who wanted her to appear in public for charitable purposes. The most persistent of these was Rebecca Craggs of Hull, secretary of a bazaar in aid of the Port of Hull Society and Sailor's Orphan Institution. The wife of a grocer and tea dealer, belonging to the Methodist New Connexion, Craggs stressed the spiritual objectives of the bazaar, and clearly believed, doubtless rightly, that a brief appearance by Grace would enormously enhance the takings. Failing to get an answer from Grace (who ultimately referred matters to her trustees), Craggs tried an indirect approach, getting a friend of a friend, Ann McGregor, to write to Grace: 'Perhaps you may shrink from the thought of being made so publick, but then think of the motive, the good of fellow creatures …' Grace was not persuaded.[54] The organizer of a Manchester bazaar 'for the relief of thousands of operatives out of employ' more modestly asked simply for autographs to be sold in aid of the funds.[55] Another organization seeking to capitalize on Grace's name and fame was the National Swimming Society, keen to enrol her as an Honorary Member. Grace agreed, and when her support for the society was reported at a meeting 'your name (as the Heroine of many ages) was received with loud, long, and deafening acclamations' – and this two years after the rescue.[56]

If it had seemed at one time likely that she might be left at the Longstone with only her mother and father for company, this proved not to be the case. Her brother, William Brooks, had been appointed as assistant to his father in November 1838, and under the terms of his contract was resident from then onwards. He married in October 1840, and he and his wife Jane, and soon a nephew for Grace, William Swann Darling, born in August 1841, were all on the Longstone. Grace's sister, Mary Ann, was widowed in April 1840 and, with Georgiann, born in July 1840, also came to live at the lighthouse.[57] The lighthouse was becoming overcrowded, so in the summer of 1842 a new house was built on the Longstone for William Brooks and his family.

There are some indications that Grace found the presence of so many family members irksome, and certainly an intrusion on her privacy. Her confidante was her sister Thomasin in Bamburgh. Mary Ann, reported Grace, could not find time to write so Grace had to pass on a request for medicine from the Bamburgh doctor. And then, in an undated letter, Grace sent Thomasin 'a silk Handkerchief which I hope you will hem and give to George with my compliments ... You will excuse me to G in not writing a few lines as I cannot find opportunity as Betsy [her sister Elizabeth Grace] came in and looked on when I was busy writing which I can assure you put me very much about and asked me what G it was, and had to tell her not to mention it but I do not need to tell you that.' This George was not her brother, but an admirer, presumably based in Bamburgh. In another letter, dated 4 February 1840, which Thomasin was asked to destroy, Grace asked her to 'let us know how George is'.[58]

There seems to be no way to identify George or to gauge how serious their relationship was.[59] Grace at some point copied out a verse:

> Love's a gentle gen'rous passion;
> Source of all sublime Delight;
> When with mutual inclination
> Two fond Hearts in one unite.[60]

But even if this was an expression of her feelings rather than her hopes, she seems to have been distinctly wary of marriage. When the Duke of Northumberland asked whether she had any marriage plans, she replied, 'I have not got married yet for they say the man is master and there is much talk about bad masters', erasing this reason for not marrying, and substituting in her draft, 'for I have heard people say there is luck in leisure'. What exactly she meant by this we can only guess. Her father, writing to the Duke, confirmed Grace's crossed out reason for not marrying. She cannot think of getting married, he said, 'for every time she goes on shore she gets a catalogue of this one and that other that has made such a bad job of it'.[61] In old age Thomasin was adamant that marriage was far from Grace's thoughts. 'She had offers of marriage but none that she entertained. She clung to her father and to her name and used to say that any husband of hers should take it.' 'Now about my sister's admirers', she wrote, 'I believe no one knew her mind better than myself. Therefore to speak candidly, I do not believe she had any one that she would taken [sic] as a Husband.'[62] Thomasin, of course, having been asked to destroy the letters referring to George, had a motive for dismissing any stories of romantic attachments. But at least we know from the references to George in the undestroyed letters that there was one of these admirers for whom she must have had some reciprocal feeling.

The one public appearance that Grace did make was in Alnwick, and that inadvertently. A crowd gathered outside Alnwick Castle when she and her father went to visit the Duchess. On coming out of the castle gate she was jostled as she tried to make her way to a relative's house. Thereafter she steadfastly refused to appear in public. When the Mayor of Newcastle wanted to make a public presentation to her, her father replied:

> You can hardly form an idea how disagreeable it is to my Daughter to show herself in publick, I believe very much from being brought up in such a retired situation she has avoided it as much as possible but you cannot believe how much she has been annoyed by it. She has consulted her friends and they all advised to keep as private as possible. She has already refused to go to the Trinity, to Edinburgh and to Hull to receive presents and she thinks with me that she could not go to Newcastle without giving offence to a great many friends who have been interested about her.[63]

She knew, almost instinctively, how she should present herself. When Howitt arrived, unannounced, Grace 'was not visible', but after he had been vetted by her father, 'the old man ... went up to her room, and soon came down with a smile, saying she would be with us soon'. Howitt and William Darling then went up to inspect the lighthouse and its machinery. When they came down they 'found Grace sitting at her sewing, very neatly, but very simply dressed, in a plain sort of a striped printed gown, with her watch-seal just seen at her side, and her hair neatly braided'. It was a carefully composed picture: nothing more appropriately feminine than sewing, the presentation of herself 'neat', and the just visible watch-seal, the Duke of Northumberland's gift, which according to report she always wore when visitors came. Grace then 'rose very modestly; and with a pleasant smile, said, "How do you do, sir?"' She was modest, and as the 'sir' acknowledges, she accepted her social position. Grace knew what was expected of her, knew what a man like Howitt wanted to see, and, on this occasion at least, conformed to it. Meanwhile Howitt was subjecting her to the male gaze, taking in her figure, her face, her character, finding 'as perfect a realization of a Jeannie Deans in an English form, as it is possible for a woman to be'.[64]

There are hints that Grace was not always so entirely submissive when confronted by visitors. John Roberts reported, from someone who knew her both before and after 1838, that after 1838 there was 'a change in her bearing ... She could be sarcastic at times, when she detailed the absurd questions put to her ... She was, he believed, honestly astonished at the noise her achievement had made'.[65]

At the same time Grace wanted to connect in some way with those who admired her. We have seen that she regarded donors to her fund as 'friends' and wanted to know the names of all of them. She wrote carefully crafted letters of thanks to all her correspondents, and not infrequently sent them in return a handkerchief or a lock of her hair. The wreck of the *Forfarshire* gave rise immediately to a rush for mementoes. Bits of the wreck itself were highly valued, the artist Henry Parker being keen to lay his hands on some of them.[66] But even more valuable was anything connected to Grace herself. The dress she wore during the rescue seems to have been cut up and distributed among the visiting artists: David Dunbar testified in 1855 that he had been given a portion of it, together with a lock of hair; another piece of it is framed in the Grace Darling Museum and inscribed 'Presented by J. W. Carmichael [the marine artist] to late James Hardy, carver and gilder, Grainger St, and by him to S. H. Farrer of Gosforth'. Henry Parker was given the cape Grace wore during the rescue and a plaid.[67] Can we begin to imagine what it must have been like for Grace to cut up and distribute her clothing in this way? She was, even if not at a conscious level, contributing to the assembling of 'relics', and to the emergence of Grace Darling as a modern saint. Locks of hair or autographs were also valued. Robert Smeddle, the agent at Bamburgh Castle, received many requests for autographs that he passed on to Grace. She found this burdensome. When in March 1839 a printer from Newcastle requested an autograph, a draft reply, crossed out, reads 'you requesting my autograph for M. L. which things I am almost tired of wrighting'.[68] A clerical acquaintance and admirer, the Reverend M. M. Humble from Chesterfield, wrote with some suitably uplifting advice, and asked her in reply to sign 'your name a few times' so that he could cut out the signatures and distribute them to friends. A sample of her handwriting sent to Mr and Mrs Sinclair of Berwick, Sinclair being the agent for Lloyd's, was described after Grace's death as this 'now precious relic'.[69]

Grace's hair, however, was the most precious of all relics. People wrote asking for it, men as much as, if not more than, women. J. G. Grant, the author and poet whose poem on Grace was published in the *Sunderland Herald*, asked for and got a small lock of her hair. The Reverend Humphrey Brown, from Kirkheaton, near Copleston, Newcastle, enclosed a few lines as a New Year's gift in 1841, and asked in return for 'a small piece of your beautiful hair (or anything else which you think proper) … as a most particular favor, and which would ever be held dear, to *sweet remembrance*'.[70] Sometimes Grace would offer her hair without being asked for it. Some ladies from Sneinton, near Nottingham, received in return for their gifts 'a little of my hair and pockett hankerchief'. Catherine Sinclair of Edinburgh, the leader of the Ladies of that town, received when all the money had been raised and accounted for, 'a small lock of my hair as a small memorandum'.[71] The newspapers had long previously reported that Grace had become almost bald in an attempt to satisfy the demand for locks. Grace's brother reported from Newcastle that there was a variety of samples of it in the barbershop he frequented.[72]

Gifts of hair were common in the age of Romanticism. A lock from a famous head, Byron, Nelson or the Duke of Wellington, was precious, and remains so – some of the Duke of Wellington's hair has recently been sold for £1,380.[73] At a different level, before the days of photographs and of easily-carried passport-sized photographs, hair, enclosed in a locket, was perhaps the easiest way of bringing to remembrance someone from whom you were parted. Hair was normally exchanged between family members or lovers. Grace, with her view that subscribers to her fund were friends, seems to have enlarged the circle of those who might be regarded as proper recipients of hair. She kept a memorandum of those to whom she had sent hair or other gifts, mostly silk handkerchiefs. Twenty-three people are recorded as having received hair in 1839, the artists or their wives prominent among the recipients.[74] These gifts connected her in a way she seems to have valued with those who were moved by her deed. By sending locks or handkerchiefs, and by providing samples of her handwriting, Grace played a role in establishing her image as a heroine: people who received some token from her could feel that they knew her.

Bibles, prayer books and other religious publications featured large among the gifts sent to Grace. They were often accompanied by earnest enquiries about her spiritual state during and after the rescue. Grace replied to these with a mixture of common sense and affirmation of her faith. 'I believe I had very little thought of any thing but to exert myself to the utmost', she wrote to one correspondent, 'my spirit was worked up by the sight of such a dreadfull affair that I can imagine I still see the sea flying over the vessel.' 'Although I am but a very weak Christian,' she replied to another, 'yet I hope to be found in that fold whose Sheapherd is Jesus Christ our Lord & Saviour ... I am at a loss to explain my self better but my parents learned me to read & wright the Church of England Catechism and the General Assemblies Short Catechism which I admire as a butiful little book.'[75]

Grace's simple faith was to be tried and tested over the next four years, most profoundly in her response to her illness and approaching death. Out of it emerged someone who had forged herself and could be represented as a Christian heroine. There was a script for a Christian death in the early nineteenth century, and Grace seems to have known it almost by instinct.

Pat Jalland has summarized the Victorian Evangelical version of a good death. 'Death ideally should take place at home, with the dying person making explicit farewells to each family member. There should be time, and physical and mental capacity, for the completion of temporal and spiritual business ... The dying person should be conscious and lucid until the end, resigned to God's will, able to beg forgiveness for past sins and to prove his or her worthiness for salvation. Pain and suffering should be borne with fortitude, and even welcomed as a final test of fitness for heaven and willingness to pay for past sins.'[76] This kind of death was impossible in the event of sudden illness or of a disease like cholera. But there was one illness, tuberculosis, that was almost tailor-made for a good death, and it was the cause of about one-third of all deaths. And it was tuberculosis that killed Grace Darling.[77]

There is no evidence that Grace's health was anything other than good until the spring of 1842. In March she and her sister Thomasin paid a visit to their brother William, recently installed as the first keeper of the Coquet Light. They got soaked on their journey back to Alnwick, and that seems to have brought on a cough that never cleared up. Not that Grace immediately became an invalid. Back on the Longstone, building the house for William Brooks was about to commence. In the meantime he and his young family were living in the main light, which kept Grace very busy, 'in a throng' as she put it.[78] On 20 June she wrote to Thomasin, sorry that she had heard that she was poorly, and recounting how 'I have never been quite free from cold since I was on shore but this last three weeks I had been worse. I think it has been influenza but blessed be God I am a good deal better ...'[79] She then wrote a long and chatty letter. But by August the seriousness of her illness could not be disguised. A friend of the family, George Shield, an artist from Wooler, invited Grace and Thomasin, now her companion and nurse, to visit, hoping that 'the pure air of our hills' would help. In September she moved to Alnwick to stay with her cousins the Macfarlanes in Narrowgate, its name alone indicating that sun and air were not its chief attractions. The Duke and Duchess of Northumberland arranged for a change of domicile in Alnwick and a new doctor, Dr Barnfather, but Grace's health declined, and most who knew her began to realize that she would die. In October she moved back to Bamburgh to the house where her uncle Marsden lived. There she prepared for death.

George Shield was her chief spiritual guide. On 16 October, four days before she died, he wrote that 'I trust in God that although your health has not been restored, that your affliction has not been without profit to your Soul ... Yes, My Dear Grace, as I said to you before strive continually during your illness to engage your mind on Heavenly subjects.' Remember, he urged, that 'the enemy of Mankind has a thousand ways to ensnare our souls and never is he more busy than when we are laid on a bed of sickness'.[80] The devil must be resisted. Grace seems to have done so. She wasn't at home on the Longstone as the good death demanded, but she was in a reasonable substitute in Bamburgh. Not all her family could be with her, but some were: her father, probably her mother, her sister Thomasin, and her elder brother William. A short time before her death, she distributed some of her gifts and medals to her attendant family. At a quarter past eight on 20 October, she asked to be raised from the pillow. Her father lifted her up and she died in his arms. The next morning he wrote to his absent children, telling them of Grace's death, and 'confident that she has obtained favour with God through her dear Saviour, I hope you will endeavour to submit to the divine will with Christian resignation'.[81]

In the obituaries of clergymen that had a dominant place in Christian magazines, the death-bed scene was too often implausibly close to the ideal. The reality was often different. We cannot be sure that Grace's death was as the family chose to remember it, but, exposed as she was to the writings of the Religious Tract Society and to the advice of men like George Shield, it is not unlikely that she fashioned her behaviour to accord with the many good deaths she had read about. She knew what was expected of her, and it was probably in tune with her own sense of how she should die. Certainly the reports of her death must have reinforced the sense that she was someone special. According to the *Berwick and Kelso Warder Memoir*, 'For some time previous to her death, she was perfectly aware that her latter end was approaching, but this gave her no uneasiness. She had been nurtured in the fear and love of God, and dependent on the merits of her Redeemer, and her hope of mercy increased as her bodily strength diminished. She was never heard to utter a complaint during her illness, but exhibited the utmost Christian resignation throughout', finally resigning 'her spirit into the hands of Him who gave it, without a murmur'.[82] In death, as in her life after her deed, she had behaved in a way that reinforced the conviction that she was a heroine. The irony was that she herself denied the heroism.

Like her death, Grace's funeral on 24 October was entirely in accord with what might be expected of the obsequies for a heroine. Bamburgh was 'crowded with strangers, both rich and poor, many of whom had come a long way'. When the coffin was carried to the grave, 'An immense concourse of people of all grades in society followed, many of whom were observed to be bathed in tears. The scene, altogether, was deeply impressive and affecting'. The coffin was carried by four young men of Bamburgh, and followed by four pall bearers, William Barnfather, her doctor in Alnwick, and a representative of the castle, Robert Smeddle, representing Bamburgh Castle and the Crewe Trustees, the Reverend M. Taylor of North Sunderland, and Dr Fender, the Bamburgh doctor. Mr Evans, Customs officer in Bamburgh was also there. The institutions and powers that Grace had been brought into contact with through her heroism were there to pay their respects at her funeral. Family members were there too, though some of her brothers were prevented by bad weather from leaving the Longstone. And, final touch, there was said to be 'a young man from Durham, who wore the mourning emblem of intimate friends of the family'.[83] Grace, it seems, had an admirer, admitted to the family confidence. Perhaps he was the George of her correspondence.

5

A Place in History

Grace's early death was of critical importance in the way she came to be remembered. Had she lived longer it is likely that memory of her deed would have faded. Her death, say in the 1870s or 1880s, would have been noted, her deed recalled, but it is doubtful if the news of it would have set in motion the celebrity that she came to enjoy in the late nineteenth century. Dying young, a maiden, her image could be preserved in the way it had been created in the years between her deed and her death. As one later writer put it, 'She died in that beautiful period of her life when all seems hallowed, so that the heart turns to her in her loveliness, beauty, innocence, and purity, and venerates her as a gem of virtue and a true heroine'.[1]

The period of thirty or more years after her death was nevertheless in some ways an interlude between the fame that came to Grace during her lifetime and a more prolonged period of celebrity after 1875. Not that she was forgotten. Foundations were laid on which a later superstructure of fame could be built. She secured a place in the history of Northumbria, in memorials in Bamburgh and the Farne Isles, and in a famous painting at the Trevelyan family home at Wallington; and, at national level, she featured prominently in collective biographies celebrating the role of women in history.

Even in her lifetime Northumbria laid claim to Grace. 'I feel proud indeed of my *county woman*', wrote Anne Potts to her nephew at Rugby school, cutting across class in a display of female solidarity and local pride, and promising to send details of the deed from the local press.[2] The person who did most to place Grace within the history of Northumbria (the ancient title was so much more evocative than a mere Northumberland) was Jerold Vernon. Grace, we are told, taught by her father, became 'passionately fond of the many legends and traditionary ballads connected with the coast'. A key part of the action of his novel, *Grace Darling, The Maid of the Isles*, takes place on Lindisfarne, and friendships established there were confirmed the next day with visits to Warkworth and Dunstanburgh. It would be difficult to imagine any three places more deeply resonating with history and legend: Lindisfarne, where Christianity took root in England; Warkworth, described by William Howitt as 'enchanted ground', the setting for one of Bishop Percy's most famous ballads, and given 'an immortal interest' by Shakespeare in *Henry IV, Part One*; and Dunstanburgh,

another castle with a ballad attached to it. At Dunstanburgh Grace recites to
the college-educated menfolk the whole of John Service's 'Wandering Knight of
Dunstanbrough Castle', a woeful ballad about a returning crusader who fails a test
to win the hand and heart of an incarcerated maiden.[3] Later writers, revisiting
this fiction, found it so unlikely or unseemly that Grace should do the narrating
that they made her an attentive listener to Reginald St Clair.[4] Either way, Grace
was made to seem knowledgeable about and entranced by Northumbria's past.
By her deed and by her death, she established a link to these heroes and heroines
of Northumbria's 'olden times'.

Grace's death prompted two ideas for permanent memorials to her and
her deed. She herself had been buried beside her brother in a simple grave in
Bamburgh churchyard. At a little distance from it, at the west end of the graveyard,
there was a proposal to erect a monument which could be seen by passing sailors.
On 17 November 1842 Robert Smeddle reported that he had been entrusted with
£10 for this purpose by Catherine Sharp, who had been so ready to offer advice
and gifts in 1838. Sharp herself was now near the end of her life – she died in
1843 – and may have had a sense of family obligation to record and reward good
conduct in Bamburgh. In 1839 she, as the 'sole survivor of the name', had had a
memorial monument erected in Bamburgh church recording the distinguished
achievements of the Sharp family over the generations, and now it must have
seemed appropriate to further remember the thoroughly meritorious Grace
Darling. Her £10 must have been supplemented from other sources, perhaps
mainly the widow of the Reverend Andrew Bowlton.[5] The canopied tomb,
which was erected in 1844, was the work of the architect Anthony Salvin, and
the sculptor C. Raymond Smith, both London-based. Salvin had a distinguished
career ahead of him: he was, for example, entrusted with the £320,000 rebuilding
of Alnwick Castle between 1852 and 1866.[6] The monument resembled a canopied
tomb of the thirteenth century, with Grace lying recumbent, her oar beside her,
in place of the sword of a medieval knight. Portland stone was used for the figure,
an unfortunate choice as it soon began to crumble when exposed to the climate
of the north east.

The choice of a thirteenth-century design for the canopy was partly a
reflection of the popularity of Gothic architecture, but it also represented a
wish to connect Grace to a longer history of the nation and of the north east in
particular. This was even more the case with the second proposal for a memorial
to Grace. There were few more important figures in the history of the north east
than St Cuthbert. Durham Cathedral is built above the spot where the monks
brought his coffin after his death. In his lifetime he had left Lindisfarne or Holy
Island for the greater solitude of the Inner Farne and there built himself a cell. It
had been in a ruinous state for one thousand years. Might it now be restored and
incorporate within it a memorial to Grace? The idea was mooted immediately

after her death by a correspondent in the *Berwick and Kelso Warder*, and by the Reverend M. Dickenson of Heighington, near Durham. In the short term nothing came of the idea. It was in some ways on odd suggestion. St Cuthbert had been notoriously suspicious of women, refusing to allow them into his church. Archdeacon Thorp, one of Grace's trustees, and the owner of the inner Farne Isles, backed the idea, however, and interested the great and good in it. The Queen sent £20 and her mother, the Duchess of Kent, £10. The Bishop of Durham gave 10 guineas, Thorp himself £10.[7] In 1848 the restoration was complete, incorporating a plain stone monument inscribed to the memory of Grace and including some lines from the poem on Grace which, as we shall see, Wordsworth had written in the spring of 1843.

By the end of the 1840s there were therefore two permanent memorials to Grace in Northumbria. Both went out of their way to connect her to the history of Northumbria, and in particular to the middle ages: if the Bamburgh tomb took viewers back to the thirteenth century, the connection with St Cuthbert linked her to the early history of Northumbria and the laying of the foundations of Christianity. After recounting a miracle associated with St Cuthbert, the *Berwick and Kelso Warder* described Grace's deed as 'a miracle indeed, performed under the mighty guidance of Him whom the winds and storms obey, and let it be held in everlasting remembrance'.[8] Grace, it seemed, might herself become a saint, the memorials places of pilgrimage.

There were other suggestions for memorials to Grace. 'W. H.', writing from London in October 1842, hoped that 'the people of Scotland' might erect a suitable monument, though with an overt message: 'nothing can so tend to purify and elevate the minds of the poorer classes', he wrote, 'as to find one of themselves thus rewarded and distinguished without reference to station in society'.[9] How, if at all, 'the people of Scotland' responded to this is uncertain. But there was at least one memorial outside Northumberland – and a long way from it. Outside St Thomas's parish church in Exeter, a stone was erected in 1845 to commemorate Grace's 'unparalleled achievement' – and restored in 1869 and again in 1911.[10]

Some ten years later, Grace became further embedded in Northumbria's history. Wallington, near Morpeth, is the Trevelyan family home. Like an even more famous Northumbrian family, the Dukes of Northumberland, the Trevelyans had come from the south. Originating in Cornwall, they moved in the sixteenth century to Nettlecombe in Somerset, and were given a baronetcy at the Restoration. Marriage in the eighteenth century to the sister of Sir Walter Blackett, Newcastle's richest man, who had no children, had led to the Trevelyans inheriting Wallington and 20,000 acres. Originally a border castle, Wallington had been rebuilt as a shooting-box in 1688, then extensively remodelled in the 1730s. Each generation of Trevelyans had to choose whether to centre themselves on Nettlecombe or Wallington.[11]

Walter Calverley Trevelyan, the eldest son and heir to the baronetcy, was in Cambridge in 1833 for the third meeting of the British Association for the Advancement of Science. Aged thirty-six, and a scientist of some distinction, he had come to exhibit fossilized saurian faeces. A keen phrenologist, he held distinctly unorthodox opinions for someone of his wealth and position: he was opposed to capital punishment, favoured state education for all children, and would not touch alcohol or tobacco – he disposed of the contents of the Nettlecombe cellar in the lake. Less unusually, he was active in schemes for improved sanitation and dwellings for the poor. Also attending the Cambridge meeting were the Reverend George Jermyn and his eldest daughter, Pauline, then aged seventeen, but already well known in scientific, artistic and literary circles. Drawn together by a common interest in natural history, Trevelyan and Pauline married in 1835. They spent the next decade travelling in Europe from an Edinburgh base. Then, in 1846, on the death of his father, Walter succeeded to the title, and by the beginning of the 1850s the Trevelyans' life had became focused on Wallington.[12]

Wallington had a central courtyard, damp and cold, and in 1852 the Trevelyans decided to cover it, entrusting the work to the famous Newcastle architect, John Dobson. Once roofed, the internal decoration became the issue. Pauline, who had met John Ruskin in 1847, had become a great admirer – 'my Master' she called him in the half-ironic style she favoured. She was also an early champion of the Pre-Raphaelites. In 1853 Ruskin, his wife Effie, and John and William Millais were guests at Wallington, a visit which was on the surface a great success, but which presaged the break-up of the Ruskin marriage, and Effie's subsequent marriage to John Millais. Pauline remained loyal to Ruskin, and when Wallington became inhabitable again in January 1855 after the alterations, he was inevitably consulted about the design for the interior of what came to be called the Central Saloon. The key role in the decoration had been given to William Bell Scott.[13]

William Bell Scott was a second-ranking Pre-Raphaelite, a close friend of the Rossettis. Brought up in Edinburgh, he became an engraver, wrote poetry, and exhibited at the Royal Scottish Academy. In 1837 he moved to London where he continued to illustrate, paint and write without securing a major reputation. By 1843 he was back north again to head the School of Design in Newcastle, a position he held for twenty years. He was, recalled a Newcastle contemporary, 'a man of great original ability and inspiring genius', who became 'a distinct force in the town at a time when strong influence in literature and art was greatly needed'. While establishing a reputation for himself in the provinces, Scott also had some success at national level, getting his poetry published and exhibiting at the Royal Academy and the British Institution.

Scott's *Memoir* (1850) of his elder brother, David Scott, was reviewed by Pauline Trevelyan, but it was not until 1854 that he had any direct contact with the Trevelyans. In 1855 he made his first visit to Wallington.[14] Scott was immediately taken with Pauline, 'my never-to-be-forgotten good angel', as he later described her, and she, in a teasing way, encouraged him and opened doors for him. That they were lovers, as was once suggested, seems highly unlikely, but there was enough in the relationship for Scott's friend, Dante Gabriel Rossetti, to write a limerick about it:

> There once was a Lady Trevillian
> Whose charms were as one in a million.
> Her husband drank tea
> And talked lectures at she,
> But she had no eyes but for William.[15]

Pauline arranged for Scott to meet Ruskin. Although Ruskin reported that 'I liked Scott very much', Scott himself was more ambivalent, and, on his own account, made the mistake of making fun of Turner's accent. He was also highly critical of Ruskin's method of teaching at the Working Men's College.[16]

After another visit to Wallington in March 1856, Scott received a commission from the Trevelyans to 'illuminate the history and worthies of Northumbria' for the Central Saloon at Wallington.[17] Scott, at Pauline's prompting, sought advice from Ruskin, but the latter's reply did little to endear him to Scott. He pleaded fatigue, and thus unable to 'think over the plan you send', offered a few comments on interior decoration, and concluded, 'So get on that I may have plenty to find fault with, for that, I believe, is all I can do. Help you I can't.' Dante Gabriel Rossetti was much more encouraging, praising the paintings as they were completed.[18] The original aim was to have heroic and historic scenes alternating, the heroic scenes being representative of one of the beatitudes. The first four paintings, taking up one wall, proceeded no further in Northumbrian history than the Venerable Bede: the Romans building their wall are succeeded by King Edfrid and Bishop Trumwine persuading St Cuthbert to be made bishop; then the Danes are seen descending on the coast, and Bede finishes his works and his life at Jarrow. The fifth painting is an historic scene, depicting border skirmishes in the twelfth century, and in the sixth Bernard Gilpin in 1570 prevents two armed gangs from attacking each other in Rothbury church.[19] What was to follow to represent the period since 1570?

In May 1859 Scott reported to Pauline that 'Sir Walter spoke seriously of throwing Grace Darling out of the series. If so who is to be in her place, and how are the four godly characters with their beatitudes, to balance the four epochs with their mottoes?' In an undated letter, presumably subsequent to this, and perhaps after some negotiations, Scott wrote to Sir Walter, 'I think you quite agreed on the propriety of Grace Darling being the fourth beatitude "Blessed are the merciful", so necessary to the scheme of the hall. I propose doing it next ...' Sir Walter had clearly had doubts about including Grace, but they were overcome.[20] Scott (and Pauline Trevelyan) had by this time formed a friendship with a near-neighbour of the Trevelyans, the young and precociously talented Algernon Swinburne. Scott and Swinburne, together with Pauline's brother, a naval commander, set off to the Farne Isles to see the scene of Grace's deed. Scott was seasick, Swinburne in his element, and much taken with William Darling.[21]

The Grace Darling painting was the work of 1860. In May William Rossetti acknowledged that 'I have always been curious to see what you make of "Grace Darling", and trust it will be in my power, as a conscientious and eminent critic, to pat your breakers on the head'.[22] Scott himself seemed in no doubt about his 'breakers': it is 'the best sea-storm ever painted', he told Sir Walter.[23] In August Pauline wrote to Scott, asking 'Is Grace Darling finished? Is she fearfully and wonderfully ugly?'[24] Understandably bemused by this, Scott thanked her for her letter 'although you say such contrary things in it – but indeed I understand them as they say dreams are to be construed – by the rule of contraries, so I dare say you very properly expect Grace Darling or rather the picture to be lovely beyond description … However that may be, I myself privately believe that a storm was never so well painted before, nor the earnest simplicity of the sailor character so well rendered.' The storm, he thought, was so much better than those of 'Turner and other cockneys', who 'put boats by the half dozen all toppling over in various directions for the sake of composition where no boat could live for a minute'.[25] This was a bold, if tactless, claim, for Pauline's 'Master', Ruskin, was the prime advocate of Turner's virtues. Pauline, knowing of Scott's seasickness, wickedly put him in his place, acknowledging the letter 'in which you go in as a great marine painter, which, no doubt, you ought to be considering your great love of the sea and your passion for voyaging upon it, so that you are a sort of a fat peaceable sea-king. Not like that "Cockney Turner", who used to go for a voyage whenever he could, and had himself lashed to the mast to watch storms when they came.' Shaken by this, and anxious how she would judge his sea painting, Scott pulled back: 'Of course when I praise my pictures I mean to be jocular …'[26] We may doubt it.

In Scott's painting, Grace's features are scarcely visible, so it is impossible to determine her ugliness or otherwise. In the manner of Carmichael, Grace and her father are tiny figures in the coble surrounded by the storm of which Scott was so proud. The human figures to whom the eye is drawn are the survivors hanging on to bits of the breaking-up *Forfarshire*, prominent among whom is the one woman with her two dead children. Scott had modelled figures in the historic scenes on his friends and patrons. When the Danes descend on Northumberland, for example, Pauline (and her dog) are clearly visible. The model for the woman in the Grace Darling picture was the new and lasting love of Scott's life, Alice Boyd, whom he had met in 1859.

Having seen the painting, Pauline Trevelyan measured out praise and criticism in equal measure. 'I like Grace Darling and it isn't nearly so ugly as I expected. – I think it is one of the best of the lot in point of composition & I think both the sea & the sky are capital.' But she was unhappy about the colour of the light falling on the faces of the survivors: 'I'll never believe these people looked that colour, never'. Fortunately 'Sir Walter likes the picture greatly better now he sees it up'.[27]

At Wallington, now a National Trust property, parents during an autumn half-term take their school-age children round the Central Saloon. It is with some sense of relief that they reach Grace Darling: the preceding pictures have required much explanation or have been passed over in silence. 'Ah, Grace Darling, now you know about her', they say, and the children with more or less enthusiasm acknowledge that they do: at last there is a scene from Northumbrian history to which they can relate. It is little surprise that the Trust's guide to Wallington features Grace Darling on its cover. The Romans building their wall, and the last painting, 'In the nineteenth century the Northumbrians show the world what can be done with iron and steel', have received most attention from art historians, but it is the Grace Darling picture, so nearly excluded from the series by Sir Walter, which most attracts the public.

The Grace Darling picture was exhibited at the Literary Society in Newcastle in October 1860, and, reported Scott, 'seems to be giving pleasure'.[28] But he had more ambitious plans for it. His portrait of Una at the Royal Academy summer exhibition of 1860 had been much criticized. Scott now hoped to rebuild his reputation by exhibiting Grace Darling at the short-lived Hogarth Club – 'it would be of great service to my character as an artist'.[29] The advice he received was that he needed to show all eight of the Wallington pictures, not just one, and that Ernest Gambart, a major entrepreneur in the art world, might take it on as a speculation. Gambart agreed, and on 29 June 1861 the exhibition opened in the French Gallery in Pall Mall. Scott, nervous on the private opening day, 'did not act the showman so far as to address any who did not seem to wish to speak to me'. He was, however, in contact with Tom Taylor of *The Times*, who seemed very positive, and kept a close eye on any notices of the exhibition.[30] In August Scott reported to Pauline that 'as a whole, I consider the exhibition a great success to myself. My Newcastle "friends" who treated the pictures as all very well in a provincial way, feel now I may pass them by without caring for their opinion'.[31] But if Newcastle now took Scott's paintings seriously, there was little sign that the metropolis was much moved. Despite pressure from Pauline Trevelyan, *The Times* never carried Taylor's piece, and Gambart proved remarkably elusive about attendance figures. The exhibition had come at the tail end of the Season and, as Scott acknowledged in his *Autobiographical Notes*, 'did little good'. On 8 September 1861 the pictures arrived back at Wallington.[32]

In August 1863, when Ruskin was persuaded to visit Wallington, Scott was

summoned from Newcastle. A space had been left for Ruskin to paint some
flowers. This he did, while advising attendant ladies on painting and thoroughly
irritating Scott – he was 'very good and sweet and kind to everybody, myself
included ...; yet he is a little nauseous', he reported to Alice Boyd.[33] After the
Wallington visit, Ruskin described Scott to his father as 'a very good and clever
man, and one of the honestest and best scions and helpers of the best part of
the Pre-Raphaelite School. He has painted for Lady Trevelyan a very interesting
series of historical pictures ...'[34] This perhaps placed Scott in the second rank,
but it was not damning. But Ruskin in fact had reservations about the paintings.
He considered the pictures, Lady Pauline told Scott, to be 'in the highest sense
of the word great works', and did not 'believe that we could have got them so
well done, take them all by all, by any other living man'. So far so good, but the
sting, and not only the Ruskinian sting, lay in the tail: although there were 'some
wonderfully skilful dexterous things', Ruskin 'does not *enjoy* them, because the
colour is not pleasant, and one colour is left quite uninfluenced by another,
and the unnecessary bits of ugliness and vulgarity annoy him as cruelly as they
annoy me (perhaps worse, though I doubt it)'.[35] Pauline and her Master were in
agreement: at the highest level the pictures were flawed.

'Man has not achieved anything more beautiful than this', Sir George Otto
Trevelyan told Steven Runciman when first showing him the Central Saloon
at Wallington.[36] It is a remarkable room, as fascinating for its insight into what
the nineteenth century thought historically important as it is as a masterpiece
of Pre-Raphaelite art. And yet the man who contributed most to the decoration
is remembered chiefly for Swinburne's vituperative response to his posthumous
Autobiographical Notes. 'As for that old miscreant "Scotus"', wrote Swinburne,
'you have already seen by this time what justice I have done upon him. [in the
Fortnightly Review in December 1892] Lying, backbiting, drivelling, imbecile,
doting, malignant, mangy old son of a bitch!'[37] Ruskin, more coldly, and in public
print, in the wake of a hostile review by Scott, had closed the door on him in 1875,
describing him as 'one of a rather numerous class of artists of whose works I have
never taken any public notice', and 'also one of the more limited and peculiarly
unfortunate class of artists who suppose themselves to have great native genius'.
After leaving Wallington in 1863, Ruskin claimed, he had 'never since sought Mr
Scott's acquaintance further (though, to my regret, he was once photographed in
the same place with Mr Rossetti and me)'.[38] Scott failed to make any major impact
as artist or poet, but he was a more significant figure than these dismissals might
suggest. Ruskin's imprimatur was vital for success in the mid-Victorian art world,
but Scott signally failed to achieve it. Isolated in Newcastle, he was in a poor
position to capitalize on his achievements. Nevertheless, the Wallington murals
were an important contribution to the Pre-Raphaelite output, and continue to
attract attention – and the one that attracts most is Grace Darling's rescue of the

survivors of the *Forfarshire*. Moreover, Grace Darling's prominence at Wallington, one of the great houses of the north east, secures her a central position in the history of Northumbria, and, given the Saloon's national reputation, in that of the nation as a whole.

Grace Darling was a national as well as a Northumbrian heroine. There is no better indication of this than the poem written soon after her death by the man soon to be Poet Laureate, William Wordsworth. The Wordsworth family had been deeply touched by loss of life at sea. In 1805 the *Abergavenny*, captained by John Wordsworth, William's younger brother, had been wrecked on the Shambles off Weymouth due to pilot error. Two hundred and sixty people, including the captain, had died. Wordsworth, his family and friends, all found it hard to come to terms with what seemed God's heartlessness. In his *Elegiac Stanzas Suggested by a Picture of Peele Castle, in a Storm, Painted by Sir George Beaumont* (1806), Wordsworth reached some kind of acceptance, acknowledging the need for fortitude in face of the disasters that punctuate life:

> But welcome fortitude and patient cheer,
> And frequent sights of what is to be borne!
> Such sights, or worse, as are before me here.–
> Not without hope we suffer and we mourn.

Wordsworth also wrote *Elegiac Verses in Memory of My Brother John Wordsworth*. These were not published until 1842. The preparation of them for publication in that year of Grace's death, must have reminded him of all the circumstances of John's death in 1805, and of the grief that accompanied it.[39] He would have been particularly sensitive to the accounts he read in the storm-tossed winter of 1842-3 of English ships being wrecked on the coast of France. The French, it was reported, were distinctly slow to come to the rescue of the shipwrecked. Wordsworth, as he put it, 'was impelled' by this to write his poem on Grace, 'and thought it well to present a contrast to the cruelty with which the sufferers were treated upon the French coast'.[40] There was, if not explicitly in the poem itself, a patriotic agenda.

Wordsworth wrote *Grace Darling* at the end of February or in early March 1843. He took the poem to Carlisle and had it privately printed, and then sent copies to friends and correspondents, particularly female ones, as the verses 'are an attempt to do honour to one of your sex'.[41] While these printed copies of the poem were being sent all over the country and to the United States, the Poet Laureate, Robert Southey, died on 21 March, and Wordsworth, after some initial hesitation, on 4 April agreed to be his successor. Two days later the *Kentish Observer*, in a notable scoop, published the poem. The editor, who had had a copy for nearly a month, congratulated himself that 'with a proper respect for the gifted writer's wish to gratify, in the first instance, his personal friends with a perusal of the verses, we abstained from laying [it] before that larger, and more comprehensive circle of friends, the PUBLIC'. But, he argued, Wordsworth had after all had the poem printed, rumours were circulating about it, and the poet had been offered the Laureateship. Now was the time for the public to have a chance to read the poem. Within two days five London papers had also published it, bringing it, one authority estimates, to a potential readership of at least 22,500.[42] Wordsworth, who acknowledged that 'it was on a subject which interested the whole nation' and seemed 'to have given general pleasure', was happy for it to be included in his *Poems 1845*.[43]

Wordsworth's poem starts with the fame Grace Darling has achieved. 'Public way and crowded street resound with ballad strains'. Her fame crosses class and reaches out across the whole country:

> A single Act endears to high and low
> Through the whole land – to Manhood, moved in spite
> Of the world's freezing cares – to generous Youth –
> To Infancy, that lisps her praise – to Age
> Whose eye reflects it, glistening through a tear
> Of tremulous admiration. Such true fame
> Awaits her *now*;

Angels in heaven will continue to celebrate Grace's 'high-souled virtues' long after they have passed from the thoughts of 'forgetful earth'. They will sing of how 'A Maiden gentle' was 'at duty's call' as 'Firm and unflinching' as the Longstone Lighthouse itself or even as the rock that centuries before had 'guarded holy Cuthbert's cell'.

Wordsworth goes on to describe the rescue through to its successful conclusion, and ends with the hope that 'some immortal Voice' will 'carry to the clouds and to the stars' praise of 'the Maiden', 'Pious and pure, modest and yet so brave, Though young so wise, though meek so resolute'. Taking further that 'fortitude and patient cheer' with which he had faced up to his brother's death, Wordsworth now sees the storm that wrecked the *Forfarshire* as an act of Providence. It was, he wrote,

> As if the tumult, by the Almighty's will
> Were, in the conscious sea, roused and prolonged
> That woman's fortitude – so tried, so proved –
> May brighten more and more!

The sea, 'conscious', both creates the conditions for, and witnesses, the acts which the storm 'called forth From the pure depths of [Grace's] humanity'. God and nature have a purpose, even when they seem most capricious: in this instance to bear witness to 'woman's fortitude'.[44]

This theme of 'woman's fortitude' was also prominent in the twenty-six page *Memoir of Grace Horsley Darling, The Heroine of the Farnes*, published by the *Berwick and Kelso Warder* in 1843. The *Warder*, as we have seen, in the person of David Kennedy, played a prominent part in the early reports of the deed. Grace's death gave it the opportunity to reflect on her heroism. It may be doubted, it wrote, whether any nation had so many examples of female 'fortitude and heroism' as our own, and they 'are equally characteristic of the daughters of the humblest as of the most wealthy and dignified classes of society in Great Britain'. For the *Warder*, straddling the border, Grace was no mere English heroine, but belonged to Great Britain. Moreover, examining the record of other national heroines who might rival Grace, Queen Elizabeth, Strafford's daughter, Rachel, Lady Russell, the Countess of Nithsdale, Lady Grisell Baillie, the *Warder* concluded that none was 'calculated to take a higher place in the estimation of mankind' than Grace. None of them, moreover, could by any stretch of the imagination be said to come, as Grace did, from the 'humblest classes'. She was being compared with aristocratic women who acted bravely to protect their menfolk. Grace alone had no motive or impulse for her act other than the wish to relieve suffering. Her deed was unsullied by any political or even patriotic motive. Her 'feeling of pity' was universal in its scope.

The *Warder*'s claim that Grace's deed had secured the 'perpetuity [of her name] through future ages, alongside of those of the most renowned of her sex', was, in the boldness of its assertions, nothing short of extraordinary.[45] Here was a local paper proclaiming that one hour of heroism by the daughter of a lighthouse keeper placed her within a pantheon of heroines higher than England's most famous queen or any of the names familiar to readers from the civil wars of the seventeenth and early eighteenth centuries. One might have expected the *Warder* to be held up to ridicule. Instead, it became the prototype for many later comparisons of Grace with other famous women – and, indeed, was frequently plagiarized.

In the 1860s and 1870s the kind of exercise that the *Warder* had initiated became commonplace. Grace was endlessly compared with and measured against other famous women. She began to feature in what became a common form of publishing, collections describing famous or noble women. The aim was to hold up to women readers examples of good conduct and fortitude, either from the national past or from the whole range of history. The prototype was Elizabeth Starling's much-reprinted *Noble Deeds of Women* (1835) in which the achievements of over two hundred women were held up for admiration under such headings as 'Maternal affection', 'Humanity', 'Fortitude', 'Self-Control' and 'Patriotism'. Grace, of course, had no place in the 1835 edition, but by 1848 there was a picture of Grace and her father in the coble on the title page, and a long entry under the heading of 'Humanity'. Only Flora Macdonald was allotted more space. Other writers pillaged from Starling's compendia. In *The Heroines of Domestic Life* (1861), Grace is one of twenty-two women ranging from Ruth and Antigone to Florence Nightingale. The editor of *Fifty Famous Women: Their Virtues and Failings, and the Lessons of Their Lives* (1864) confined her or himself, with the exception of Poccahontas, to medieval and modern Europe. A good half of the selection is made up of monarchs or aristocrats, and Grace's only British contemporary is Charlotte Brontë – not even Florence Nightingale makes this list. Hannah More, Jane Austen and Charlotte Brontë feature alongside Grace in Charles Bruce (ed.), *The Book of Noble Englishwomen: Lives Made Illustrious by Heroism, Goodness, and Great Attainments* (1875), the stories of thirty-seven women whose names 'will never be erased from our national story'. Grace is there, too, in Joseph Johnson's *Brave Women: Who Have Been Distinguished for Heroic Actions and Noble Virtues; who have exhibited fearless courage; stout hearts; and intrepid resolve* (1875).

The entries on Grace in these compilations do not pretend to any originality. They are sometimes copies of each other or of the *Berwick and Kelso Warder*'s booklet. Bruce, for example, acknowledges that his account of the deed is by kind permission of Messrs W. and R. Chambers, who had included an account of Grace in *The Book of Days* (1863–4). What is important about these publications is not the manner of the telling of the story but rather the company that Grace was keeping. She had become one of the famous women in world and national history, perhaps most comparable, if to anyone, to Joan of Arc. Her contemporaries or near-contemporaries in British history include writers, most commonly Charlotte Brontë, who had taken on the hue of sainthood with the publication of Elizabeth Gaskell's biography,[46] social reformers like Elizabeth Fry of prison fame, and, amongst the living, Florence Nightingale. Whereas the others had whole lives of striving and goodness to celebrate, Grace's inclusion was dependent on a few hours in a short life, together with her exemplary conduct in the years leading up to her death. Moreover, taking up the language of the *Berwick and Kelso Warder*, Grace alone found a place 'amongst the annals of those who, although holding humble stations in life, have yet exhibited traits of natural greatness that would grace the occupiers of the loftiest positions in society'. Conservatives loved to trace 'the annals of humble life', looking for goodness and heroism, where, as Thomas Arthur put it, 'they are least expected'.[47]

We can only guess who read these books: mainly women presumably, though many of the compilers were men. There is nothing in their format or language to suggest that they were for children. They were designed with young women of the middle classes chiefly in mind. Sometimes they are prefaced with reflections on women's roles and duties of a thoroughly conventional kind. Mrs Octavius Freire Owen in 1861 (and she was happy to repeat the words in a new edition in 1877) wanted to 'teach women to endure – her chief lesson in this life! – and unselfishly to support others – her main prerogative!'[48] The editor of *Fifty Famous Women* asked 'What is really *woman's work*?' and moved to reflections on the links between heroism and duty. Heroism was 'the performance of duty under difficult and exceptional circumstances'. That, by implication, was why Grace was a heroine: she had done her duty. And for those who might not be faced with the challenge of saving the shipwrecked, 'there is such a thing as fireside heroism, – the daily endurance of trial, and the exercise of self-denial, all the more difficult, because the objects to be gained by them are small, and their surroundings humble'.[49] Joseph Johnson agreed: the bravery of women was best seen at home, often in the endurance of difficult domestic circumstances; indeed he wrote his book in part to give strength to women whose husbands had, in some unspecified respect, failed.[50]

It was in these decades that the seeds were being sown of the women's movement for emancipation. Can we assume or deduce that readers might have taken from these compilations of heroism a different message than that set out in the prefaces? Perhaps, but on the face of it the message is that women should brace themselves for a life of duty, endurance and self-denial, and neither seek nor expect any change in their social and political subordination. Grace's life was being shaped to convey these very messages, and it did so repetitively, and in the very best of company.

Grace's death forced contemporaries to think through how they wanted to remember her. As in the immediate response to her deed, the initiatives came entirely from the upper and middle classes. From Mrs Sharp, whose gift set in motion the erection of a memorial much more striking than the one to her own illustrious family. From Archdeacon Thorp, who had the vision of linking Grace to the hallowed life of St Cuthbert – and who won the support of the Queen for his plans. From Wordsworth, the poet laureate in waiting, laying to rest his own grief for his brother, and impelled to write because of the reports he had read of French indifference to suffering British sailors. From the Trevelyans, creating a Pre-Raphaelite interpretation of Northumbrian history in which Grace, if only after debate, forms a striking image. And from the numerous compilers of books in which Grace finds a place in a global and national history of famous women. After this, it was impossible she would ever be entirely forgotten: the memorials were there, in stone, in prose and in paint. What could not be anticipated was that in the late nineteenth century Grace would be catapulted to a fame perhaps even greater than that thrust upon her in her own lifetime.

6

The Age of Celebrity

For thirty years after her death the memory of Grace at national level was sustained in compilations of women's heroism and duty aimed at a middle-class and largely adult female readership. In the last quarter of the century Grace's name and deed achieved almost universal recognition, something that was kept alive through the early decades of the twentieth century. Moreover, she was not only a heroine but also a celebrity, someone whose name and image had become so familiar that they helped to sell consumer goods. How and why did this happen?

Up to 1875 there was no single-volume account of Grace that was easy of access and had the appearance of reliability. *Grace Darling, Heroine of the Farne Islands: Her Life, and its Lessons* by Eva Hope, first published in 1875 by Adam and Company, and in subsequent editions by Walter Scott, both publishers operating from Newcastle and London, was to change all that. 312 pages long, priced at 3s. 6d., it was to be the single most important means of sustaining and spreading the name of Grace Darling in the late nineteenth and early twentieth centuries. Edition after edition was produced – the Grace Darling Museum holds at least six. How did the book come to be written and who was Eva Hope?

Until 1875 most people knew what they knew of Grace from memories which went back to the 1830s and 1840s or from one or more of the collections in which her heroism was briefly proclaimed. They in turn were largely dependent on the *Berwick and Kelso Warder*'s 1843 *Memoir*, or on what might be culled from Jerold Vernon's *Maid of the Isles*, neither easily available. Thomas Arthur was the first to attempt a more sustained account. Nothing is known of him except that 1875 was a prolific year for him: his only two books bear that date, the second being *The Life of Billy Purvis, The Extraordinary, Witty, and Comical Showman*. Purvis was a well-known travelling showman in the north east, but Arthur's account of him was derivative and is, in the opinion of the modern authority on Purvis, 'a very inferior piece of work'.[1] The same criticism can be made of Arthur's biography of another, and very different, person of fame in the north east, Grace Darling. His sources were, as he stated, what he could glean by talking to people in and around Bamburgh, the *Memoir*, *The Maid of the Isles*, the *Newcastle Chronicle*, and a brief account in M. A. Richardson's *The Local Historian's Table Book, of Remarkable Occurrences, Historical Facts, Traditions, Legendary and Descriptive Ballads, etc.,*

etc., connected with the counties of Newcastle-upon-Tyne, Northumberland and Durham (1846), the latter a scrap book in which Grace occupies seven pages in volume 5 of the Historical Division. Arthur also acknowledged that Grace's elder sister, Thomasin, 'kindly gave all the assistance in her power', and the book is dedicated to her. Thomasin sent him a poem about Grace, and probably gave him a few other hints, but he clearly did not have access to the family papers.[2] Arthur's *The Life of Grace Darling, the Heroine of the Farne Isles*, 124 pages long, was first published by Adam and Company in Newcastle, in 1875. Ten years later, in 1885, it came out under the imprint of the Religious Book Society. It is almost entirely plagiarized from Vernon, and although he ignores the Spanish and London scenes in Vernon, he assumes that the passages in which Grace appears are true.

On 1 December 1875 Alexander McCallum from the Felling-Gate Printing Works in Gateshead wrote a long letter to Thomasin Darling. He had, he wrote, 'had the supervision and care of Mr Arthur's edition of Grace Darling through the press'. This had given rise to 'an earnest desire to make Mr Arthur's work the foundation of a superstructure which would more beautifully and more effectively bring out the admirable home-training which you and the other members of your family received from your worthy parents in your island home, and to which Grace owed, under God, that virtue and heroism which has made her name a household word, and endeared her memory to the hearts of the pure and the virtuous in this and other lands'. McCallum now wanted 'the principles and truth and love' which lay at the foundation of this home-training to be 'amplified and enforced' so that human hearts 'may be touched and stimulated to noble deeds and Christian living'. 'With this object in view', he went on,

> I have been successful in recommending to the Firm and securing the services of a Lady of great intellectual ability and Christian worth, who has been for a considerable time before the public, but who, for private reasons, wishes to remain *incog* in the meantime. The lessons of the life and death of Grace, with all the accessories of notices of your parents' courtship, marriage and early home – and the various events that occurred during the progress of the years in the history of your family will be given in a refined and interesting form.

McCallum then outlined the chapter headings and concluded

> that the volume in progress bids fair to be a noble tribute to the memory of your sister and her heroic deeds – a worthy memorial of all that is lovely and Christlike in her and your venerated parents. And more than all this, if it should prove the instrument in God's hand, by its lessons and its teachings, of leading souls to Jesus, shall we not admire the leadings of that Providence which has conduced to such a result. I should esteem it a favour if you would kindly furnish any scraps of information which may have suggested themselves to you or which you may be in possession of at as early a date as possible.[3]

McCallum, it seems, while seeing Arthur's book through the press, became aware of its inadequacies, or at least saw it as a missed opportunity for bringing souls to Christ. He then somehow persuaded his firm to enter into a contract for another book on the same topic. His chosen author was born Mary Ann Hearn in 1834, the daughter of a shoemaker and later postman in the small village of Farningham in Kent. The Hearns were Strict and Particular Baptists, impoverished, and hostile to the Church of England. Mary went to school only when she was nine or ten when a nonconformist school, run by the British and Foreign School Society, opened in the village. She was an able student, and at the age of eighteen went to Bristol as an assistant teacher. Summoned back home again to help run the home – her mother had died when she was twelve – Mary now encountered a new Baptist pastor, the Reverend Jonathan Whittemore, who in 1857 launched the *Christian World*, and in 1860, the year of his death, the *Sunday School Times*. Mary contributed to both, writing under the name, suggested to her by Whittemore, of Marianne Farningham. She continued teaching, first in Gravesend, then in Northampton, which became her permanent home, until in 1867 the new editor of the *Christian World* took her on full-time. Marianne Farningham wrote for every number, in prose and verse, and often collected together her contributions and published them as books. She was unbelievably prolific – as even she acknowledges in her appropriately entitled autobiography, *A Working Woman's Life*. Her thousandth contribution in verse for the *Sunday School Times* was published in 1879. Her most successful book, *Girlhood*, again from the *Sunday School Times*, was in a fourth edition by 1869.[4]

Marianne Farningham was a very well known name in the world of nonconformist Christian publishing. She had moved away from the Strict Baptism of her childhood to a broad-minded acceptance of other Christian traditions, but without losing her deep Christian faith. This was manifest in the enormously successful Sunday School class she taught over many years in Northampton. The girls who came to her class – and were often invited to her home – were aged from sixteen to twenty, many of them young workers in the Northampton shoe industry. There was clearly a rapport between teacher and taught: perhaps Mary Ann Hearn was able to draw on her own remarkable childhood and adolescence to inspire the young of Northampton – though she is too tactful to suggest this.[5]

McCallum's approach to Marianne Farningham was a shrewd one. Her name on the cover of a book on Grace Darling would immediately commend the book to those who read her weekly in the *Christian World* and the *Sunday School Times*. The prospective author was delighted with the idea. But what McCallum had not reckoned on was that Marianne Farningham would think that that name belonged exclusively to her two journals. She must have a new name for the Grace Darling book and any others she might write for Adam & Compay. Eventually they settled on Eva Hope – as Farningham put it, 'about the weakest we could have found' – with an agreement that any subsequent books would appear as 'By the author of "Grace Darling"'. There were subsequent books, on General Gordon, 'Our Queen', Abraham Lincoln and James Garfield and H. M. Stanley, none of them as popular as her first, which, as she says, 'had a very large sale, both at the time and afterwards'.[6]

Eva Hope had no time for research on the ground, being mainly dependent on what she could find in the British Museum, which meant chiefly Vernon. 'A relative – an aunt, I think – gave me a lock of Grace Darling's hair', she recalled, 'and some particulars of her family reached me, so that I had a most enjoyable time while writing my first biography.'[7] McCallum's letter may have produced from Thomasin Darling 'some particulars of her family', but by that time the book was effectively written and probably in proof: McCallum wrote to Thomasin on 1 December 1875 and the book was published in that year. Hope, who never set foot in the north east, made some elementary geographical errors which later writers seized on. Mention Eva Hope in circles who know about Grace Darling and you get at best a resigned shrug and a raising of the eyebrows: Hope, it is implied, and correctly, perpetuated some of the fictions with which Vernon had embellished his tale.

Hope's book was indeed, as McCallum had stated, a 'superstructure' built on Arthur's 'foundation'. But where Arthur had plagiarized Vernon directly, with an occasional change of word or sentence structure, Hope took the Vernon/Arthur version of Grace's life, and, for the most part, reimagined it in her own words. Where Vernon/Arthur have descriptions of events, Hope tells them through imaginary (and, it must be admitted, often stilted) conversations within the Darling family. Occasionally she also excised or fundamentally altered passages that failed to conform to her overall project. Here, for example, is Vernon describing Grace at the age of sixteen:

> Grace Darling was rather beneath than above the ordinary size of women, of a slender and graceful figure, whose easy and airy movements bespoke a light and happy heart. Her countenance was remarkable for an expression of good-humoured vivacity; her dark-brown hair waved in sunny ringlets; her complexion partook of that delicate shade of pink, often admired in sea-shells; while her soft hazel eye beamed with an expression of benevolent feeling.

Arthur's only amendment to this passage was to replace the opening 'Grace Darling ...' with 'The lovely Grace ...' Hope, by contrast, wants to convey, not the burgeoning sexuality of an adolescent, but the character that lies beneath and shines through the physical appearance:

> there was an easy winning grace, and guileless sweetness of manner, about the simple true-hearted lighthouse maiden, that won its way to all hearts. There is no such beautifier as thoughtful goodness; and the amiable character, and clear understanding of Grace

Darling, shone through her hazel eyes, and added to her loveliness. Grace was rather beneath the ordinary stature, and her figure was slender and graceful. She had a wreath of sunny brown curls, and a delicate clear complexion, which revealed the quick emotions of joy and sorrow that moved her. She was rich, too, in having a fund of good common sense ...[8]

This was the kind of role model which Hope wanted to present to her readers, gendered but not sexualized; later we are told that 'Grace Darling was not what is called beautiful; but she had a pleasant face, and she made no wrong use of it'. And even in what looks a positive description there is a veiled warning: the 'delicate clear complexion' signalled to the informed reader, as Hope reminds us when she comes to Grace's death, that the seeds of consumption are germinating.[9]

This reworking of Vernon/Arthur underscored the two features of Hope's book which distinguished it from everything which had preceded it: it was imbued with Christianity and, addressing girls and women, it reflected at length, rather than in passing, on what constituted goodness in a woman. Hope drew a Christian message from almost every incident in Grace's life and in the wreck of the *Forfarshire*. She divided those on the soon-to-be-wrecked ship into the happy ones for whom 'death by drowning was ... only a short swift passage to the heavenly land, where "*there shall be no more sea*"', and the others who 'little knew' when they went to sleep,

how the angels wrote above their cabin, 'There is but a step between thee and death.' With busy brains, planning all sorts of work for future years, and dreaming of worldly success and prosperity, they laid down to sleep. While the night yet lasted came the terrible cry, 'Behold, the bridegroom cometh: go ye forth to meet Him.' And what terror and affright the message caused, only He knew who looked down from Heaven into the souls of the men and women. Was it not a pity that they had not thought of this before? If only they had been His friends, they would not have feared to see His face.

Too late. For them, there was 'nothing but hopeless desolation'.[10]

Grace dies the perfect Christian death. 'She knew that she must die, but she was not afraid of death ... She was ready to go, and was only listening for the welcome voice of the messenger "to fly away and be at rest". "Do not mourn for me", she says to her family; "'I am only exchanging this life for one far better ... in dying, I go to be with Christ, my Saviour." 'Her quiet death-bed was so hallowed a scene, that as we turn from it we cannot but think of the home to which she has gone, where the good and illustrious of all ages and all lands have met together. And there may it be the privilege of the writer and readers to greet her when this life is over.'[11]

With this prospect before them of meeting Grace in Heaven, readers were enticed to read on in the next chapter where Hope preaches 'several sermons', taking texts from the last chapter of the Book of Proverbs, which, we are assured,

Grace 'must often have read, and with which she must have been very familiar'.[12] The sermons address Hope's other concern, how to be a good woman. The book had opened, not with the birth of the heroine, but with a chapter on 'Woman's Work'. A woman's work, Hope asserts, 'is that which she sees needs doing', be it the prison visiting of an Elizabeth Fry, the nursing in the Crimea of a Florence Nightingale, or the rescue of the shipwrecked of a Grace Darling. All of these were answering to a call, higher than anything society expected, to God. Women, the author hoped, might rise from reading of Grace's life 'with a stronger determination than ever to become unselfish, useful, and devoted. Are there not lives yet to be saved? Are there no wrecks as awful as those which are caused by ships crashing among rocks, or stranding upon dangerous sands? ... There is work enough for all willing hands, and the women of Great Britain can do no unimportant part of it.'[13] The rescue itself prompted Hope to drive home the message: 'May hundreds of thousands of girls, alike in humble or lofty positions, be taught by it to be self-forgetful, brave, and eager to save others. And may many noble Englishwomen arise who shall have reason to thank God for the lesson which they learnt from the life of the heroine of the Farne Isles, Grace Darling!'

The sermons from the Book of Proverbs provided a more extended opportunity to reflect on what it was to be a good woman, and how to achieve that status, and the encouraging message was that 'there is not a girl who reads these pages, but can become that most valuable treasure – a good woman. It is possible to every one of them to attain to that degree of excellence to which Grace Darling reached. They may not ... have the same opportunity of saving life by going out over the stormy waters to the rescue of the perishing; but they can be, if they cannot do, the same.' To do so, a girl will need to be strong, and have 'plenty of fresh bracing air, and out-of-door exercise'; she will reach out to help the poor; she will learn 'to say kind things well' and not to gossip; she will scorn idleness; and she will 'not be satisfied with less than the best'.[14]

'I am perhaps half a socialist', wrote Marianne Farningham in her autobiography. 'One of the people myself, my sympathies are frequently with them.' In party political terms she was, 'of course', as she says, a Liberal. She served on the Northampton School Board, and expressed her support for the Salvation Army, temperance movements, youth organizations and the NSPCC. In the late 1870s she became a lecturer on such topics as 'The Women of To-day', and 'The Rush and the Hush of Life', touring the provinces and staying with leading Nonconformist families, amongst them the Cadburys in Birmingham – and was successful enough at this to provide herself with the funds to buy a house.[15] In *The Life of Grace Darling* this political and public side of her life is expressed in her contempt for the frivolities and luxuries of life amongst the well-to-do. The Grace Darlings of tomorrow will not be 'the produce of ball-rooms, where the air is poisoned by gases, and where women spend nights in scenes of excitement and gaiety … if the women of the next generation are to be strong and healthy in mind and body, they should be taught to despise, rather than to covet, the dissipations, the shams and frivolities, the dress and fashion, of modern society'. But if Eva Hope had no time for 'modern society', and was happy to assert the equality of all people before God, there was nothing she wrote which even hinted at a reordering of society, or at the desirability of using your talents to rise in the social scale. People should accept the position they find themselves in for there were always opportunities to do good: 'Poor women help the poor, even more than the rich do'. Grace, thankfully, was never tempted to respond to the offers of marriage from the well-to-do which supposedly came her way: 'One feels glad to know', comments Hope, 'that all the praise did not make her other than the humble British girl.' Put more positively a few pages later on, Grace, like Hope herself, 'was one of "the people", and did not aspire to leave their ranks. Her sympathies were with them; and she asked nothing better than to spend her life among them.' There was a message here, as blunt as could be, for the Sunday School girls who provided the most likely readership for the book: aim, above all, to be good, and display that goodness in the sphere in which you find yourself. The social order is taken as a given, the Duchess of Northumberland much praised for her role in helping the Darlings, and Grace herself properly 'humble'.[16]

Hope was writing against the background of considerable public discussion of women's proper role. Some women were campaigning for equality with men, wanting to open up opportunities for women in education quite as much as in politics. Others accepted that men and women had different characteristics but wanted to see women's special aptitudes being used in the public sphere, particularly in philanthropy. Hope herself is more condemnatory of some of her own sex than she is of men, but in this she can be seen as sharing some of the impatience of reforming women with ideas and practices they had inherited. She has no time, for example, for idle women, nor did she have 'any other feeling than scorn for women who, not being really afflicted with disease, are useless'.[17] But in two other key respects she offers no support, implicit or explicit, for what might be described as proto-feminist concerns. First, there is no mention of the possibility that girls might through education, as indeed she herself had, rise to positions of self-realization and influence. We think of this period as one in which Samuel Smiles's advocacy of self-help and of the desirability of using your talents to the full was dominant. Hope, in holding up Grace Darling as a role model, lends no support to such ideals. Secondly, there is no hint in Hope that the separate spheres, public for men, private for women, were anything other than natural. Two chapters conclude resoundingly with passages on the importance of home for women: 'It is at home that there is opportunity for the display of all that is sweet and good in the female life and character; and it is there that true goodness shines the most brightly. Let English girls remain attached to their own home-circles …' And later, 'Let the women of England remember that their power is in their love, and that the homes they know shall surely be bright or dark, sad or happy, as they shall make them, by their meek or gentle spirit, and unselfish, devoted affection … Women should understand that their home-life is the most important, and give to it their devotion and love.'[18]

There is one other theme that shines through Hope's book, though she has here little to add to what she had read in Vernon and Arthur: Hope's Grace is a lover of the history and ballads of Northumbria. History has its lessons to tell, and Grace is rooted in it. Hope herself devotes nearly thirty pages to 'Ancient Northumbria', telling a story of progress wrought out of struggles: 'It is because our fathers fought that we possess so many privileges.' For Grace as a young girl, 'the legends and traditions of heroic Northumbria were most dear to her heart', and her reading of them implanted in her 'the heroic spirit'. These ballads were infinitely preferable to novels, indeed we are assured that it 'is morally certain … that Grace Darling had not read many novels. The effect of doing this is to make girls dream, rather than do'. The sites of ancient Northumbria are as dear to Grace as the ballads: pages of the book describe fictional visits by Grace and her friends to Lindisfarne, Warkworth and Dunstanburgh, where the ruins, and the legends associated with them, draw forth ruminations on the lessons they hold for today: thankfulness for progress, inspiration for action. Grace, who has read about, and witnessed the sites of, ancient heroism, was thereby made ready for her own heroic act, ready to take her own place in the history of Northumbria.[19]

It is difficult to read Hope's book now without imagining that even at the time of its publication readers must have been tempted to skim whole chapters – no one surely could wade through the potted history of Northumbria or the equally long history of shipwrecks. But set aside these faults of structure, and set aside the inaccuracies that Hope inherited from her sources, and it becomes possible to understand the attraction of the book for the readership at whom it was aimed. From Grace's life story, told now more vividly than ever before, clear lessons were spelt out. It was the perfect book to give as a prize, and often was. Men as well as women received it as a prize. A plate in one copy tells us that John Edwin Turner of Crossley Hall, Openshaw, received it as his Regular Attendance Prize at the Sunday Afternoon Men's Own Bible Class. What he made of it, we can only guess. For it was girls for whom Grace was held up as role model. Her transgression of gender boundaries in persuading her father to go out to the rescue was justified by the motivation that drove it, a conviction derived from her home training that you should succour fellow humans in distress. But surrounding this one act of heroism, was another kind of heroism, the one appropriate to most girls, an uncomplaining devotion to home, family and duty. If you wanted to be a 'good woman', follow Grace's example, live a Christian life, and eschew the snares set by modern fashions and modern society.

The books by Arthur and Hope were both dedicated to Thomasin Darling in identical words: 'This volume is respectfully dedicated to Miss Thomasin Darling, the beloved sister of the heroic Grace Darling, in recognition of her Christian character and amiable disposition, by the author.' This might suggest that the Darling family had in some way authorized or approved the books. Thomasin, as we have seen, had given some assistance to Arthur, but there is no obvious evidence that she responded to McCallum's plea, on behalf of Hope, for information about Grace's childhood. After her father had died in 1865, Thomasin had become the guardian of the family's reputation. Thomasin herself had been devoted to her father – her diary which covers the last twenty years of her life from 1865 to 1885 soon becomes little more than an annual entry recording the anniversary of her father's death and her abiding sense of loss.[20] She must have read the Arthur and Hope volumes with some bewilderment: here were Vernon's fictions, errors and misrepresentations amplified for a new generation of readers. She alone, in possession of the family papers, was in a position to present a more accurate account but lacked the skills necessary for the job.

Thomasin in the 1870s was running a boarding house, Wynding House, in Bamburgh. Mary Baird was to describe how as a child she had spent summers in Wynding House where they were warmly greeted by 'Miss Thomasin Darling, the old sister of the heroine Grace, a kindly body, unattractive in appearance, and rather alarming at first sight; but to us she was everything that was interesting and romantic, and her cooking is something to remember!' The house was somewhat old-fashioned, the dining room 'smelling strongly of mice', the sofas 'harder than any ever made', but it provided a memorable base for family holidays – and for contact with Darlings. 'Old Miss Carr', for example, was the pew-opener, and, 'like everybody else, was a connection of the Darling family'.[21]

Among the visitors to Wynding House were the Atkinson family from Harrogate, Daniel Henry Atkinson and his sisters. Daniel Atkinson, who had retired from being what he described as an 'old Leeds cropper', was dabbling in local history.[22] Thomasin turned to him to set the record straight. In 1880 Hamilton, Adams & Co. of London published *Grace Darling; Her True Story. From Unpublished Papers in Possession of Her Family*, seventy-four pages long. No author's name was appended, but it was the work of Atkinson and Thomasin – 'our book' as she called it. It is explicitly designed to correct the inaccuracies that had entered into many accounts. For example, it points out that Grace could not have heard the cries of the survivors on their rock, half a mile away and in a gale. It puts into the public domain for the first time some of the letters Grace and the Darlings both received and wrote in the aftermath of the rescue. Atkinson was certainly determined to make it as factual as he could. In 1878 he had left his first draft with Thomasin for her comments, and added a series of searching questions. She was delighted with the outcome: 'I know as long as [I] live it will be a source of Pleasure to me, as it has now done justice to a Beloved Parent as well as my dear Sister.' Thomasin's parents were in some ways more in the forefront of her mind than Grace. Of her father she wrote to Atkinson, 'If you had known him I believe you would [have] loved him. Likewise you have noticed my Dear Mother in your manuscript being left alone at the Longstone.' Atkinson himself may have felt a little frustrated. He was dependent on what Thomasin chose to tell him or the letters she showed him, and did not have a free run of the manuscripts. There was, she wrote to him in 1878, probably more she could send him, 'only when I go amongst the Pappers and letters it rather trys my feelings. I have never looked at any since you left until I received your letters.' Atkinson had lifted a burden from Thomasin's shoulders in compiling and publishing the book – her gratitude shines through their correspondence – but he must have wondered if there was more hidden away.[23]

With the publication of *Grace Darling: Her True Story* in 1880 a phase in writing about Grace Darling comes to an end. Within the space of a few years, Arthur's book had prompted Hope's, and the two together had led to Atkinson's reply. Atkinson himself was to put himself further in the Darling family's debt by publishing William Darling's journal in 1885, and by continuing as the guardian of the family's reputation through the 1890s, but there were to be no further publications on Grace with any claim to originality until 1932. The many people who wrote about Grace in the half century leading up to 1932 based their work on what had been published between 1875 and 1880; and the book they chiefly relied on was not the *True Story*, which seems to have had very limited circulation, but Hope's *Grace Darling, Heroine of the Farne Islands: Her Life and its Lessons*.

Words on their own were not enough to sustain and enhance Grace's reputation. A commanding image was required. The paintings done during Grace's lifetime were mostly portraits done after the event or seascapes with the coble centre-stage but small. An action picture of Grace rowing was needed to bring home to people what it had been like in 1838. Thomas Brooks (1818–91) had been born in Hull, but worked in London as a genre painter, frequently exhibiting at the Royal Academy. He was influenced by the Pre-Raphaelites, and in the late 1860s and 1870s painted many marine dramas. Daniel Atkinson in an undated letter mentions hearing that Mr Brooks the artist was going to visit Bamburgh for 'his intended painting' and offers his assistance. Since the letter also refers to permission to use material from *Grace Darling; Her True Story*, it seems that the painting cannot predate 1880. Yet there are prints of the painting that bear the date 1868. Whichever the correct date, Brooke's painting became well-known through an engraving by George Zobel.[24] Brooks's painting shows Grace, without her father visible, rowing with two oars. Probably the scene is intended to show the crucial moment when William Darling had leapt ashore, leaving Grace to control the coble. Grace's hair is loose, her sleeves rolled up, the boat is awash with water, but no one could be in doubt of the determination in Grace's face and posture.

Brooks's painting was the template for all future representations of Grace. Her clothes or hairstyle might be changed (and frequently were) but her posture remained the same, the hands firmly gripping the oars. Brooks's painting was copied, engraved, sold as a 'stevengraph' (a woven silk card), reproduced for a card game and on a Staffordshire mug, and formed the basis for the representation of Grace in Arthur Mee's *The Children's Encyclopedia*.[25] It is a romantic and compelling picture, making Grace come alive again for the generation of readers who were now being brought up on Hope's book. Most people who carry a mental image of Grace see her in some version of Brooks's painting and imagine that she rowed out on her own to the rescue.

Music was perhaps the most immediately evocative way of remembering Grace. A number of ballads, as we have seen, were composed immediately after Grace's deed. One of them, by George Linley, seems to have had enduring popularity. 'This very highly popular song' appears, on its own, as a broadsheet, at the price of 1d., in the Poet Box, dated 'Saturday Morning, July 24, 1858'. It also went further downmarket. It is included in another, undated, broadsheet, printed by J. Catnach, together with three other ballads. In these, and other versions, some of the words were changed. They conspire to give a very different version of Grace than Linley's 'gentle girl' whose 'heart beats lightly' after she has accomplished the rescue. She becomes, in one version, 'Grace Darling, that gallant young female so bold', 'brave' and 'undaunted', and it is not her heart that beats lightly, but her 'swell'd bosom' or, in another rendering, 'sweet bosom'. The opening line in one version, 'I pray give attention to what I will mention', is capped by a closing toast:

> Here's a health to that damsel, that gallant young maiden,
> Grace Horsely [sic] Darling, that maiden so bold.

These verbal changes, and the conventional opening and closure, place these broadsheets in a long and vibrant tradition of popular song, hawked on the streets. Songs recounting stories about rescues, such as Grace Darling's deed, were 'the most popular stories of all'. Apart from the most refined version of 1858, it is difficult to date them; the Bodleian puts one at about 1845, and they seem to belong to the mid-century years, perhaps stretching into the 1860s. They are evidence that the upper classes were not completely successful in their attempt to control Grace Darling. She was, at some level, a popular heroine, 'gallant and bold', not gentle and modest, as the upper class version of her demanded. [26]

The ballad that can be traced in its descent from George Linley was replaced in the later nineteenth century by what is now known as 'The Grace Darling song'. It was through this latter song that many people, from Kenneth Williams to Jessica

Mitford, came to know about Grace. The chorus was the highpoint:

> And she pull'd away, o'er the rolling seas,
>   Over the waters blue.
> Help! Help! She could hear the cry of the shipwreck'd crew.
> But Grace had an English heart,
>   And the raging storm she brav'd;
> She pull'd away, mid the dashing spray,
> And the crew she saved.

With the Mitford family in full song on the Hebridean island of Inch Kenneth, boats from neighbouring islands, so it is said, would put out to see what was wrong when they heard the 'Help! Help!' The final verse exhorts singers, in an imperial age,

> Go, tell the wide world over,
>   What English pluck can do;
> And sing of brave Grace Darling,
>   Who nobly saved the crew.[27]

The words and music of the song were almost certainly by Felix McGlennon (1856–1943), a prolific songwriter who has nearly 400 entries in the *Catalogue of Printed Music in the British Library*: yet curiously the Grace Darling song is nowhere to be found among them. It is just possible that McGlennon provided the music for a song that was already in circulation as a broadsheet. It is more likely, as with the Linley ballad, that the movement was the other way, that McGlennon was indeed responsible for both words and music, and that the printers of broadside ballads picked it up.[28] Its date remains uncertain, but certainly not later than the 1880s, for on one broadside it appears with a song that can be firmly dated to 1889. As with the earlier ballad, there are minor variations, the most significant being the substitution of 'British' for 'English' in the line 'What ... pluck may do'.[29]

The Grace Darling song seems to have remained popular until the 1930s, then being forgotten. Constance Smedley reported in the mid-1930s that 'until a few years ago, songs about Grace Darling were heard in pantomimes as patriotic songs', but implied that that time was now past. When the Grace Darling Museum opened in 1938, it obtained copies of the words and music from Denmark, there being apparently no local knowledge of it.[30] In the 1970s folksong collectors recorded versions of it from four men and two women, most of them remembering the chorus only, though one singer, who had learnt it from his mother, managed it all.[31]

Words, an image and a song laid the foundation for the fame and celebrity that surrounded Grace Darling in the later nineteenth and early twentieth centuries.

If she had been in large part the preserve of the well-to-do in her lifetime and in the decades after her death, her reputation now expanded far beyond that to encompass the nation in its entirety. Of course she had always had at least a toehold in aspects of popular culture in her lifetime and beyond, as shown by the panoramas, the Staffordshire figures and the broadside ballads. In the north east, too, her deed appealed to parts of the community where Dukes of Northumberland had no sway. In a poster for the Temperance Hall, Hartlepool, in 1861, there was a 'grand mechanical representation' of 'Grace Darling and the Wreck of the *Forfarshire* Steam Ship'. As befitted the venue, Grace shared the bill with a representation of 'The Life and Labours of that Eminent Divine, The Rev. John Wesley'.[32] Nonconformists who allowed themselves an evening of pleasure could go and relive Grace's rescue.

The first sign that Grace was reaching a wider public was her inclusion, in about 1890, in William McGonagall's *Poetic Gems*. The poem is a dramatic rendition of the wreck and rescue written in the execrable verse that was McGonagall's staple. With it he toured the concert halls of Scotland, reminding us that Grace Darling's heroism had as much resonance in Scotland as in England. Grace was 'modest and lovely', but also 'that heroine bold'.

> Grace Darling was a comely lass, with long, fair floating hair,
> With soft blue eyes, and shy, and modest rare;
> And her countenance was full of sense and genuine kindliness,
> With a noble heart, and ready to help suffering creatures in distress.

Her deed 'to the end of time, will never be forgot', and 'for her equal in true heroism we cannot find another'.[33] Grace, who, in early versions of the rescue, had her hair tight in curlers, was now being reinvented as a lass with 'long, fair floating hair', a more romantic picture, and one that may have been derived from Brooks's painting.

By the end of the century Miss Vesta Victoria was singing 'He Calls Me His Own Grace Darling' in the London music halls, in the cockney accent that was compulsory in the depiction of the working class. The song tells of a girl in love with a fisherman, the chorus going:

> And he calls me his own Grace Darling
> He says that I'm his pet,
> I've filled each *plaice* within his *sole*
> That ain't no *cod*, you bet;
> When he asked me if I loved him,
> I said, 'What 'O! not 'alf,
> Why, I likes you just for your whiskers
> 'Cos they tickles me and makes me laugh'
> And he laugh.[34]

If Grace Darling could sell seats in the music hall, she was also capable of adding value to more prestigious articles and occasions. 'Grace Darling' signalled all good things, and advertisers were quick to sense the advantage of association with her. As Jessica Mitford put it, 'Grace Darling's name, like those of Jenny Lind and Fanny Kemble, appeared on a large variety of items – pens, shoes, fireplace implements, hearth tidies, door-stops, napkin rings, soap, chocolates, and all kinds of decorative tableware.' There was a Grace Darling rose, one of the first Hybrid Teas, introduced in 1884. Cadburys sold Grace Darling chocolates, as did Rowntrees. Lifebuoy soap in 1898 had Grace in the coble rowing while her father was about to throw a lifebelt to the unseen survivors.[35] In these advertisements the picture of Grace is clearly derived from Brooks's painting. Chocolate and soap were two of the most heavily advertised products in the burgeoning consumer market of late nineteenth- and early twentieth-century Britain. The use of Grace in them could be effective only if potential purchasers immediately recognized Grace, and associated the product with all the good qualities that Grace had come to embody. The advertisements made a deliberate appeal to women, who were the vital element in the consumer boom.[36]

Grace Darling's name also had its appeal to men. The most obvious sign of this was in the naming of boats and ships. Pride of place must go to the *Grace Darling*, registered in Dundee, that set sail from that port on 18 December 1838 to embark on a long voyage that took in St Domingo and Trieste before ending up in Liverpool on 21 September 1839.[37] Closer to home, there were, not surprisingly, lifeboats named after her, at Holy Island and North Sunderland. But there were also all too many Grace Darlings that ended up in some kind of trouble: a bark from Dundalk, sailing from New York, and parting from its cable in 1848; a sloop, its mast broken at the mouth of the Humber, in 1851; a schooner lost near Llanelly in 1853; a bark from Blyth running ashore at Aberdeen, with most of the crew drowned in 1874; a smack run down and sunk at the mouth of the Ribble in 1895; a British steamer aground near Adelaide in 1910; a steam herring drifter from Yarmouth sinking after a collision off Scarborough in 1911; a British schooner, laden with fish, a total loss off Newfoundland in 1919.[38] These barks, sloops and schooners, known to us only because they were involved in some accident, were workaday ships. They do not feature in Lloyd's Register of Shipping, nor indeed, on a spot check, do *Grace Darlings* at all. The name seems to have been used for small cargo and fishing vessels.

There were other land-based, uses of Grace Darling's name appealing primarily to men. Some of them were of an improving kind. There was a temperance charity in Northumberland, the Grace Darling British Workmen, founded in 1871, supported by Lord Armstrong. The Grace Darling Lodge of the Ancient Free Gardeners in Seahouses, formed in 1869 and dissolved only in 1948 with the coming of the welfare state, was of benefit to the wives and families of members, but the members themselves were all men, meeting in pubs in Seahouses (but with no intoxicating liquor during the meetings). Less obviously improving was the Grace Darling Inn, in or near Manchester, the focus in 1910 of a compensation claim after it had had its licence removed.[39]

So appealing was Grace Darling's name that it was even used to promote some rather shady ventures in the City of London, the Grace Darling (Broken Hill) Silver Mines Ltd, incorporated in 1889, and the Grace Darling Purchase Syndicate Ltd, incorporated in 1897. The former, with a nominal capital of £155,000 in £1 shares, planned to work the mines in Victoria, one indication among many, as we shall see later, of the resonance of Grace's deed in Australia. The latter, with a nominal capital of only £10,000 in £1 shares, had nevertheless a more extensive remit – to acquire land 'in any part of the world' in order to exploit mineral rights, or, as the company put it, 'To prospect for, open, work, explore, develop, and maintain, gold, silver, copper, coal, iron, and other mines, mineral and other rights, properties, and works ...' No lack of ambition there. Capital for the Grace Darling Purchase Syndicate came from the Gresham Gold Exploring Syndicate Ltd, the New Zealand Reward Syndicate Ltd and the Colthurst Syndicate Ltd. In these two Grace Darling City of London firms, the heroine's name seems to be being commandeered for the finance imperialism of the later nineteenth century. Even the magic of her name, however, was unable to bring success. Only seven shares were paid up in the Grace Darling (Broken Hill) Silver Mines Ltd, the shareholders being two accountants, two clerks, a cashier, a self-styled 'gentleman' living in Tottenham and the company secretary. The addresses, in Peckham and Upper Holloway, seem to take us into the world of Mr Pooter rather than of Cecil Rhodes, and after letters sent to the company office were returned 'Gone away', the company was dissolved by the Companies Registration Office in 1893. The Grace Darling Purchase Syndicate wound up its affairs with greater decorum, but after an even briefer life span. In 1899 it announced that it could not 'by reason of its liabilities, continue its business'.[40]

A later, and also unsuccessful, commercial use of Grace Darling was the Grace Darling Hosiery Company Ltd, incorporated in 1921. Based in Burnley, the company was formed with 'the object of acquiring and carrying on the merchanting portion of the business of Hosiery Manufacturers and Hosiery Merchants', its formation probably a sell off by J. and J. Cryer of Lyons Mill, Littleborough of that part of its business. The shareholders, entirely local, were grocers, bookkeepers and builders. By 1927, however, Wilfred Cryer, one of the directors, was a publican and the company had ceased trading, the 'accumulated losses', according to the accountants, 'largely the result of a period of extreme stringency in trade'. In short, the company fell victim to the inter-war economic depression.[41]

In the late nineteenth century there were anniversaries of Grace's deed and death to commemorate: 1888 was fifty years after the deed, 1892 fifty years after her death. Local newspapers gave Grace some attention in 1888. The *Newcastle Daily Chronicle*'s 'special reporter' spoke to various people still alive who remembered the Darlings in the 1830s, including the artist John Reay, and concluded that Grace's deed was one 'which Northumberland will not willingly let die', hardly a ringing endorsement. But there seems to have been little, if any, notice of the jubilee at national level.[42] In Dundee, however, an enterprising publisher, John Leng, capitalized on the jubilee to put into book form David Pae's *Grace Darling, the Heroine of the Longstone Lighthouse; or, The Two Wills. A Tale of the Loss of the "Forfarshire"*. Pae was one of the most widely read authors of fiction in Victorian Scotland, writing serial novels for the weekly press. His *Grace Darling* must have appeared in this form some years before 1888, for he had died in 1884. The book is another long fiction about Grace, a reworking of Jerold Vernon, except that, where Vernon had taken them off to London and Spain, Pae confines his characters to Scotland. Grace and the Darlings play rather less part in the book's 426 pages than they had in Vernon, and are quite incidental to the main action. Like other writers, Pae cannot help thinking that Grace was lucky in her death. 'Removed in her youth, her beauty, her pure maidenly innocence, the fame of her heroic deed undiminished, a more glorious memory of her would be left than if she had lived many uneventful years and passed gradually but naturally out of human recollection.'[43]

There was much more attention at both local and national level in 1892. From London 'Flora', a columnist for the *Echo*, used the anniversary of Grace's death to reflect on progress. The contemporary enthusiasm, she thought, was 'somewhat exaggerated and fulsome'. 'It speaks volumes for the strides made by girls and women within the last fifty years that deeds of heroism on their part are becoming so familiar as to excite little more notice than when performed by men.' Nevertheless, 'Grace Darling will … remain for ever as an inspirer and forerunner for the more developed womanhood of the future', and it suggested that 'the womanhood of England' might erect a statue to honour Grace. The *Shipping World* agreed that there should be a national memorial: 'Grace Darling's fame needs no extolling to the people of England. The story of the Northumbrian maid's exalted courage is a fireside talk; her name is dear to the English heart.'[44]

The *Newcastle Daily Chronicle*, the premier newspaper of the north, gave full attention to the anniversary, with poems on Grace's death. A lengthy comparison of her with other 'so-called heroines' (Queen Elizabeth, Joan of Arc, Marie Antoinette, women pirates, and others) concluded that Grace belonged to 'the higher class' of heroines, like Florence Nightingale or, apparently unable to think of any other heroines in the same class, like Father Damien with his work among the lepers. Of Grace's place in history there was no doubt: 'By acclamation, Grace Darling has been classed among the heroines of history.'[45] The *Alnwick and County Gazette*, which rejoiced that 'half a century of homage' had been paid to Grace, referred to the efforts of H. J. Burn of Newcastle to instigate a national memorial and, as a conservative county paper, offered suitably cautious comments on the message that Grace's deed might have for modern women. 'Though brave, she was refined. At this time when the advancement of women's status is being pleaded, urged and demanded on every platform, it is to figures like that of Grace Darling to whom we must turn for illustration; and from characters like hers that we must draw arguments for the concession to women of a higher place in the world.'[46]

Comparing the *Echo* and the *Alnwick and County Gazette*, we can see that Grace is becoming caught up in the contemporary discussions of the 'woman question'. To the one she was an admirable forerunner, someone whom today's 'more developed womanhood' should remember and honour. But the world had moved forward, and women should be asserting a more prominent place in society and politics than was within the compass of Grace Darling. For the *Gazette*, on the other hand, Grace Darling embodied precisely the qualities that women should honour: gentleness, refinement and a willingness 'to sacrifice themselves in a genuine love to help their distressed fellows'.

Amidst all this reflection on the lessons that Grace's life might have for the late nineteenth century there intruded a long and bitter dispute on what had actually been involved in the deed in 1838. Between 29 October 1892 and 14 January 1893 (when the editor announced that 'This controversy might conveniently end now'), the *Newcastle Weekly Chronicle* carried no fewer than thirty-five letters on Grace's deed. The correspondence revived the simmering suspicion in North Sunderland that Grace's so-called heroism had not amounted to very much at all. William Wylie fired the opening shot. He claimed a familiarity with the Darlings and with Grace. 'I have rowed with her many a time. She was a canny lass … a fine young woman. Many a time she had made us our porridge.' But there was no danger in mounting the rescue, the sea, sheltered by the Harcar rocks, 'as calm as could be', and it was 'foolish to say "Old Bill", as we used to call him, jumped into the sea'. The North Sunderland boat, by contrast, in the open sea, was 'in great danger'.[47] This brought immediate ripostes, some disputing the facts, others simply looking to bring the debate to an end. 'We must remember we are treading on hallowed ground', wrote one. 'North-Country folks', said another, 'will always be proud of the name of Grace Darling, and will ever look upon her as a heroine and one worthy of the title she so nobly won.'[48] 'There are few Northumbrians', wrote John Robinson from Newcastle, 'who will not have felt a blush of shame at the attempt to detract from the fame of our Northern heroine, Grace Horsley Darling, more especially as the attack has been made by a Tyneside correspondent.' 'All nations', he went on, 'have their heroines; and the two whom Englishmen most delight to honour are Grace Darling and Florence

Nightingale. Their glory will never fade, and they will ever be held as the brightest stars in the world's galaxy of noble women.'[49]

Amidst all this furore about and declamation on the nature and extent of Grace's heroism, one thing stands out. Not one of the thirty-five letters was by a woman. When John Robinson wrote that 'Englishmen' delighted to honour Grace Darling and Florence Nightingale he may not have intended the word to exclude women – or indeed the Scots – but this was very much a male debate in its language and assumptions. Consider the contribution by W. Parker Snow from Bexley Heath. Inspired by revisiting press cuttings of the deed that he had assembled in 1838, he reflected on 'how many thousands of her sex do the same, or some daring deed akin to it'. There are heroines everywhere, he thought, from Sisters of Mercy to mothers at home, from Florence Nightingale to 'explorers, such as Mrs Pearcy in the North, and, permit me to add, my own lately deceased brave old wedded partner of over fifty-three years in the far South'. But he ended this roll call of heroines, of whom 'Grace Darling was but a symbol', by urging that they must not be forgotten 'if we are to remain a manly people'.[50] Heroines, confusingly, contribute to manliness. In the language of the time 'a manly people' were contrasted with 'an effeminate people', but the chief gauge of manliness in this comparison was performance in warfare. Heroines were being judged by masculine standards.

Other letters in the correspondence reflected on the way in which Grace's deed had been disparaged locally. 'Low Light' from Blyth had visited the area thirty years previously and had been astonished at the attempts to lessen the credit due to Grace. He put it down to envy, adding 'The envy of the men was taken up by the women with redoubled force, almost amounting to spite, from the thought that the heroine had taken the credit and rewards that should have gone to their husbands'. He had visited again in 1880 and found a better attitude, but now it seemed that 'the spirit of envy and spite that hurried this brave girl into her too early grave' was still alive. 'Reiver', writing from Leeds, amplified this account of 'the deep-rooted envy of the village communities along the Farne coast … From a lengthened sojourn in their midst, envy was a characteristic which particularly struck me; and, Northumbrian as I am, I am ashamed to note it … Not even in the grand work of rescuing shipwrecked mariners did I see that jealousy between village and village, even for one moment, lapse; nay, it was then that it seemed most emphasized, and marred all noble purpose.'[51]

There were attempts in the correspondence to reconcile the warring parties. James Robson, who had gone out in the North Sunderland boat, it was claimed, had never been known to 'utter one word in disparagement of Grace Darling. On the contrary, he has always spoken highly of her, and given her praise for venturing out on such a stormy morning'. James Cuthbertson from Beadnell suggested that there might be a dinner or supper for the present crew of the

North Sunderland boat, many of them descendants of those who had gone out in 1838, and for George Darling and James Robson, the two living representatives of the main families. 'It would warm the hearts of those two old men to know that kindly feelings are still entertained for them, and it would also cheer those younger and trusty friends who are ever ready to respond to the call of duty.' The editor said he was happy to receive subscriptions for such a dinner, but there is no record of it being held.[52]

Certainly George Darling could have done with something to warm his heart. With Thomasin now dead, he was the protector of the Darling name, but no more able than Thomasin to act in public: the family was once again indebted to Daniel Atkinson. He it was who responded to claims from Batty's agent, Mr Sylvester, in the Alnwick papers, and from the Robson family in the *Newcastle Weekly Chronicle*. Sylvester's 'eronious statements', according to George Darling, included the statement that Grace died of a broken heart. Nonsense, said George: 'poor dear creature she was in her happiest Element when she was where her Father and her mother were'.[53]

Atkinson was not the only writer leaping to Grace's defence in 1892. A much greater figure than he, Algernon Charles Swinburne, wrote his 'Grace Darling' in the summer of 1892. Most of the great Northumbrian families, the Dukes of Northumberland, the Trevelyans, the Greys and, in the twentieth century, Lord Armstrong, were to play a role in securing remembrance of Grace Darling, and to them can be added the Swinburnes. They could trace their Northumbrian family and estates back to the thirteenth century, and had been given a baronetcy in the seventeenth century for their loyalty to the Stuarts. At Clapheaton they had a substantial house with gardens laid out by another famous Northumbrian, Capability Brown. Swinburne's grandfather, Sir John, a well-known figure in Northumberland, was a radical in politics, and a friend of artists. It was said of him, Swinburne noted with pride, 'that the two maddest things in the north country were his horse and himself'.[54] Swinburne's father, the second son, pursued a naval career, rising eventually to become an admiral. From early childhood Swinburne was a lover of the sea. One of his earliest and happiest memories was of being held up naked in his father's arms, 'then shot like a stone from a sling through the air, shouting and laughing with delight, head foremost into the coming wave'.[55] In his teens he made contact with the artistic and intellectual coterie that gathered at nearby Wallington, and was championed by Pauline Trevelyan.

When William Bell Scott was commissioned to paint Grace Darling for the Central Saloon at Wallington, Swinburne accompanied him on the trip to the Longstone. The memory remained with him. In 1882 he chided Scott, fearing that 'your recollection of our excursion to Grace Darling's lighthouse will not include anything so agreeable as the lovely view of three blue herons on the ledge of a sea-rock to which I remember that I vainly though urgently called your attention, then distracted by sea-sickness'. In October 1892, sending the poem ('which has been very successful in MS') to Edward Burne-Jones, and wishing that he could have sent it to Tennyson before the latter's death, he again recalled the trip to the Longstone, and asked, 'Didn't you ever when a boy think how you would like of all things to keep or live in a lighthouse? I do to this day. Of course I mean if it's some miles out to sea and difficult to get at.' To William Morris, again enclosing the poem, he recalled meeting William Darling, 'a splendid old Norse – or Northumbrian – hero', a shrewd attempt to win Morris's sympathy and approval.[56]

Swinburne's poem is a paean of praise to Grace, to the north, and to the sea. In the first verse Swinburne establishes his northern credentials, and places Grace on a pinnacle:

> Take, O star of all our seas, from not an alien hand,
>   Homage paid of song bowed down before thy glory's face,
> Thou the living light of all our lovely stormy strand,
>   Thou the brave north-country's very glory of glories, Grace.

The bulk of the poem describes the storm, and asks:

> Who shall thwart the madness and the gladness of it, laden
>   Full with heavy fate, and joyous as the birds that whirl?
> Nought in heaven or earth, if not one mortal-moulded maiden,
>   Nought if not the soul that glorifies a northland girl.

'Sire and daughter', 'Maid and man', their names 'are beacons ever to the North'. Northumberland, 'our mother', never brought forth

> Children worthier all the birthright given of the ardent north
>   Where the fire of hearts outburns the suns that fire the south.

And Grace will be remembered. Perhaps alluding to the aspersions cast on her heroism, Swinburne saw her fame lasting 'till earth be sunless'.

> Now as then, though like the hounds of storm against her snarling
>   All the clamorous years between us storm down many a fame,
> As our sires beheld before us we behold Grace Darling
>   Crowned and throned our queen, and as they hailed we hail her name.
> Nay, not ours alone, her kinsfolk born, though chiefliest ours,
>   East and west and south acclaim her queen of England's maids.

So Grace belonged to all of England (no mention of Scotland), but chiefly to the north. If we are looking for a romanticization of northern England – and we

THE AGE OF CELEBRITY

shall encounter further examples in the twentieth century – Swinburne's poem can stand as a key foundational text. Swinburne, remembered as an aesthete as well as sexually deviant, here stands firm for a north that bred a tougher kind of person than the, by implication, effete south. And, as with Wordsworth, the storms that rack the coast are a positive, not a negative; they are the elements that bring forth in a Grace Darling the courage that can flourish only in a harsh environment. The poem ends with the Darlings and the sea in symbiotic unity. Swinburne remembers how at 'the hearth once thine' he had 'touched thy father's hallowed hand':

> Thee and him shall all men see for ever, stars that shine
> While the sea that spared thee girds and glorifies the land.[57]

When Tennyson died on 6 October 1892, there was much speculation that Swinburne would succeed him as Poet Laureate. It is an extraordinary coincidence that both Wordsworth, who became Poet Laureate, and Swinburne, who was seriously considered for the post, wrote poems on Grace Darling in the weeks immediately before the post was vacant. Grace Darling, a national heroine, was an entirely suitable subject for a Poet Laureate. It would be wrong, however, to suppose that either Wordsworth or Swinburne in any way wrote to canvass their cases. Swinburne would almost certainly have refused the offer if it had come to him. His 'Grace Darling' was in manuscript by the end of July 1892 and 'well approved of all round', but it was not published until nearly a year later, in the *Illustrated London News* in June 1893. In the same month, 'at Swinburne's expressed wish', the poem was privately printed. Someone making a bid for the Laureateship would surely have rushed into public print such an obviously patriotic poem.[58]

Swinburne was writing for adults. And there were other more conventional ways in which writings on Grace continued to address an adult or near-adult market. The collective biography genre, so common in the 1860s and 1870s, survived into the late nineteenth century, and Grace continued to be well represented. She is there in *Everyday Heroes: Stories of Bravery During the Queen's Reign 1837–1888*, published by the Society for the Propagation of Christian Knowledge. The book celebrates not military and naval heroes but rather the heroism of those 'who have devoted themselves to the good of their fellow-men'. Grace is ranked alongside John Howard, Elizabeth Fry, William Wilberforce, Thomas Clarkson, the Earl of Shaftesbury and Florence Nightingale, her name shining forth 'with particular lustre … in the annals of female heroism'. Grace can be found, too, in F. J. Cross's *Beneath the Banner: Being Narratives of Noble Lives and Brave Deeds* (1894), with the reflection that her name was 'now a household word', and in Rosa Nouchette Carey's *Twelve Notable Good Women of the XIXth Century* (1899), where, rather more effusively, in the chapter on Grace, we are told that 'no name has been more tenderly enshrined in the hearts of thousands', and that 'her best memorial is in the countless hearts that still love and cherish her'.

These books might have been appropriate for older adolescents, but none was so explicitly aimed at the teenage and young adult market as Eva Hope's *Grace Darling* had been. Hope's book, however, started a process that then gathered pace, a progressive lowering of the age at which the young were introduced to Grace Darling. The process was similar to that for fairy tales. Initially aimed at adults, fairy tales came to be thought suited to a younger and younger readership. And those who read fairy tales in the nursery, or had them read to them, just like those who now learned about Grace Darling in childhood, retained the memory through adulthood.

The lowering of the age range is clearly in evidence by the end of the century. The story of Grace Darling was a hardy annual in the *Girl's Own Paper*, readers in 1880 being told, in words that seem to come straight from Eva Hope, 'to do first the duty that lies nearest to you, until you have done that, be satisfied not to look further'.[59] In Annie Craig's *Golden Deeds Told Anew* (1897), or Marianne Kirlew's *Twelve Famous Girls* (1897), the simplicity of the language, and the fact that the publisher included at the back of each book a 'Catalogue of Illustrated Books suitable for Libraries, Rewards, and Presents', bespoke an even younger readership. Children were again unmistakably the market for the forty-seven page *Grace Darling: A Story of Shipwreck and Heroism* (1896), one of a series of children's books priced between 1d. and 3d. The book was plagiarized from Thomas Arthur and Eva Hope, but its format and binding place it clearly among juvenile literature. We can see the shift to a child market in the rewriting of one sentence. Arthur had plagiarized, almost unchanged, from Vernon: Grace, he had written, 'now lingered on the verge of girlhood, and the gay and thoughtless child was fast emerging into a graceful but noble woman'. In 1896 this became, 'She now lingered on the verge of girlhood, but at length the simple and artless girl emerged into a thoughtful and noble woman'.[60] Change the adjectives, prolong the shift from girl to woman, and you have both a new market and a new morality. The last thing girls in this new literature should be was 'gay and thoughtless'.

This shift of Grace Darling to the children's market coincided with a huge expansion of the market for juvenile literature associated with the spread of elementary schooling. School was not the only place where children heard about Grace, but it was the most important one. Much of the teaching was done through general reading books of collected stories for the lower standards, and Grace often featured in these. Her story can be found, for example, in *Longmans' New Readers, Standard IV* (1885), where it is sandwiched between entries on 'The Bison' and 'The Otter'. Her deed, children were told, has made her name as 'familiar to our ears as household words'. The emphasis was on her heroism, and on the ways in which Grace's heroism differed from conventional views.

> The mention of a heroine is apt to call up the picture of a tall and stately girl with dark, flashing eyes, and perhaps a little 'manliness' of voice and manner: but nothing could be more unlike Grace Darling. She was a fair-haired comely lass of twenty-two, with soft blue eyes, and a shy, timid manner. Her figure was of middle height, and by no means striking; but her face was full of sense, modesty, and a true kindness of heart.

In short, children could aspire to be like this 'lass', not least because amidst all the praise that came her way, 'Grace never forgot the modesty which is the true handmaiden of heroism'.[61]

Grace also found her way into History Readers, for example *Simple Stories from English History for Young Readers* (1893), *The Complete History Readers: Standard I: A First Book of Stories from History* (1904) and Macmillan's *New History Readers* (1905). In the first of these, with sixty-seven simple short chapters from the Celts onwards, Grace's near contemporaries are John Howard and John Lawrence (prison and slavery reformers), Nelson, Wellington, the Stephensons, the English in India, General Gordon and Queen Victoria ('A Good Queen'). Children learned that 'there was a brave deed done by a girl named Grace Darling that we all ought to hear of and copy, should we ever have the chance'. After reading the story, they had to write out and learn by heart, 'It was a noble deed, and we honour her name and think of her as a heroine'. National pride pervades these stories from English history, with heroes held up as embodiments of innate English virtues. Grace's name 'will never be forgotten, because English people prize noble deeds above all other things'. Although 'it would take a very big book in which to write an account of all the heroes of English history', Grace and General Gordon seem to head the nineteenth-century cast list. 'Every boy and girl', the children read, 'should be proud that Gordon was an Englishman, and should say to themselves: "I also will be a hero as Gordon was"'.[62] Grace Darling and General Gordon are exemplars of all that is best in the English: children should not only learn about them, they should also copy them.

The message was drummed home even more forcefully in *Grace Darling: An Action Scene for School Concerts* (1907), where Grace overcomes the fears of her timid father:

> With thunder crash upon the air
> The billows leapt and tossed,
> *Her father shouted in despair*
> 'Turn back, or we are lost'
> But prayerfully his heart she cheered,
> And plied her oars again.

The finale beat home the theme of woman's courage.

> And hearts with pride on land and sea
> Still at her mem'ry glow,
> How brave a woman's heart can be
> Her noble deed doth show.

The girls pictured in the accompanying stage directions in their 'Dress-Blue serge skirt, white sailor blouse, blue and white spotted neckerchief, tied carelessly with knot on shoulder, sleeves rolled up to elbow, and bare feet', looking more appropriately attired for a hornpipe than a sea rescue, seem to be aged about eleven. Performing it must have been a stirring, and memorable, experience. Whether children learning the piano were equally inspired to be confronted with the *Grace Darling Waltz* (1909) is a moot point.

The half century straddling the end of the nineteenth and beginning of the twentieth centuries saw Grace Darling at the pinnacle of her fame. She was held up as a heroine whom the young should aim to emulate, and she was a celebrity whose name and image were immediately recognizable. In a period when the 'woman question' was being hotly debated, and when, in the age of imperialism, there was heightened national awareness, the uses to which her name could be put were numerous.

Women's position in society was under constant discussion, brought to a head by the suffragists and suffragettes. People were looking for female role models. For those sympathetic to a new role for women, Grace was a pioneer who, in the circumstances of the 1830s, had done something that lay far outside the bounds of accepted and acceptable female behaviour. But, for such people, the world had now moved on. While Grace could be honoured for what she had done, young women of the late nineteenth and early twentieth centuries lived in a different world and faced new challenges. Grace Darling was of strictly historical interest, admirable in her day, but hardly any longer of much immediate relevance. For more conservative thinkers, Grace Darling had greater appeal. The courage displayed in her deed was wholly praiseworthy. Equally so was her comportment in its aftermath, her continuation in her domestic role at the Longstone, and her modesty amidst the flattery. Eva Hope's book, with its emphasis on the primacy of women's domestic role, made Grace immediately appealing to those alarmed by the claims of feminism. It is a simplification to imagine a world divided between advocates of women's cause (good) and reactionary opponents of it, mostly male and upper class (bad). There were many women and men looking for a compromise, a world in which it was perfectly possible and desirable for a girl or young woman to display the courage of a Grace Darling, within an overall acceptance of a division of roles between the sexes, with women mainly in the domestic sphere. For such people Grace Darling was a perfect exemplar, of immediate contemporary relevance, not merely some uplifting story from the past.

Her contemporary relevance was all the greater when set against anxieties about the future of the nation in the age of imperialism. A dominant motif in the writings about Grace in this period is the claim that 'her name is dear to the English heart', 'tenderly enshrined … in the countless hearts that still love and cherish her'. Her deed was, for the English, 'fireside talk'. She came, in an imperial age, to stand for a certain kind of Englishness, and one with which the people could identify. The empire was thought of largely as a male enterprise, and male heroes – missionaries, explorers, pioneers, generals – were easy to find: Livingstone, Havelock, Gordon, Kitchener, Baden-Powell and Scott of the Antarctic. But what role were women to play in imperial Britain? Some women, such as Mary Kingsley on her travels in West Africa, acted as though they might do the same as men, but a much more comfortable role to majority opinion was that they should, as wives and mothers, help their menfolk, or find some role in furtherance of empire that was distinctly feminine. Florence Nightingale, the nurse, fitted the bill exactly. So, in a different way, did Grace Darling. For in her deed Grace Darling showed that women, particularly English or British women, had physical courage the equal of any man's, but in her behaviour that such courage was entirely consistent with a traditional womanly modesty, and devotion to home and family. In a period of acute alarm about the future of the race, when mothers were being blamed for the carelessness and indifference that led to the premature deaths of so many babies, or, if middle-class, for their failure to accept their duty to produce children at all, Grace Darling was a model of traditional and desirable feminine behaviour. Of course she herself had no children, but, in her absorption in domestic and family duties, she displayed the qualities that the nation was thought to need.

So successful was the propagation of her name and image in the schools and Sunday schools of the period, and so appealing was her deed and life to the children and young women who heard about it, that advertisers had, in Grace Darling, a name and image ready at hand. In this way she became a celebrity, a name that could be used to promote both the obvious (a rose or chocolate), but also the unlikely (a mining company or a pub). In the late nineteenth and early twentieth centuries there were no limits to the fame of Grace Darling.

7

'Our National Sea-Heroine'

In 1929 Grace Darling's coble went on display at the North-East Coast Exhibition in Newcastle. It attracted considerable attention, and the interest aroused led, after many hiccups, to the opening of a museum in Bamburgh in 1938 to house the coble and other relics. In 1932 Constance Smedley published the most important twentieth-century book on Grace, *Grace Darling and Her Times*, and she herself spearheaded the Grace Darling League, a campaigning body designed to make Grace 'our national sea-heroine'. The centenaries of the rescue in 1938 and of Grace's death in 1942 led to plays, broadcasts and reflections on the significance of the deed for the twentieth century. Grace Darling's name and deed remained unsullied in the public consciousness for a further twenty years before, in the 1960s, the heroine began to be toppled from her throne. There were, however, signs before then that she no longer held as prominent a position in national culture as she once had.

The coble was the crucial element in the campaign for a museum memorial to Grace Darling: no coble, no museum. The boat in which Grace and her father rowed out to the rescue had been made in Berwick in about 1828 and was named 'The Darlings'. After the rescue, Grace's father continued to use the boat until about 1856 or 1857, when he passed it on to his son George, Grace's younger brother. George repainted it, replacing some rough timber and sending the pieces off to gentlemen who might appreciate them, and then used it for some years for fishing from Seahouses. By 1873 its condition made it impossible to use it any longer for fishing, and George, who had, as he put it, 'a sincere respect' for the coble, offered it up for sale. He had repaired it the previous summer and it was, he claimed, 'in such a condition that it will do for a Gentleman'. [1]

Colonel John Joicey of Newton Hall, Stocksfield-on-Tyne, and MP for North Durham, was interested. The Joicey family had made its fortune in coal. John Scott, probably acting on the family's behalf, entered into negotiations, and arranged with George to come and see the coble, but then backed off. George, under the impression that Scott was still interested, refused to sell to a clergyman acting on behalf of the Duke of Northumberland, but was then distinctly grieved to hear that Scott thought the coble too big. George's new assertive tone – he had previously been deferential, anxious not to cause offence, acknowledging that 'I am only a poor man' – seems to have worked: the boat was sold to the Joiceys. [2]

Until 1913 it remained in their possession. They kept it on their ornamental lake, and then, when it was no longer sound enough to lie afloat, in a shed. In the 1880s it made trips, quite frequently, to exhibitions: Tynemouth in 1882, London in 1883, Liverpool in 1886, Newcastle in 1887, Glasgow in 1888.[3] It is possible that it was planned to exhibit it in America in 1893 when David Grant in Dundee, the last living survivor from the wreck of the *Forfarshire*, wrote that he had 'never heard who was to go to America with the boat but I would not be able to go as I am very frail'.[4]

In 1883, Scott having got in touch with him again, George Darling let it be known that he still had the oar that Grace had used: 'It was no use in working the boat when you got her nor yet much to look at but I always preserved it as a memorandum of her so that if you should meet with any Gentleman in your travels that would wish to purchase it I have made up my mind to part with it as I have other little things that was in the boat at the same time.' Scott felt that he ought to have got the oar with the boat. Darling would have none of this, but was willing to let the oar accompany the coble to London for the exhibition, with a price tag of £65, to be returned to him if not purchased. Aware now that he had parted in 1873 with an increasingly valuable piece of property, he told Scott that 'Had I had the boat now one hundred pound [presumably the sum he received] would not have bought her'. Scott, we may assume, wanted to ensure that the oar remained with the boat, and eventually came to an agreement with Darling to buy it for £40 on condition that it remained in possession of the Joicey family. Unless there was more than one oar at his disposal, George must have been beaten down to £20, for in December 1883 he acknowledged receiving £20 from G. S. Buck, Esq., 'for oar used by Grace'.[5] George Darling also seems to have kept the mast and tiller, eventually disposing of them to Daniel Atkinson, the author of *Her True Story*, and a man to whom the Darlings were increasingly indebted for the protection of their reputation.[6]

For twenty-five years after the last exhibition in Glasgow in 1888 the coble seems to have been out of public view in the shed in the Joicey grounds. In 1913 Colonel Joicey's daughter, Lady John Joicey-Cecil, vested formal ownership of the coble in the RNLI, with the proviso that it must remain in Northumberland.[7] The RNLI's assumption of ownership was of critical long-term importance. Henceforth Grace Darling and the RNLI were to be inextricably linked, the RNLI being anxious to use the association with Grace for publicity purposes but also conscious of its responsibility for the coble. The latter's history over the next sixteen years remains obscure. A home was found for it in the Marine Laboratory at Cullercoats, at the mouth of the Tyne. How far it was open to public viewing we do not know. It was the exhibition in Newcastle from May to October 1929 that was crucial to further development. The attention it attracted was, as the *Life-boat* commented, 'hardly surprising when it is remembered that Grace Darling is Northumberland's special heroine, and that every Northumbrian child knows her story'. At the end of the exhibition a company which had had a neighbouring stand offered to pay for the coble to be repaired and strengthened, and this was done.[8] The Marine Laboratory was short of space and unwilling any longer to house the coble, so a new home had to be found. It had been hoped to place it in Bamburgh church, but the bishop refused permission – there were limits to the process of Grace's canonization. Lord Armstrong came to the rescue. He agreed to provide a separate site near the church, to house the coble in the meantime in Bamburgh, and to launch an appeal for funds.[9]

Between 1929 and the opening of the Museum in 1938, the centenary year, there were four main players in the bid to provide a new home for the coble: Lord Armstrong; the RNLI, in the persons of the Secretary, Lieutenant-Colonel Satterthwaite, and the Publicity Secretary, Charles Vince, in London, and the District Organizing Secretary in the north east, Captain W.J. Oliver; Constance Smedley and the Grace Darling League; and the people of Bamburgh. Relationships between the four were, to put it mildly, fraught.

Lord Armstrong, born in 1863, was the son of John William Watson of Adderstone Hall, Belford, and named after his father. He was also the great-nephew of the first Baron Armstrong, the great Newcastle industrialist who had died in 1900, leaving John Watson as his heir, but without a title. Along with much else, Watson inherited Bamburgh Castle which his great-uncle had bought in 1894, and Cragside, the house built for him near Morpeth. Watson's new wealth was large enough to demand a title to go with it, and in 1903 he became Lord Armstrong of Bamburgh and Cragside. Soon after succeeding to his fortune, however, Armstrong seems to have lost a large portion of it through ill-judged investments. 'For long', wrote *The Times* obituarist in 1941, 'he was a prominent figure in the public life of Northumberland', a major in the Northumberland Hussars, a county alderman, and active in charity work. He was also a crossword addict and (unexpected, this, for a peer) successful with the football pools.[10] But one senses that he was neither particularly popular nor energetic. Certainly he showed no urgency in launching the appeal for the coble. After the exhibition in Newcastle in 1929, it was taken to Bamburgh and housed in what was variously described as a coach house (Armstrong) or a disused stable (critics) in the grounds of Bamburgh Castle. The coble could be seen on application to the porter's lodge at the Castle, though how far this information was made available must be in doubt.

The RNLI, now the owner of the coble, was increasingly irked by Armstrong's delays. The RNLI dates back to 1824 when Sir William Hillary initiated the National Institution for the Preservation of Life from Shipwreck. The history of the institution in its early years gave little hint of the established place in national life it was later to acquire. The 1840s marked a nadir in its level of activity, with no appeals for money and no reports. In December 1849, however, twenty men were drowned in the Tyne while trying to rescue a wrecked crew, and this stirred people into activity. In 1851 the Duke of Northumberland took on the vacant post of President, and in 1854 secured a change of name to the Royal National Life-Boat Institution. For the following fifteen years there was a subsidy from the government, but thereafter the RNLI depended on charitable donations from the public. And its place in public life and public affection grew.[11]

Grace Darling did not feature in the RNLI's publicity in the second half of the nineteenth or earlier twentieth century. True, there was a boat named after her, and the very occasional and second-hand account of her deed in the *Life-Boat*.[12] But there was no concerted effort to link Grace's name and fame to the ongoing task of raising money for lifeboats across the United Kingdom. The acquisition of the coble in 1913 remains wrapped in mystery: was it an unwanted gift? Did the RNLI have any perception of what ownership of the coble might in future entail, or what opportunities it would offer? It seems doubtful. But after the Newcastle exhibition, and the public interest in the coble, the RNLI could not afford to do nothing. The public would blame the RNLI if Armstrong's promise to house the boat was not fulfilled.

Three years after the exhibition in Newcastle had closed, Satterthwaite felt that 'we cannot leave matters indefinitely as they are at present', and asked Oliver in the north east 'if you think there is any hope of Lord Armstrong completing the business'. If it was going to be impossible to get Armstrong 'to collect the small sum necessary to provide the house', could the coble be put on display in Bamburgh Castle? Oliver was blunt in reply:

> Lord Armstrong will never be of any value to us and we should therefore take a very firm attitude with him. If you will let me go and see him I will tell him that if he does not intend to do something the coble should be offered to the Seahouses people who would probably jump at the chance of having it there. I think that would put him on his mettle and we would get some satisfactory solution of this little problem.

Oliver had no doubt that the money required (£300) could be easily raised locally if there was the will to do it. The YMCA, he said, had asked Newcastle businessmen to raise £2,500 for boys' clubs and over £4,000 had been subscribed within a week.[13] Perhaps, in the conditions of the depression in the north east, boys' clubs may have seemed to have more urgency than a home for Grace's coble. Armstrong himself, however, had not been entirely inactive. By the end of 1932 he had collected about £40 towards a building to house the coble. Lady Armstrong had given permission for a ball to be held in Bamburgh Castle, with some of the proceeds going towards the housing of the coble – but this had had to be called off on the grounds that the electric light in the castle was too weak. The dim light in the castle was indeed aptly symbolic of Armstrong's approach. In May 1933 he was still thinking the time unsuitable for launching an appeal.[14]

Meeting in May 1933, Satterthwaite and Armstrong spent most of their time discussing the new player in the field, the Grace Darling League. The league had held its inaugural meeting in March at the Dorchester Hotel in London. Constance Smedley was its founder and inspiration, and perhaps its sole active member.[15] She was also the person who did most in the 1930s to keep alive and to further the memory of Grace's deed. The daughter of W. T. Smedley, a chartered accountant and philanthropist in Birmingham, she had the misfortune at the age of two to sustain serious injuries in a fall down the stairs. She was thereafter, as she put it, 'shut off from all forms of physical exercise except driving'. Or, as contemporaries described her, she was a 'cripple'. Educated at King Edward VI High School in Birmingham, and then, after two years of illness, at the School of Art, her 'primal desire', she wrote, 'was for adventure and experience'. Given her physical disability, she translated this urge into writing: plays, children's books and novels poured from her pen, forty-two publications over a lifetime. As a young woman in the early twentieth century, she was drawn to feminism, and became 'a convert to Women's Suffrage, and even a champion of the Suffragettes'. In 1907 she published *Woman: A Few Shrieks! Setting Forth the Necessity of Shrieking till the Shrieks be Heard*, a book which, she says, did not go down well with the old guard of suffrage campaigners. She probably made little attempt to ingratiate herself with her critics. In her *Reminiscences*, published in 1929, she wrote that her inability to remember faces 'gained me a most unjust reputation of being snobbish and exclusive'. Paradoxically, that reputation was probably enhanced rather than diminished by her acknowledgement that 'I was and always shall be incorrigibly ungenteel'. Smedley could evoke strong reactions. One correspondent told Jessica Mitford, 'I disliked Constance. She was dogmatic, bossy, ruthlessly righteous and alarmingly energetic'. The Duchess of Northumberland, however, if a little worn down by the persistence of Smedley's demand for further archive material, 'thought her most interesting and very charming'.[16]

Smedley's feminism took a practical turn. Aware of the difficulties of women struggling to maintain a professional life in a world of bed-sits, she conceived the idea of a network of Lyceum clubs where such women could meet, socialize, and advance the status of women in the world of arts and letters. From 1903 to 1909 she devoted much of her energy to organizing the clubs. Twenty years later she could congratulate herself that the International Lyceum Club was 'the most important woman's club in the world with its ten thousand members and club-houses in more than thirty capitals in both hemispheres'. Then, in 1909, she married the playwright and artist Maxwell Armfield, and moved to Gloucestershire, where they hoped they could give scope to their interest in fantasy in art and literature.[17]

Politically, Smedley is difficult to pigeonhole. She was influenced in her feminism by Philip and Ethel Snowden, both of them suffragists and also socialists, but that did not prevent her describing herself in 1909 as 'a broad-minded Conservative'. Cotswold slums converted her to Liberalism, but she purported to see good in all parties. In the First World War she was in touch with the Union of Democratic Control, indicating opposition to the war. In 1915 she and her Quaker husband went to New York. After seven years there, her next big step, after some years in the New Forest, was to move to London in 1927 to open the Greenleaf Theatre Studio.[18]

If in public Constance Smedley appeared overbearing, in private things were different. In early 1930 she and her husband were 'down to £3 and lots of bills', Smedley was chronically ill, and she was struggling to reconcile her ambition with the ideas of Christian Science which now occupied much of her thoughts and time. 'See everything I do must be in the right spirit', she wrote in her diary. 'Not in the spirit of levity, of exultation, of scorn, of fear, of doubt. But in the spirit of temperance, sobriety, gratitude, humility, courage, hope, certain trust in good.' Were these latter qualities not very precisely the ones that Grace Darling exemplified? Certainly Smedley was soon thinking of a play on Grace Darling for Sybil Thorndike. Two visits to Northumberland in the summer of 1930 and the autumn of 1931 set her up for something more ambitious.[19] Smedley, wrote the Marchioness of Aberdeen in 1931, 'came under the glamour of Grace Darling when she was visiting Northumberland last year'. This chimes with Smedley's own account in her book. 'The desire to find out all about' Grace, Smedley tells us, came from a visit to Bamburgh, 'and the discovery of wide unpopulated distances; a coast almost uninvaded by charabanc or bungalow; stretches of hill and park land; silence, stillness; above all, a great remoteness. In a Bamburgh farmhouse a collection of Grace's letters, simple and natural, in a fair and flowing script were found …'[20] The charabanc and the bungalow stood for all that Smedley and many like her found most distasteful about the modern world in which they lived. Grace Darling, Bamburgh and the Farne Isles seemed to offer Smedley a chance of retreating to and recreating a world devoid of such modern monstrosities. She was captivated by what she was uncovering in the archives, and unable to fulfil her publisher's wish for 'a very modern, racy story, without too much detail – like a Lytton Strachey or Maurois biography. But this style is going out of fashion, and people are beginning to demand documentary evidence.' The problem, however, was one of tone quite as much as of evidence. Smedley was aware that she might not be writing 'quite ironically enough, but I have gained such an affection for these curious Victorian people'.[21] In short, as the Marchioness of Aberdeen had seen, Smedley was smitten. Grace offered hope not just for the nation, but for Smedley herself.

Grace Darling And Her Times, published in 1932, and 288 pages long, was the first book to take full account of the range of published and unpublished material available. It remains, and will remain, an invaluable source. The amount of material Smedley accumulated, some of which has disappeared since she wrote, threatened to overwhelm, and the book as published is a distillation of a much longer first draft, which, as her husband wrote after her death, 'was found too cumbersome to publish, and she had then, tired as she was, to start all over again'.[22]

The 'crusader' of the *Reminiscences* was not content with nostalgia; she wanted to draw from the past lessons for the present. The first of these is a surprising one: dukes, pre-eminently the Dukes of Northumberland, had played and continued to play a vital role in British history. 'Few people outside their own county know anything about the splendid work the 1st, 2nd, 3rd, & 4th Dukes accomplished for our Coast & Seas – & also for our country', she told John Oxberry, the Secretary of the Society of Antiquities in Newcastle. Her aim was to remedy this ignorance. The role of the Dukes in promoting safety at sea was highlighted, and their political role, not least that of the eighth Duke who had supported far-right causes in the 1920s, ignored.[23] Contemplating a book on the third Duchess after recovering from 'the immense strain' of the book on Grace, Smedley told the Duchess how 'We want men and women like these to be in people's minds today – people who honestly and seriously *tried to do their* duty. That's why I'm so keen on them.'[24] A centrepiece of the book describes the visit of Grace and her father to Alnwick Castle in December 1838. Here, for lack of the documents on which most of her book is properly based, Smedley gave full rein to her imagination, describing the meeting of the humble Darlings and the condescending but benign aristocrats, imagining the feelings which each side felt. The passage ends with an extended set of similes which, if the word in the context can be excused, gives something of the flavour of Smedley in full flow:

> Compared to the homely rusticity of their visitors, one sees the Duke as a great golden King William Pear, suavely swelling, ineffably mellow, with his consort, a glowing Peach, highly coloured, luscious, but with a firm and tangy kernel; while William Darling has the texture of a russet apple, hard, sound, flavoursome, and Grace in her smooth-spoken invincibility and her sweetness appears a hazel plucked from the green branches in the hedgerow; the Duke and Duchess so urbane and mellow, the Darlings so homely and yet so full of savour – the savour of common life with courage and decorum.

The country, it was implied, needed the qualities both of aristocrats and of common people, and in the interaction of the Darlings and the Northumberlands there was a model of a society functioning effectively. 'The study of the lives of the First Dukes of Northumberland', Smedley concluded, 'shews them to have performed their duties as Peers as satisfactorily as the Darlings executed theirs as light-keepers. Such people meet on common ground ... The friendship of the two families in such vastly different stations is unique, but how like they were in their standards and their values! Grace Darling and her father will be for ever united in history's record, but so must be Grace Darling and her Guardian and his Duchess.'[25] It seems likely that readers were being invited, at the crisis point of the economic difficulties of the inter-war years, to draw lessons for the politics and society of their own day. Smedley makes no allusion to the present in her book, but one feels she may have reverted to the Conservatism of her youth.

The second theme that emerges from the book, and from Smedley's other writings and activities in these years, is a concern for the sea, and all to do with it. 'The awful apathy of the public to the sea', Smedley wrote, 'is just a call for Grace, once more, and the House of Northumberland.'[26] The book was dedicated 'To all Lightkeepers and Lifeboatmen', and came embellished with a foreword by Commander Stephen King-Hall, who, after a distinguished naval career, had turned to writing and broadcasting, and was famous for his weekly broadcast on current affairs in the BBC Children's Hour. Smedley's concern stretched beyond safety at sea. With the collapse of world trade in the aftermath of the First World War, she worried about the merchant marine and about the overall position of the country with its dependence on imports. She wanted to focus the attention of the country outwards towards the coast and the seas, to make Grace a 'sea-heroine', her deed a 'seamark' in history. Grace, she asserted 'will never be forgotten as long as British seamen sail the ocean. Her name is sacred to them.'[27] The present and future of the country, it was implied, was dependent on those British seamen sailing the ocean, with Grace their talisman.

If the seas and the oceans were one way in which, Smedley thought, British history needed to be reimagined, another was the need to be more alert to the role in national history of 'the North'. Smedley, whose life had been spent in the south or midlands, became, as she was aware, enraptured by 'the North'. Concerned as the publication date neared that there appeared to be no press notices in the northern papers, she confessed to Oxberry that 'My admiration for the North is so profound, that I may have erred in overestimating the value of the characters' lives & the events may not seem as important to the North as to me'.[28] For Smedley 'the North' meant the north east of England, from Hull to Berwick. There was another north, Scotland, to the north of 'the North'. On a day trip in 1930 Smedley recorded 'Tremendous thrill at having been to Scotland at last', but her outlook was English, not British: 'the North' stops at the border with Scotland. And her 'North' did not include, far less focus upon, as it did for George Orwell in *The Road to Wigan Pier*, the industrial and urban north of Manchester, Liverpool or Bradford. Smedley's 'North' was rural and largely empty of people, marked, in late November, by a 'latent savageness' and a 'surpassing loneliness'.[29] All this stood in implicit contrast to a never-mentioned South, softer, crowded with people and buildings. Britain (or England) needed an infusion of northern values, as embodied in the Darlings and Northumberlands.

What of Grace herself? Could she be presented as a role model for modern girls in the way Hope had been able to do in the 1870s? Grace's limitations, Smedley tells us, were those of her time and class. 'Where the girl of to-day', she wrote, 'faces publicity with courage, sanity and humour, Grace allowed herself to be literally pestered to death.' But on the positive side lay achievements and qualities that deserved to be remembered and treasured. 'As for Grace', she wrote,

> we owe to her deed reforms innumerable for the benefit of all who go down to the sea in ships; and to her life, a standard of cheerfulness, unselfish love, and content with simple duties faithfully performed. She and her father are akin to "The Unknown Warrior" in that she is typical of the thousands of men and women of their class who live equally devoted lives, happy, hard-working, heroic in hardship and peril, with no desire for praise. Grace's deed brought her into light but she became, and remains, our National Heroine, because she represents the common virtues of humanity.

Smedley's Grace is in fact remarkably similar to Hope's, despite her contempt for Hope's 'airily unsubstantial accounts'.[30] But Grace now became not so much a role model as a representative of a 'class' of men and women (not the 'class' of Smedley or her readers), who stand for essential qualities in national life and for humanity as a whole. How comforting in the early 1930s to think of that class (the working class) as 'happy, hard-working, heroic in hardship and peril ...'

Smedley told Oxberry that her publisher, Hurst and Blackett, 'desires the history of Grace Darling & her family & the Dukes of Nd to be in every Library'.[31] Publishers, like authors, have their dreams. Smedley herself did everything she could to promote the book, even persuading the Duchess to go with her son to Seahouses for a photo opportunity to provide publicity: 'It is awfully good of Her Grace', wrote the bemused photographer, 'to be taking so much trouble to further the interests of Mrs Armfield's book.'[32] Reviewers were polite if not enthusiastic, most being puzzled that a simple deed of heroism could lead to such a large book.[33] The book can hardly be said to have taken the country by storm. It sold only 390 copies in the first year of publication.[34]

Publication of *Grace Darling and Her Times* by no means exhausted Smedley's enthusiasm for Grace. In 1933 she was still looking for any outlet for publicity, bombarding the provincial press. All too often she met with rejection, from the BBC, from Arthur Mee, from an educational publisher. 'Grace obsesses me and feel exhausted', she acknowledged. But Grace also soothed her amidst much depression and illness, perhaps a more effective remedy than Christian Science, though she would have denied any division between the two. 'Tried to realise unity with Source as I felt a little tired', she wrote, 'and poems about Grace flowed into my thought. Several came. I wrote one down.'[35] After her death in 1941 Maxwell Armfield told Satterthwaite how 'My wife was not at all herself for some time: actually I feel that the research, etc. on Grace was a great strain on her'. She 'was never quite the same', he thought after the effort involved in writing her book on Grace.[36]

Eventually she found a responsive publisher for a book for children, *Grace Darling and Her Islands*, published by the Religious Tract Society in 1934. The society had published two of Smedley's earlier books, *The Emotions of Martha* in 1911 and *Ruth's Marriage* in 1912, and it may have been this connection which accounts for the choice of the society as her publisher in 1934. Any religious message, which might have been expected from such a publisher, is distinctly muted. The focus is on Grace's love of birds, on the happiness and healthiness of her childhood in the open air, and on the importance of the sea in the national life of the country. Grace herself becomes emblematic of the nation. Her album, Smedley tells us, had been recently found. The first poem is, appropriately, 'To the Sea'. The front page is decorated with a wreath of roses, there are three poems mentioning roses, and there is a full-page picture of very bright pink and crimson roses. It looked 'as if the rose, our national emblem, was our heroine's favourite flower'.[37] That 'national emblem' was of course English, not British.

The Grace Darling League gets a page to itself at the end of the book, its aims neatly reinforcing the message of what has come before. Grace Darling was to be established 'in history as our Sea Heroine'; a Memorial Museum was to be built at her birthplace, 'on the ground already provided by Lord Armstrong'; and interest was to be promoted in 'our shipping and navigable waterways'. In other formulations this latter aim expanded to arousing public interest in 'maritime inventions and experiments and in British achievements for the safety of life at sea' and securing support 'for institutions benefiting seafarers'. An exhibition of paintings and other souvenirs of Grace Darling was to tour the country raising money for a memorial at Bamburgh 'and a proper shelter for her historic rescuing boat, which was now housed in a disused stable'. The league was to have a finite life of five years, ending therefore, it must have been hoped, in triumph in the centenary year.[38]

In the weeks before the league's opening Smedley had frequent contact with the RNLI, trying to secure its support, both financial and moral. Other institutions, too, were approached: Lloyd's, the insurers, the Navy League, the British Coastal Commission, the Royal Empire Society and Benevolent Societies for Marine Purposes. The hope was that they would provide the £1,200 to £1,500 which it was estimated was required for the travelling exhibition – at which sponsors would be able to exhibit in proportion to their donations. The exhibition was to be organized by the Art Exhibition Bureau. The RNLI quickly disabused Smedley of any idea that it could provide financial backing for the exhibition, nor did it want to be associated in any way with 'propaganda for other societies, such as the Navy League ...'[39] Smedley refused to be brushed off. She was looking, she said, for cooperation between organizations, convinced that 'it is of the utmost consequence to arouse and maintain public interest in the Sea. A massed effort may effect this.' The RNLI's assurance of 'moral support' was not enough. Investment by the RNLI in the exhibition would, Smedley urged, 'be the cheapest and I think most profitable Appeal the RNLI has ever issued – and my book will turn many to you ... Your organization is so dependent on the seamen of the coast that you well may co-operate with the movement for getting back to our seas again in which Grace (God bless her) will lead.'[40] Smedley meanwhile was writing articles praising the RNLI, and stressed that as the league was going to work 'for the Safety and Mastery of the Seas (not in a spirit of truculence and anti-foreigner but of conquest by pluck and skill) the RNLI's example and record (no lives lost at sea this year) is of great importance'. Subscriptions for the RNLI, she noted, had gone down in 1931 and 1932: 'It seems to me we've got to make a great push for 33. *Grace will do it.*'[41]

Confronted with this barrage of letters, Satterthwaite attended a private meeting of the league in April. None of the charities present offered any financial help for the proposed exhibition. Satterthwaite himself expressed his personal sympathy for the objects of the league, but was not willing to appear as a patron. In face of this rebuff, Smedley displayed a sublime ability to turn a defeat into victory and to rewrite the immediate past. 'I never thought of and never liked the idea or the responsibility of your financial co-operation', she wrote to Satterthwaite the next day, 'and I feel much free-er now to do what I can – little or much.' And she promised him that she still stood by a previous agreement that she would donate to the RNLI money from the trade show of a proposed film on Grace.[42]

At intervals over the next few years Satterthwaite was asked to cooperate in Smedley's ideas for raising money and publicity for Grace. They ranged widely. Oak trees or groves of oaks were to be planted throughout the empire in memory of Grace.[43] Three one-act plays about Grace, suitable for amateurs, which Smedley had written, were to be promoted, including a matinee performance with Dame Sybil Thorndike and Dame Madge Kendall, both patrons of the league.[44] A former whaler, the *Grace Darling*, was to tour coastal resorts in the summer of 1935. The ship, which had been fitted up for dancing, lectures, music and drama, was under the command of Miss Borthwick who had had a hospital ship in the First World War. The hope was that mayors in the towns to be visited would provide some subsidy.[45] Another round of play readings was planned for 1937, with the possibility that Victoria Hopper, a film star and the wife of Basil Dean, would take Grace's part, and bring with her 'Basil Dean's publicity organization, too'. And if not Victoria Hopper, then Anna Neagle.[46]

Most of these ambitious schemes came to nothing. One exception, with the RNLI lending support, was the planting of an oak tree in Battersea Park on 24 November 1934. Also involved was the Green Cross Society, an organization formed to plant memorial trees after the First World War and boasting the support of both Stanley Baldwin and Ramsay MacDonald. The tree itself came from Northumberland, and was presented by the Lord Lieutenant, Sir Charles Trevelyan. A RNLI boat came up the Thames, and its crew performed the planting – they were pictured standing round the oak, holding their oars aloft, with some young naval cadets to the rear. The Merchant Navy was also represented.[47] In 1949 the Conservative MP for Berwick on Tweed, Brigadier Thorp (the Thorps had an association with the Darlings going back to Grace's time) worried that the tree might be damaged in the construction of buildings for the 1951 exhibition, but assurances were given by Herbert Morrison. Willie Gallagher, the Communist MP, then intervened to ask that, if the tree was damaged, could it be replaced with 'a statue of the lady's famous descendant, Sir William Darling' (laughter). Sir William Darling, MP for South Edinburgh, reminded the House that 'Grace Darling died a spinster' (loud laughter).[48] Had Grace and everything and everyone associated with her become a joke? Not quite. It was perhaps the tree that led, in 1953, to a Special School that had been relocated in Battersea to being named the 'Grace Darling School'.[49]

The Battersea Park oak was the only one to receive any publicity and perhaps the only one ever planted. Surviving the 1951 exhibition, and now in its maturity, in summer its dark leaves stand out against the dominant London planes bordering the Thames, but few probably pause to try to decipher the decayed sign that is the only obvious reminder of the Grace Darling League. In 1938 Constance Smedley was still hoping that trees would be planted in ports throughout the empire in time for the centenary of Grace's death in 1942. The Duke of Northumberland had evidently agreed to plant one in Gibraltar.[50] But whatever may or may not have happened in Gibraltar, the empire-wide tree planting, like most of the Grace Darling League's schemes, came to nothing.

Great hopes petered out into non-events. A play reading in the Burlington Gallery in London 'left us very considerably in arrears'. At another, 'everyone was so busy with the play-reading, and the audience was so few, that no-one could be found to take a collection'.[51] Satterthwaite and the RNLI carefully distanced themselves from schemes that might bring the institution into disrepute. While offering some support to Smedley, whose enthusiasm was hard to resist, they assured their RNLI colleagues in the field, who occasionally wrote in for guidance about the league, that it was best to keep at a distance. 'The heads of the League', the Scottish Organizing Secretary was told in October 1935, 'are very enthusiastic but not at all businesslike, and though, of course, we have given the League our sympathetic support, the Secretary has had to be very careful in dealing with its attempts to bring the Institution into what have not been very practical schemes'. The Organizing Secretary for the south west was assured by Satterthwaite that he had as far as possible kept out of the arrangements for the whaler, which 'I

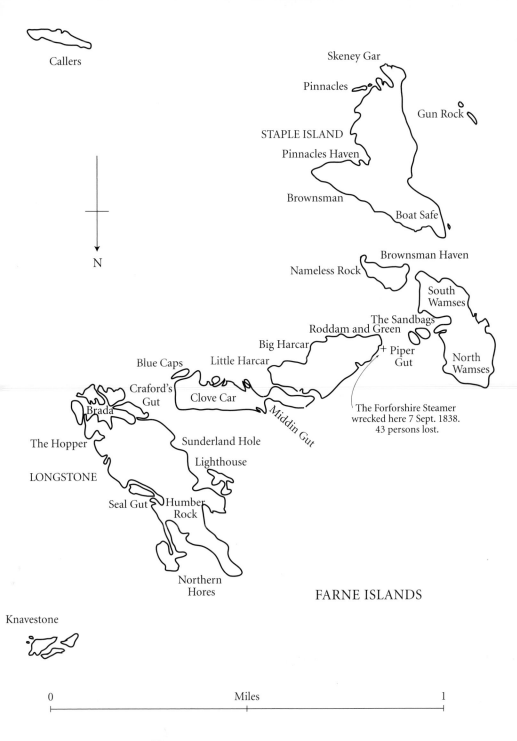

Callers

STAPLE ISLAND

Skeney Gar

Pinnacles

Gun Rock

Pinnacles Haven

Brownsman

Boat Safe

Brownsman Haven

Nameless Rock

South
Wamses

The Sandbags

Roddam and Green

Big Harcar

Piper
Gut

North
Wamses

Little Harcar

Blue Caps

Craford's
Gut

Clove Car

Middin Gut

The Forforshire Steamer
wrecked here 7 Sept. 1838.
43 persons lost.

Brada

Sunderland Hole

The Hopper

Lighthouse

LONGSTONE

Seal Gut

Humber
Rock

Northern
Hores

FARNE ISLANDS

Knavestone

0	Miles	1

1. Map of Farne Isles.

2–5. Henry Perlee Parker, Portraits of Grace Darling and of her father and mother: Parker, an established Newcastle painter, spent a week with the Darlings in November 1838, and did at least four sketches of Grace as well as portraits of her mother and father, and scenes of the rescue. In the one where Grace is looking to the right she is wearing the cape she had on during the rescue. She gave this to Parker, who named his baby daughter Grace. *(Photographs by Eddie Ryle-Hodges)*

6. David Dunbar, bust of Grace Darling: David Dunbar arrived in Bamburgh from Newcastle on 6 October 1838, and by 27 October was advertising finished casts at one guinea each. He also did three versions of the bust in marble, this one commissioned by the Bishop of Durham, Edward Maltby, and now in the National Portrait Gallery. Dunbar, it was said, made Grace in profile, look like Napoleon. *(Photograph by author)*

7. Thomas Musgrave Joy, portrait of Grace Darling. Joy was commissioned by Lord Panmure to paint this portrait and a scene of the rescue. On the proceeds, he was able to get married – and he was soon commissioned to paint portraits of the Prince of Wales and the Princess Royal. Panmure donated the paintings to the Seamen's Fraternity of Dundee in 1842. *(Dundee Museums and Art Galleries)*

8. John Wilson Carmichael, 'The Rescue'. John Wilson Carmichael had built up a reputation in Newcastle as a marine painter much influenced by J.M.W. Turner. This version of Grace and her father rowing out to the stricken *Forfarshire* was painted before Carmichael visited the Longstone. For a later and more accurate version, see the dust jacket. The idea that Grace rowed standing up is taken to extremes in plate number 10.

9. William Bell Scott, 'Grace Darling Rescuing the Men of the Forfarshire'. William Bell Scott was commissioned by Sir Walter and Lady Pauline Trevelyan to paint scenes of Northumbrian history for the Central Saloon at Wallington. The painting of the rescue dates from 1860. Grace represents one of the beatitudes, the merciful, but the eye is drawn away from the tiny coble to those about to be rescued, in particular the one woman, modelled here by Scott's mistress, Alice Boyd. *(Wallington, The Trevelyan Collection (The National Trust), © NTPL/Derrick E. Witty.)*

GRACE DARLING

BALLAD.

Written and Composed by

GEORGE LINLEY.

The heroic Conduct of Grace Horsely Darling, who, with her Father rescued nine Persons from the Wreck of the Forfarshire Steamer, has furnished the subject of this Ballad. The cries of the sufferers were heard by this young female during the night, but the darkness was such as to prevent any assistance being rendered. At Day-break, notwithstanding the storm was still raging, the old Man assisted by his intrepid Daughter, launched a small Boat, each plying an Oar, and after many dangerous and desperate efforts succeeded in safely conveying to the Lighthouse Nine of the surviving Crew.

Nothing but the pure and ardent wish to save the Sufferers from impending destruction could have induced these two humane beings to enter upon so perilous an Expedition, fraught as it was with the imminent hazard of their own lives.

Sta Hall.

Price

LONDON.
Published by CRAMER, ADDISON & BEALE,
201, Regent Street & Conduit St.

10. Grace Darling Ballad Written and Composed by George Linley: Ballads to celebrate Grace's deed were numerous. George Linley's perhaps had the longest life – versions of it were still being printed twenty years after 1838. Grace's clothing and posture here show the licence given to artists in depicting the rescue. *(Photograph by Eddie Ryle-Hodges)*

11. Staffordshire pottery: Staffordshire pottery, now a collector's item, was cheap and mass-produced, casts being reused for different purposes. This representation of the rescue, with the lighthouse prominent, and Grace and her father curiously still and composed, would have graced many a mantelpiece. In the twentieth century, Maurice in P.D. James's *Innocent Blood* (1980) has a copy of it, along with figures of Nelson, Wellington, Victoria and Albert. *(The Potteries Museum and Art Gallery)*

12. Royal Doulton Figure of Grace Darling. Produced for the 150th anniversary of the deed, designed by Eric Griffiths, and in a limited edition of 9,500, this statuette was memorably described by Jessica Mitford as representing Grace as 'a composite of Elizabeth Taylor and Snow White'. *(Photograph by Eddie Ryle-Hodges)*

Above: 13. Thomas Brooks, Grace Darling.
Painted at least thirty years after Grace's deed,
Thomas Brooks's painting became the model
for all later renderings of the deed. It seems to
represent the moment when William Darling
has gone ashore on to the Big Harcar, but
many people assumed that Grace was alone
in the coble all the time – her father was
airbrushed out of the rescue. *(Photograph
by Eddie Ryle-Hodges)*

Right: 14. Lifebuoy soap. In the consumer
market of the late nineteenth century, women
were key buyers, and soap high on their list of
purchases. The portrayal of Grace is modelled
on Brooks's painting – but at least William
Darling is also present. *(The John Johnson
Collection, Bodleian Library)*

15. The coble in the 1930s. Lord Armstrong looked after the coble in the years before the opening of the Museum in 1938. Much blamed for keeping it away from public gaze in a 'disused stable' he here had it taken out into the open for the benefit of photographers, only to be criticised for not even keeping it under cover. The massive walls of Bamburgh Castle loom in the background. *(RNLI)*

16. Grace Darling's tomb: Erected in Bamburgh churchyard soon after Grace's death in 1842 and designed as a canopied tomb of the thirteenth century, the stone crumbled away, and the tomb had to be redesigned and rebuilt in the later nineteenth century. Even after that, there were complaints of neglect. *(Photograph by Eddie Ryle-Hodges)*

need not tell you that I cannot regard … as a very efficient and economical way of raising funds'.[52] But there remained a certain loyalty towards Smedley. When District Organizing Secretaries complained in 1937 that they had in a matter of days received from Smedley four telegrams, one letter and a gramophone record to be collected at midnight, and thought she might be unbalanced, they were told: 'I do not think that Miss Smedley is in any way unbalanced, but she is a great enthusiast.'[53]

Smedley was fully alive to the necessity of involving 'the North' in any campaign to promote Grace and her deed. She delayed the launch of the league because 'the North feels we must await the return of the Duchess [of Northumberland] and so do I before further steps are taken'. She wrote an article for the Newcastle *Sunday Sun*, promoting the Grace Darling League, explaining that, since Grace was a 'national heroine', 'it is fitting that the desire and preliminary activity should come from the capital of the nation, London'. In any case, she flattered her readers, 'Grace is already established in the North. Every child knows of her deeds and loves her name.' The outcome of the league's activities should be that 'the great Epic of the North will be shewn in its full significance as one of the seamarks in our history', and that 'we shall recognise the part the North has played in British history a little more clearly'.[54]

What the people of Bamburgh, the fourth player in the drama of the coble, made of this we cannot be certain. They were caught in the crossfire between Armstrong and his critics, each uncertain as to what Smedley might be up to. At the end of 1934, Smedley reported to Satterthwaite what she had been told by a member of Bamburgh Parish Council. There had been a committee in Bamburgh to raise money in 1929, some stimulus provided by the arrival of Smedley in the winter of 1931, the coble better housed in the aftermath, a second committee formed, and then, as she put it, 'the suppression of the inhabitants' activity by 3 or 4 local people – of course Lord A's friends'. 'The inhabitants', she went on, 'have wanted to collect from summer visitors & the Parish Council have discussed the matter – but could not move because of the "Committee" instituted. Nor is the boat, theirs. They are all aggrieved at the attacks *on them* & say visitors go away thinking the wreck exaggerated & Grace in no way remarkable.' Smedley herself, privy, it seems, to information about these Bamburgh committees, had promised to give the member of the parish council who had approached her 'full information about Lord A & the committee when I am free and able to do so'.[55]

It was doubtless interaction between Smedley and people in Bamburgh that led to the suggestion that Thomasin's old house, the Wyndings, should become a memorial to Grace.[56] Armstrong, Satterthwaite reported, was 'quite well disposed' to the suggestion. His agent, however, saw difficulties. William Dixon, the tenant (and also, for most of the 1930s, treasurer of the parish council, and as a descendant of the Darling family, perhaps Smedley's informant), had lived there all his life, and his father before him. The conversion of the house, or part of it, into a museum would interfere with lettings to summer visitors. Armstrong's lukewarm welcome for the idea now shaded into disapproval. He was 'not enthusiastic about Miss Smedley buying it, even if she manages to propitiate Mr Dixon. I am doubtful whether there are enough genuine relics to fill a room, and I must add there seems to be no local enthusiasm.'[57]

These exchanges were punctuated by press reports about the housing and condition of the coble that roused Armstrong's suspicions about Smedley and her associates. Armstrong was sensitive to complaints that the coble was not properly cared for, but his efforts to allay the worries tended to backfire. He arranged for the coble to be taken out into the open to be photographed – but then found subsequent press reports claiming that the boat was not even kept under cover. In September 1933 he summoned W. J. Oliver, the RNLI's representative in the north east, to come and look at it. A year later Satterthwaite was assuring Armstrong that neither the Grace Darling League nor the RNLI had had anything to do with further critical reports in the north country press. The reports, riposted Armstrong, were inaccurate, 'but only a repetition of a remark made by Miss Smedley and published as such about a year or two ago'.[58] Mrs Gardiner, the chairwoman of the Grace Darling League, wrote to Armstrong with various proposals on 15 December 1934, and complained bitterly to Satterthwaite on 4 January 1935 that she had not even 'received the courtesy of a reply from him'. 'It is only with the greatest difficulty', she went on, that 'we are keeping back a public outcry about the boat since it was handed over to the RLI [sic]'. A report in the *Sunday Express*, with a photograph of the coble, 'evidently emanated from Bamburgh', Smedley reported to Satterthwaite. 'I knew nothing of it. It will serve to rouse the inhabitants further – but it is lamentable.'[59] Relationships between the league and Armstrong were frosty, Satterthwaite the confidant of both sides. Armstrong agreed to meet the latter to discuss the League's proposals, adding that 'I may say that although I have never met Mrs Gardiner, who I think is the same person as Miss Smedley, and have no wish to do so, I have helped her with material … but I do not think any substantial museum of Grace Darling Relics could be got together.'[60]

All sides did, however, agree on one idea for fund-raising. In the summer of 1934 Professor C. P. Darling, late of the Royal Military Academy at Sandhurst, had agreed to make an appeal to members of the Darling family and name in the United States and the Dominions. Armstrong thought the idea 'worth consideration', Satterthwaite was willing to assist, and hoped that Armstrong might hand over to Professor Darling the sum already raised. But like so many other projects for fund-raising this one seems to have run into the sands.[61]

Positive progress towards rehousing the coble and creating a museum began to be made at the end of 1935, and probably owed most to Charles Forster, recently returned from Wiltshire to his native Bamburgh. Forster (no mere Foster, as Oliver pointed out) was a name of weight in the north east, and in Bamburgh in particular. He persuaded Armstrong to preside over a meeting in Bamburgh, where it was agreed to set up a committee to raise funds. The idea was that the coble would be visible through glass and that there would be an adjoining room for relics, open on Bank Holidays. Armstrong himself insisted that the coble needed to be enclosed to guard against souvenir hunters, 'and this is more so with Americans who may come here'. Lady Armstrong graced the occasion, but her presence did not secure a large turnout, or, as we shall see, may have prevented one. 'It was a great pity', reported the *Berwick Journal*, 'that with such interests at stake, that the attendance was not larger'.[62] There was evident local ambivalence about the role that Armstrong had and would play.

After the meeting, Forster wrote to Satterthwaite at the RNLI seeking assistance and cooperation, and explaining that 'Before calling this public meeting I got in touch with the Grace Darling League informing them of what was proposed and asking them what steps, if any, had been taken by the League towards the object we had in view. I gathered that the League looked with favour on my suggestion that Bamburgh should proceed as proposed.' Forster and Satterthwaite, it turned out, had encountered each other at the Horse Guards during the war, Forster serving with the Tyne Electrical Engineers. This doubtless facilitated a cordial and productive relationship. Oliver, the RNLI man in the north east, met up with Forster and reported to Satterthwaite that 'The Grace Darling League have made attempts to take the credit of this Movement, but have offered no help. Please keep them in the dark as to what is being done.'[63]

Forster and Oliver set about fund raising. They wanted to, and did, get the signature of Colonel Harold Robson, of Lesbury House, Lesbury, thinking that it would 'counterbalance the disadvantage of Lord Armstrong's. An attempt was made to draft the letter so as to avoid having to have the latter's signature, but it could not be done nicely as after all he is the Lord of the Manor.'[64] The problem with Armstrong lay not only in his activity, or lack of it, as Lord of the Manor, but also in his third marriage in 1935, in his early seventies, to Kathleen England. The exact nature of the problem is not entirely clear. Perhaps the marriage ensued too soon after the death of Armstrong's second wife in 1934. Perhaps there was an embarrassing disparity of ages. The new Lady Armstrong was, on the face of it, entirely respectable, the daughter of a clergyman, and working for a local cancer charity. But rumours accumulated around her: her father was a bookkeeper; she had been a chorus girl on the London stage; she was a prominent and rather loud presence at social gatherings and parties in Newcastle. Whatever the reason, as Oliver reported, 'Lord and Lady Armstrong are not being received by the County at present ... The Duchess [of Northumberland] refused to meet the girl before marriage and people are now waiting to see if she will receive her as Lady

Armstrong. Lady Armstrong has suggested to Major Forster that she should give a dance in the Castle for the Appeal but as no one would dare to go the latter is in a very awkward position.'[65] Eventually the Duchess was persuaded to come on board the appeal, donating £5 after Oliver had explained to her that, given his local position, it had been impossible to sideline Armstrong.[66]

The RNLI threw its weight, and eventually money, behind Forster's initiative. It agreed to 'undertake the custody of the house, provided the cost involved is raised locally'; it drafted an appeal leaflet which a meeting in Bamburgh happily approved; and, eventually, in September 1936, it agreed to pay £200 to meet the shortfall from local fund-raising. In March 1937 came confirmation that Armstrong was willing to gift a site, just opposite the church, for the museum.[67]

These positive moves, and the approaching centenary, may have motivated a last burst of activity from Constance Smedley. 'After a long silence we have heard again from Miss Constance Smedley', reported Charles Vince of the RNLI in August 1937. But Smedley and the league had by now lost any credibility they may have had. The RNLI was 'cautious about being drawn into the activities of Miss Smedley and the League'. Oliver in the North 'had quite a long talk with the Duke of Northumberland and he tells me that I can turn down any suggestion she makes regarding getting his help, without troubling him. He sees no point in encouraging this woman if, to use his words, we are not going to get anything out of it.'[68] Oliver did suggest that the league might contribute £200 towards the museum of relics (as distinct from the housing for the coble), but Maxwell Armfield, Constance's husband, acknowledged that that 'seems rather fantastic to us at the moment ...'[69] Smedley herself was showing distinct signs of strain. In a letter to Vince, with the writing all over the page, she ends, 'Now Mr Vince, you and Colonel Satterthwaite never admit defeat, & nor do I – the British lose all battles but the LAST!!'[70] In June 1938, with the centenary little more than two months ahead, Smedley had a long telephone conversation with Satterthwaite, the latter reporting to Oliver that

> She appears to be in touch with Lord Armstrong regarding celebrations to take place at Seahouses and in London on the 8th September ... In this connexion, apparently Lord Armstrong is likely to approach both the Duke and Duchess of Northumberland, and I made it clear to Miss Smedley that we could not actively co-operate. I did not tell her that I scarcely expected that the Duke or Duchess would very readily agree to anything Lord Armstrong suggested.[71]

The centenary celebrations took place without, it seems, any participation by Smedley or the League. Yet it is fair to ask what kind of celebrations of any kind there would have been without Smedley's championing of Grace Darling in the 1930s. The league itself never came near to fulfilling its agenda and ultimately served to discredit Smedley, but her research and her books, and her ceaseless championing of Grace, gave the cause a level of publicity and plausibility which it would not otherwise have had. Without Smedley, Lord Armstrong might never have been prodded into any kind of activity. The RNLI might not have committed itself so strongly to the campaign for a museum had Satterthwaite not been constantly reminded of the cause by Smedley. The people of Bamburgh might not have had the tenacity to negotiate their way through the intricacies of local politics consequent on the unpopularity of Armstrong without Smedley goading them into action. These are all imponderables. To most of those involved Smedley was a thorn in the flesh, though perhaps a salutary one. Satterthwaite had a soft spot for her, and offered encouragement for her more practical schemes, but had to be careful not to compromise the RNLI's position. Armstrong had little time for her, and, as we have seen, no wish to meet her. To the Duke of Northumberland, she was, with all the weight that the phrase carries, 'this woman'.

On 21 July 1938 the great and good of Northumberland assembled in force in Bamburgh for the opening of the museum. The ceremony began with a service in St Aidan's church, conducted by the vicar, the Reverend G. R. Wilkinson, who was also honorary treasurer of the Bamburgh Grace Darling Memorial Committee. Every seat in the church was occupied, many stood in the aisles, and outside hundreds listened to the service that was relayed by loudspeakers. After the service, the Bishop of Newcastle and the clergy of the diocese led a procession across the churchyard to the door of the museum. There Major Forster told the story of the rescue, and Lord Armstrong handed over the title deeds of the site to Sir Godfrey Baring, the RNLI's chairman. As he did so, Sir Charles Trevelyan, Lord Lieutenant of Northumberland, raised the RNLI's flag on the mast above the museum. The Bishop of Newcastle then dedicated the building, and the Duke of Northumberland unveiled a memorial plaque on the north wall. Presented with the keys of the museum by the architect, the Duke then unlocked the door and declared the museum open. The coble, repaired once again, its name now *Grace Darling*, stood behind a panel of glass on a bed of sand from Bamburgh beach. 'Relics', whose existence sceptics had doubted, had been given or lent. About three thousand people were reported to have taken part in the ceremony, among them members of the Darling family, the mayors of Tynemouth, Berwick and Morpeth, and the crew of the North Sunderland lifeboat.[72]

In 1838 the aristocracy, led by the Duke and Duchess of Northumberland, had set themselves up as the guardians of Grace and her reputation. One hundred years later they reaffirmed that role, burying their differences for the day in a public display of solidarity in memory of Grace. Closely associated with them was the church. Grace's deed was celebrated as an act of Christian courage, her life as one of Christian devotion, St Aidan's church in Bamburgh the natural centre for any ceremony. Dukes, bishops, baronets, lord lieutenants and mayors assembled to give thanks for Grace's deed and life, and to open a permanent museum of the coble and other relics. They were all male. The person who had done most to keep alive Grace's reputation, a woman, Constance Smedley, was not there.

Seven weeks later, on Wednesday 7 September, Bamburgh celebrated the centenary, organized by the Joint Seahouses and Bamburgh Centenary Committee with the indispensable Major Forster as chair. After a short service in the church, wreaths were laid on the Grace Darling memorial in the churchyard by Lord Armstrong, Captain Oliver for the RNLI and Mrs J. Jepson, a great-niece of Grace. Also present were three great-nephews and a great-great-niece. In the afternoon every available motor boat took parties out to the Farne Isles, the weather deteriorating and the sea unfortunately becoming 'very choppy'. From a press photo, it looks as if there were about fifty 'pilgrims', as they were called. Then people 'poured into the Seahouses cinema' for films about bird life on the islands and lifeboats. In the evening there was another service in the church with a large congregation and a sermon by the Archdeacon of Lindisfarne.[73]

The centenary of the deed received some notice in the press, on the radio and on Pathé News, where cinema audiences would have seen it, but it was by no means overwhelming. The *Newcastle Weekly Chronicle* carried the reminiscences of R. W. Clark, who had known Thomasin, whose 'prominent front teeth … lovely grey ringlets, … and graceful gait are all imprinted on my mind', and who 'stuffed my pockets with cake, apples and nuts after I had sung hymns to her'. Thomasin would then tell the young Clark about Grace, though most of his stories sound improbable. But the centenary event itself was reported without much fanfare. This included a letter from 'A Graceless Hiker', lamenting the failure of buses and trains to provide transport to Bamburgh and Seahouses.[74] The centenary was very much a local event, hardly testimony to any national awareness that it was a hundred years since Grace's deed.

The BBC carried an account of the opening of the museum. It also broadcast two plays: in May, from the Regional Studios in the Children's Hour, came *Grace Darling*, by Lawrence du Garde Peach, one of the pioneers of radio drama and a frequent contributor to Children's Hour; and in September, *Longstone Light* by Mary D. Sheridan. Its most ambitious effort came a year later in July 1939, with a two-hour play on television, *The Fame of Grace Darling*, by Yvette Pienne, starring the young Wendy Hiller. It was, reported *The Times*, 'an ambitious production, with a long cast and clear interpolations of film', the theme that 'the intrepid Grace … was literally killed by the kindness of her admirers'. Starting well, it tailed off after the rescue. Pienne's script survives, but not the television play itself. I wrote to Dame Wendy Hiller for her memories, only to find myself, two days later, reading her obituary.[75]

The Times reflected on Grace at the centenary both of the deed and of her death. The theme in both, perhaps written by the same hand, was that the fame that had accrued to Grace had to be seen in the context of the 1830s. 'The moment was opportune for acclaiming female virtue. A girl had just ascended the Throne, endowing maidenhood with fresh romance and dignity; Florence Nightingale was just starting her career; *Oliver Twist* had just been published. The humanitarian movement was fairly launched; the growth of steam transport had been marked by an increasing number of wrecks ... Only a spark was needed to kindle the fires of pubic imagination.' As for Grace herself, as part of a lighthouse family, 'Her courage was not exceptional, her modesty not unusual, her good sense typical of her day'. By 1942 it was confident that 'any one of us may shake hands any day with a woman as heroic as Grace Darling'. Even in her own day 'Grace Darling was not the only woman ready to face untold labour and almost certain death as a matter of course'.[76] The heroine's stature was hardly enhanced by these reflections. Most other papers passed over the centenaries of deed and death without a mention. The *Manchester Guardian* in 1938 noted that Grace 'became a national heroine and was to be held up to children as a model of womanly humanity and bravery for the next hundred years', but this suggested that her time was now over, and she was not mentioned in 1942. Neither the *Daily Mail* nor the *Daily Herald*, at opposite ends of the political spectrum, gave any attention to Grace in either year, and the *Daily Telegraph* contented itself with a filler in September 1938 announcing that the Grace Darling League had had to postpone, because of illness, a planned ceremony in Battersea Park to present the oak tree to Sea Rangers, Sea Scouts and Sea Cadets.[77]

There were other signs that all was not well. The effort to raise a relatively small sum for the establishment of the museum had been protracted. Smedley at an early stage of the campaign thought of abandoning the approach through an appeal via patrons of distinction and going direct to the public and the press. Perhaps it might have been better to have done so. There is a telling comparison with the campaign to build a memorial to David Livingstone at his birthplace of Blantyre. Launched in the unpromising year of the general strike, 1926, it was nevertheless successful, most of the money coming from small donations from Sunday school and Bible classes in Scotland. Blantyre became, in the words of the leading campaigner, 'a place of pilgrimage, a shrine', attracting 90,000 visitors a year.[78] If Eva Hope's Grace Darling still held sway in the Sunday schools, perhaps there would have been a similar response to the appeal for a memorial to Grace. As it was, there was no real attempt to raise money from the mass of the population. Grace Darling remained the possession primarily of the elite.

An indication of the limitations of Grace's appeal is that, in the age when cinema was at its height, no one took the opportunity to make a film of the deed. True, there had been the television play, but that by definition had been for a small audience. Commercial films had been discussed. There were rumours that Basil Dean was going to make one with his wife, Victoria Hopper, playing the part of Grace. But nothing came of it, and Dean does not give it a mention in his autobiography.[79] The Grace Darling League often talked of a film, hoping that a successful play might give filmmakers the encouragement they needed to invest in the project. The Duchess of Northumberland politely refused the use of Alnwick Castle for filming, but that did not spare her from further attempts to enlist her help.[80] But again, nothing happened. There were difficulties in the story, as the comments on the television play suggested: it was good up to and including the rescue, but a disappointment thereafter. If making a film, did one end with Grace's death, a downbeat conclusion after the drama of the rescue? Perhaps that put off filmmakers. Whatever the case, the medium which would have best maintained and spread Grace's reputation in these years contributed nothing to that cause.

It is possible that something else put off the filmmakers. The Grace Darling story was increasingly becoming something for children. As Stephen King-Hall noted in the foreword to Smedley's book, 'the memory of this simple sensibly minded girl still flourishes to a considerable extent in the nurseries and schools of our land'.[81] Adults might have been persuaded to attend a film about her only with difficulty. The ceremonies for the opening of the museum and for the centenary featured adults and were attended by adults, with children conspicuous by their absence, but these were of course very much Bamburgh occasions, remembering events in local history. Elsewhere it might have been difficult to assemble adults to hear about Grace Darling. In marketing terms, she was now sold almost exclusively to children, at every level of sophistication.

Both the rescue and her death, caused, we are told, by the fact that she did not open her window at night, were strongly featured in Arthur Mee's *Children's Encyclopaedia*. Constance Smedley, as we have seen, had quickly followed up her adult book with a version for children. Children keen on history would have encountered Grace occupying 'an undisputed place among the nation's heroines' in *Hutchinson's Story of the British Nation*.[82] In the 1930s, and up to 1957, she had a prime spot in the much-reprinted *Girl Guiding: A Handbook for Brownies, Guides, Rangers, and Guiders*, where, not surprisingly, the message is that the 'sort of thing' that Grace did 'can only be done when a girl has trained herself as the Guides try to do, to be plucky, to be hardy, to keep cool, and to know what is the right thing to do – and to do it at no matter what risk to herself'.[83] A very different message comes through in J. A. W. Hamilton's *Twelve Clever Girls* (1937), where Grace's courage is, perhaps blasphemously, seen as only marginally inferior to that of Christ: 'The little boat was in great danger, but Jesus went all the way to Calvary, knowing that there he must die for us … Do you love Him? Has He saved you?' As if to make Grace's story more apposite for the child readership, she is here described as 'still very young' and looking 'almost like a child'. She looks very young, too, in the 'Heroine of the Storm', a three-page cartoon rendering of the story, Grace's heroism made all the greater by the fact that at the outset she is lying 'sick in the lighthouse'.[84] Not only ranked as one of twelve clever girls, Grace was also to be found within the covers of E. H. Farrance's *Twelve Wonderful Women: The Romance of Their Life and Work* (1936). Her name still had sufficient magic to sell *Grace Darling's Tales*, a Ladybird publication of 1938, made up of stories about girls without any mention of Grace. Other children's books were C. Fox Smith's *The Story of Grace Darling* (1940), thirty-four pages long in an Oxford University Press 'Great Exploits' series, and, belying its title, for it was riddled with errors, Eileen Bagland's *The True Book About Heroines of the Sea* (1958).

At the end of the 1950s Grace Darling's reputation was sealed in the world of childhood, her heroism much admired. Schoolchildren of that decade across the country were told her story, and of all the heroines with whom they were presented many have told me how Grace was the one who made most impact on them. In the 1950s heroes and heroines, many from the Second World War, some contemporary like the conquerors of Everest, could be lauded without hesitation. Her story was told and received at face value, a simple story of courage that no one could deny. Among adults, however, Grace's hold was much less secure. The elite, certainly in Northumberland, paid homage to her, as they had always done, but her popular appeal had been on the wane for some years: the song about her was now rarely sung; she was not so much of a catch in advertisements (though Brasso were offering her in a Reward Card that appears to date from these years); and she had lost her hold in popular culture. Would she survive the remainder of the twentieth century with all the social and political changes that, on the face of it, posed a challenge to a simple narrative of heroism?

8

Disgrace and Recovery

In early June 1963 the District Organizer for the RNLI in the north east reported to headquarters that Commander Phipps Hornby, the Honorary Curator of the Grace Darling Museum, was keen to celebrate the 125th anniversary of Grace's deed (which would fall in September). Phipps Hornby had in mind a church service and the laying of a wreath. 'If a celebration of this anniversary is unavoidable', wrote the District Organizer,

> I suggested a much more attractive idea would be a Ball at Bamburgh Castle, possibly in period costume, or at least some social gathering in the Castle, to celebrate the rescue. There seems to be no reason to introduce a dirge in memory of Grace Darling, we are not commemorating her death and a dreary celebration will not achieve anything. The Commander, somewhat alarmed, has promised to give the matter further thought.

Phipps Hornby's further thoughts extended over five weeks, but the net result was that he felt unable to do anything other than lay a wreath – and that he duly did. Lady Armstrong evidently agreed to a cocktail party at Bamburgh Castle, but I have seen no evidence that it took place.[1]

The episode, trivial as it may seem, marked a change in public attitudes to Grace. Until the 1960s the remembrance of Grace in Bamburgh had been intimately linked with St Aidan's church. The church itself had a window dedicated to her, and gave shelter to the first statue of her lying recumbent – it had had to be brought under cover to protect it from further deterioration. As you enter the church by the south door, it immediately confronts you. And in the churchyard the reconstructed memorial to Grace stands prominent among the more modest gravestones of the citizens of Bamburgh. The opening of the museum in 1938, which might have been an entirely secular affair, was centred on the church. Phipps Hornby, Honorary Curator since 1952, was dedicated to securing an accurate account of what had happened in 1838, and perhaps thought of it as a quasi-religious duty. A costume ball, or even a cocktail party, was outside his realm of imagination. If Grace had in some senses become a saint in the way Bamburgh and the nation remembered her, the District Organizer was setting in train a process of decanonization. Where might it all end?

Richard Armstrong's *Grace Darling: Maid and Myth* (1965) was the first and most potent sign that Grace might be disgraced. A review of Constance

Smedley's book in 1932 had taken from it the lesson that Grace was 'a great Victorian in whom even the present age cannot detect feet of clay'.[2] Three decades later Armstrong found the feet of clay. After serving in the Merchant Navy, Armstrong 'sailed in tramps, liners, colliers and tankers', and 'under four different flags'. Almost certainly, if the fiction he wrote is any guide, he had served an apprenticeship as an engineer in Lord Armstrong's Elswick works.[3] His book has the benefit of being written by someone who was knowledgeable about ships and the sea. He was also keen to pick up on what he saw as errors in Constance Smedley's account while acknowledging his debt to her. But his major contribution to thinking about Grace in the later twentieth century was to suggest that there were financial motives for the Darlings' rescue attempt, and to engage in some psychologizing of the relationship between Grace and her father.

Armstrong argued that the versions we have of William Darling's journal have been severely edited. Darling himself 'transcribed and revised' the journal when he retired in 1860. This copied version, held in the Northumberland Record Office, was the main source of the published version of 1886, edited by Thomasin's friend and collaborator Daniel Atkinson. The original version, however, was evidently available to Atkinson (though it has now disappeared), and he claimed that 'The variations between the transcript and the original are slight, and in the main verbal only; but both have been used for this publication'.[4] Unimpressed by this assertion, Armstrong argued from the unevenness of the entries in these two surviving versions that much has been cut out, and he suggested that crucially what has been excised was almost any mention of the bounties available to those who mounted rescues, or of the income to be gained from salvage. William Darling, he argued, had been a wild young man, much addicted to smuggling. Although marriage and responsibilities had helped turn him into a pillar of respectability, he was still alert to the ways he could supplement his Trinity House salary, and felt no compunction about entering such episodes into his journal. But, by the 1860s, he had evidently come to think that too open an admission of this might be damaging to his reputation.[5] Armstrong thought that a quarrel about bounties was at the root of the deep antipathy to the Darlings felt in North Sunderland.[6] What all this amounts to is that the pure act of humanity that so many contemporaries conferred on Grace was contaminated by awareness that there was money to be made out of the wreck of the *Forfarshire*.

Equally important, Armstrong argued that the bond between Grace and her father was exceptionally strong. Much of this was pure speculation. Armstrong argued that the birth of the twins in 1819 'must have pushed Grace out of the centre of the stage right into the wings'. But, far from being neglected, she became

> her father's ewe lamb ... It would be to him she turned for comfort when plagued by an aching tooth, for first aid and the easing of pain when she barked her knees or bumped

her head, for refuge when a life that was always bewildering came at her too fast and the sadness of it was too big for her small heart to hold. She would spend a lot of time with him in the lantern and about the storerooms of the lighthouse, watching him at work; he would take her with him on short expeditions in the coble when the weather was fine; he would produce little treats for her – bits of cake, knobs of sugar, a measure of dried fruit in a twist of paper – out of the pocket of his huge jacket; and his big hands would wipe her nose when it ran and then wrap her up against the wind with clumsy tenderness.[7]

The conditional tense is the only indication that all that is written here was a product of Armstrong's imagination. Although the passage seems to be focused on Grace's childhood, it is giving readers hints of the nature of the relationship between Grace and her father as she grew older. Those 'big hands' with their 'clumsy tenderness' suggest a degree of emotional dependence that warped the lives of both of them.

At the age of nineteen, perhaps 'by some kind of unconscious emotional blackmail', Grace accepted a life on the Longstone: she 'turned away from life and, refusing its challenge, incarcerated herself in the lighthouse tower which became for her both refuge and prison'. Armstrong was writing in the ripple of the anti-Victorianism generated by Lytton Strachey and his followers in the 1920s. The Victorians, it went almost without saying, were sentimental, hypocritical and happy to turn a blind eye to the kinds of subjection, the 'self-immolation' in Armstrong's words, that many women endured. He aimed to unpick the 'idealized, almost sanctified relationship between [Grace] and her father' that has been handed down. Grace, claimed Armstrong, was utterly dependent on her father, and his authority was 'instant and absolute', the father displacing on to the daughter his anger at his own dependence on Trinity House and Bamburgh Castle. Grace, 'shy and timid', but also in some ways 'devious', worked the refuge or prison of the lighthouse to her advantage, taking from the world what she wanted and putting up the shutters when anything menaced. Emotionally, as Grace's mother, so much older than her father, 'withdrew deeper into the wings', Grace moved centre stage, the father and daughter relationship developing in new ways. William, 'man being what he is, … would develop an increasing emotional dependence on her; and she, consciously or otherwise, would do all she could to foster it'. But there were 'inner tensions, and especially the ultimate frustration of the most powerful urge in her', her sexuality.[8] Armstrong stopped short of suggesting incest. But, perhaps even more dramatically, he argues that the inability to resolve the inner tensions led to Grace's death.

Armstrong claimed that Grace's cough of the early summer of 1842, and the invalidity conferred upon her, provided her with an escape from the inner tension of her relationship with her father, and from the conflict she felt between her true self and the role she was so often obliged to play as national heroine. Grace learned that she could use illness to escape tension. Subconsciously, she then developed other symptoms 'to reinforce the cough', until eventually the cough and the other symptoms became real. She retreated from the challenge that the world had thrown at her by making her a heroine, and took the only exit available, death. Grace, 'a simple girl with limited resources', lacking the strength of character to enable her to ride the role of heroine, already before 1838 withdrawn into the refuge or prison of the lighthouse, eventually 'reasserted her basic human right to be herself alone in the only way left to her'. She died. There is not a mention of consumption.[9]

Armstrong was not the first to suggest, as Mr Sylvester of Batty's circus had put it, that Grace died of a broken heart. But he was the first to put this in the language of psychoanalysis. Grace, he seemed to be suggesting, needed an analyst to help her sort out her relationship with her father and her reaction to the fame thrust upon her. Far from being the simple heroine of the Farne Isles, an exemplar for schoolchildren, she had become alluringly similar to another heroine who, some think, found release from intolerable pressures in death, Diana, Princess of Wales. And just as biographers conjecture about Diana, so Armstrong conjectured about Grace. He teased away at the little evidence he had, but, as one reads him, it is difficult not to think that he had reached his conclusion before he embarked on his analysis. In the climate of the time, he brought to bear on the Victorian Grace the psychoanalytic gaze of the twentieth century; like Florence Nightingale after she had been subject to Lytton Strachey's scrutiny, the heroine would never be the same again.

Armstrong's book, just over 200 pages long, was tailor-made for the 1960s. Where Smedley, over thirty years previously, had sought to reimagine Grace as 'our national sea heroine', and did so at inordinate length, Armstrong had no patriotic agenda, but sought rather to unmask the dynamics of relationships on the Farne Isles and their coastline. His underlying assumption was that the Britain of the 1960s had outgrown the stage where it needed to turn individuals like Grace into symbols of national heroism and goodness; the time had come to think through what their lives were really like. Armstrong's Grace still displays courage, but as a human being she is flawed, in retreat from the challenges of life, unable to break away from the emotional and other demands her dominant father places upon her. Armstrong was not the first to suggest that the pressures of being a heroine were too much for Grace to bear, but he did sow other seeds that in time would germinate and grow.

The first of these was the suggestion that William Darling and Grace had a particularly strong father and daughter relationship. In the early 1980s Peter Dillon, a playwright in the north east, took this to what was its logical conclusion. At an early stage of his *Grace*, a stage direction for William Darling and Grace reads, 'cuddle unfather/daughterly'. Grace says, 'I love you, father', and her father replies, 'And I love you'. Soon there is another stage direction: 'they kiss on the lips'. Like any lovers, they have their tiffs, William on one occasion striking Grace, but at the end, on Grace's deathbed, they are reconciled. If incest is one theme of the play, another is the opportunities a range of characters (William Darling, Smeddle of the Crewe Trustees, Johnstone of the *Berwick and Kelso Warder*, the Duke of Northumberland) discern and hope to profit from. All of them have feet, or more than feet, of clay. Smeddle, for example, promotes the Grace Darling story to distract attention from the farce of the inquest and then flirts with Grace, who in turn has a soft spot for him. There are no heroes or heroines in Dillon's *Grace*. First performed at the White Swan Hotel in Alnwick on 22 July 1982, right under the nose of the Northumberlands' castle, it depicts the Duke as a pathetic character, ruled by his wife, and constantly picking at a spot on his face. From its première the play went on two regional tours.[10]

Jill Paton Walsh is a major writer of children's books, and her 1991 novel, *Grace*, could be guaranteed to attract attention. It elaborates on the other seed sown by Armstrong, that there was money for the Darlings in the rescue. As she explained in her 'Author's Note', the first part of her book tells the story of the shipwreck and rescue 'as exactly and truthfully as I can', whereas the second part is 'more free'. Anyone writing about Grace faces a problem of dramatic structure. The narrative builds up to the climax of the rescue on 7 September 1838. How do you hold the reader's attention for the four-year decline to death? Paton Walsh's solution was to imagine Grace haunted by a nightmare in which the nine people rescued from the rock turn into nine golden sovereigns. She explicitly supports Armstrong's emphasis on the importance of bounties. 'My daughter read for me in the Archives of the Crewe Trustees', she writes, '… and in their account books, and in numerous newspaper reports of shipwreck, she found very sufficient evidence for everything Richard Armstrong has to say on the matter.' When Grace's mother tries to dissuade William and Grace from rowing out to the rescue, William says, 'Whist, woman … Think of the premiums. That will stiffen thy courage'.[11]

Dillon and Paton Walsh built on and elaborated aspects of Armstrong's book. Take the three together, and they present a picture of Grace and of the circumstances of the rescue far removed from the panegyrics of the nineteenth and early twentieth centuries. There is for all of them a remaining core of heroism on display in the night of the rescue, but events and relationships before and after are murky, and sometimes tawdry. Grace might have become in these accounts more of a human being, and less of an icon, but it is difficult not to conclude that she was in some ways diminished, if not disgraced. If that was to be her fate, it was one shared with many other icons in Britain's recent past. Some, like Sir Henry Havelock, with his statue in Trafalgar Square, were simply forgotten, unacceptable heroes because of their association with events that were now simply embarrassing – in Havelock's case, the Indian uprising of 1857. Others,

like General Gordon, Florence Nightingale, and Robert Baden-Powell, attracted,
as Grace began to, the attentions of psychoanalysts, revealing much more complex
individuals than the first generation of biographers had allowed. As Britain, in
the last quarter of the twentieth century, fell into a bout of amnesia with respect
to empire, anyone whose heroism was connected with it was consigned to some
level of oblivion. And no one, once subjected to the piercing eye of the analyst,
or the rewriting of history, ever fully recovered their pristine reputations. There
was, for most of these staple heroes and heroines of the nineteenth century, no
easy way back. Could Grace buck the trend, and recover from disgrace?

Surprisingly, yes. A key factor was the museum in Bamburgh. It had some
shaky moments in its early years, but it survived. It closed during the war years,
and some of the more valuable items were removed for the duration. Forster
kept an eye on things, however, opening occasionally, for example on 20 October
1942, the centenary of Grace's death. But in November 1944 Forster moved south,
and arrangements for keeping the museum open in the post-war period proved
difficult. W. J. Oliver, the RNLI District Secretary, explained to headquarters in
September 1945 that

> You have to consider the people involved. First, you have Miss Marshall – a large
> bespectacled old schoolmarm with a moustache which would do credit to any young
> officer – horrified at the modern behaviour of young and old. Then we have the hordes
> of people coming into Bamburgh, not the type that visited the place in pre-War days,
> but a noisy crowd who think nothing of bringing their children with them, not to see
> the place, but simply to find beer and cigarettes.[12]

This culture clash was not easily resolved. Miss Marshall, a retired headmistress,
now custodian of the museum, and succeeded in the task by her sister, hardly
seems to have given a welcome to visitors, and Oliver, doubling up as curator,
probably brought to the task neither the time nor the expertise that Forster had.
A breakthrough came in December 1952 with the appointment of Commander
W. M. Phipps Hornby as Honorary Curator. He was to remain in post until 1969,
and his influence extended beyond that. His early years as curator were critical
ones. In the four years 1949–52 the museum's revenue had averaged £136 per
annum. In 1953 it dipped to £89, rising to only £90 in 1954. In June 1954 there
was talk of closure, or of handing over the museum to the County Council, or
of accepting a subvention from the RNLI. In the event there was a marked rise
in takings to £327 in 1955, and thereafter the trend was upwards. For the years
1956–60 it averaged £332, for 1961–65 £423, for 1966–70 £639. By 1962 the
finances and prospects were sufficiently good for an extension to the museum
to be agreed, the work being completed in 1964.[13]

Phipps Hornby took a dim view of most of what passed for scholarship on
Grace Darling. He devoted much time to identifying the errors in Constance

Smedley, and, in due course, Richard Armstrong, the latter's book 'wholly unsatisfactory'.[14] Send him, as one student did, a dissertation on Grace Darling, and, together with congratulations, you were likely to receive eleven pages notifying errors. I have sometimes, while writing this book, imagined him at my shoulder, shaking his head as he spots an error, and feeling a perverse satisfaction where I have unearthed some piece of information unknown to him. He himself made a notable contribution to scholarship with his 'Grace Horsley Darling, 1815–1842: Northumbrian Heroine', published in the *Mariner's Mirror* in 1968. It is a meticulous examination of the evidence on the events leading up to the wreck, on the rescue, and on its aftermath. With Phipps Hornby at the helm, the RNLI could be confident that the museum was fulfilling the critical function of preserving the evidence that had been donated to it, and adding to it where he was confident that the material on offer was genuine.

A naval qualification for the curator was continued into the 1970s with Commander Dunn succeeding Commander Phipps Hornby. Phipps Hornby, living in Berwick, had always been conscious that he was held in some suspicion in Bamburgh as an outsider, and, perhaps remembering the fiasco over the 1963 celebration of the 125th anniversary of Grace's deed, felt that 'things have changed much in Bamburgh over the last few years'. But he offered Dunn much advice.[15]

There is a gap in the museum records for much of the 1970s, but the tone of the annual reports in the 1980s was consistently buoyant. Annual reports are of course showpieces, which may conceal as much as they reveal. Such figures as they contain, however, tend to bear out the optimism of the writing. In 1979 it had been possible to remit £3,000 to the RNLI. In 1982, donations totalled £4,656, and sales £2,727, a considerable advance on the sums Phipps Hornby had been able to report in the 1960s. The guide to the museum by W. A. Montgomery and M. Scott Weightman went through edition after edition, 10,000 copies being sold in 1981. As to number of visitors, in 1980, 'Although we do not count numbers, there was a definite impression of more people than ever coming through'. 1983 started quietly, but 'there was a considerable surge of visitors in the latter part of June, and this continued up to our close'. There was, it was felt, 'increasing general interest in the Grace Darling story, as witnessed by the considerable number of film makers (TV and Educational) and the writers who have come to us for information. If all these efforts materialise, there could be a glut'. The 1984 report noted 'the continued interest of children in the Grace Darling story'. In 1985 the curator was 'delighted with the growing interest of schools and pupils in the Grace Darling story and I have had considerable correspondence both from all over the country and abroad'. In 1987 visitors were 'on the increase', and there were 'many visits from camera crews, play writers and authors all wishing to take part in the celebrations next year'.[16]

Two aspects of these reports stand out. The first is the extent to which the media were now turning to the museum for help. The Grace Darling story was a hardy perennial for TV and radio. In 1959 D. J. Saint produced a programme for the Home Service on 'Grace Darling, a Brave Woman'. The Home Service returned to the topic in 1963, using Constance Smedley's book for 'The Grace Darling Story'. In 1971 there was a radio discussion of a Grace Darling play at the Newcastle festival.[17] On television, presumably in response to Richard Armstrong's book, *Tonight* had a feature on Grace 'who after all might not have been heroic'. More recently, in 1989, Alan Titchmarsh headed a visit to the Longstone Lighthouse for *Daytime Live*, and *Look North* has regularly featured the heroine.[18]

The second theme to stand out in the reports is the appeal to children of the story of Grace Darling. Children's television programmes have found rich material in Grace. Valerie Singleton told 'the story of Grace Darling' on *Blue Peter* in 1965, and again in 1968.[19] *Jackanory* had a programme on Grace in 1966. *Blue Peter* featured her again in 1988 and 1996.[20] Even more important have been the children's books on Grace.

The modern era of writing for children on Grace started with Joanna Dessau's *Amazing Grace*, a historical novel, first published in 1980. Dessau was a remote descendant of the Darling family – her grandfather was the great-grandson of William Darling's elder brother, Robert. Dessau tells the story through the eyes of William Darling, Grace's sister Thomasin, and then Grace herself. The influence of the Armstrong book is apparent. The North Sunderland boatmen are angry because they have been deprived of a bounty by the Darlings' precipitate rescue. There is considerable stress on the strength of the father and daughter relationship – though not a hint of incest. And the fuss made over her deed makes Grace ill as early as the Christmas of 1838. Like any writer on Grace, Dessau is faced with moments in the story when no one really knows what happened. For Dessau it was William Darling who made the decision to row out to the rescue, Grace then offering to accompany him.[21]

Helen Cresswell's *The Story of Grace Darling*, a Puffin book, is more conventional in approach. Dedicated 'to the brave men of the Royal National Lifeboat Institution, past and present', and with some of the proceeds, in this 150th anniversary of the deed, going to the RNLI's Grace Darling Appeal for a new lifeboat for the North Sunderland station, the book explores the nature of heroism. Over half the book's seventy pages paint an imaginative but not implausible picture of Grace's childhood. The theme is Grace's growing awareness of her destiny and her attempts to conquer her fears. After the dramatic episode in December 1834 when Logan was saved through the efforts of her father and brothers, Cresswell reflects that 'It was as if all her life fear had been snapping at her heels, and now, for the first time, she turned and faced it': Grace realized that if her brothers were not present at the lighthouse, it was she who would have to go out to the rescue. She was therefore psychologically prepared for what she had to do in September 1838. What she was not prepared for in any way was the fame that descended on her. It killed her, invading 'her inner self'. Cresswell's book has a clear message for her readers. Courage is facing up to and overcoming the fears that we all have. Do this, and each of us can be a hero or heroine. Go out to the Longstone, Cresswell tells us, and visit Grace's room, 'and you might decide, as I myself have come to believe, that Grace Darling was not a heroine simply because of that one famous deed of courage on 7 September 1838. She lived as a heroine every day of her life.'[22]

Exploration of the nature of heroism runs through no fewer than six books on Grace Darling for school use published in the 1990s. Given the pressures from the 1980s onwards to refocus history teaching on the story of the nation, one might have expected these books to promote Grace as an English or British heroine. But that is not the case, nor is there much highlighting of her Christianity. The emphasis, rather, is on the nature of heroism, and on the moral issues thrown up by it. Children are being asked, 'What would you have done if you had been on the Longstone in the early hours of 7 September 1838'? 'What would it have been right to do?'

The way this is done is adjusted according to the Key Stage that is being addressed. In Jenny Lloyd's Grace Darling (1996), in Developing Reading Skills at Key Stage 4 (ages fourteen to sixteen), a lot of first-hand evidence is presented in an open-ended way, inviting readers to make up their own minds. A similar authenticity for rather younger children runs through Clare Chandler's Grace Darling (1995) in a 'Life Stories' series, and through Channel Four Learning's Grace Darling 1815–1842 (1998) in their 'Famous People' series. In the first of these, Grace is in the company of Louis Braille, Christopher Columbus, Guy Fawkes, Anne Frank, Mahatma Gandhi, Helen Keller, Martin Luther King, Nelson Mandela, Florence Nightingale, William Shakespeare and Mother Teresa. Channel Four Learning's other 'famous people' in the series are, amongst the women, Cleopatra, Boudica and Mary Seacole (fast dethroning Florence Nightingale as the Crimean War heroine), and, amongst the men, Leonardo da Vinci, Guy Fawkes, George Stephenson, Alexander Graham Bell, Mahatma Gandhi and Neil Armstrong.[23] Guy Fawkes, Mahatma Gandhi and Grace Darling alone make both lists, a trio who don't seem to have much in common.

Tim Vicary's Grace Darling, first published in the Oxford Bookworms Library of True Stories in 1991, and reissued in 2000 as a Keystage 2 book (ages seven to eleven), is a 'True Story' only in the loosest sense – facts are garbled to suit the need for a storyline. But it is done to place heroism under the spotlight. After they have finished the story, readers are asked to agree or disagree with various statements, giving explanations. These include, 'Thomasin Darling didn't want

Grace and William to go to the rock. She was right because it was a very stupid and dangerous thing to do', and 'Grace Darling was a famous heroine only because she was a young woman. William Darling, David Donovan, and Thomas Buchanan were also heroes'. *Grace to the Rescue!* (1995), by Margaret Nash, addresses still younger children. The focus is entirely on the rescue, and Grace's courage. Nash ends with Grace going off to the mainland to look for spring flowers, bearing with her a gold locket given to her by those she has rescued; it has nine hairs in a circle, one from each of the survivors. Heroism is the theme, death taboo.[24]

If media portrayals of Grace Darling in the late twentieth century focused on children, adults were not entirely neglected. The two most notable contributions came from people with established reputations on the left, Jessica Mitford and Tony Benn. Born in 1917, Jessica Mitford was the fifth of the six famous Mitford girls, daughters of Lord and Lady Redesdale. While two of her sisters, Diana, who married Oswald Mosley, and Unity, who was besotted with Hitler, were drawn to the right, Jessica was from her early days a rebel on the left. At the age of twelve she opened a 'running away account' at a bank; at eighteen she was subscribing to the Communist newspaper, the *Daily Worker*; at twenty she ran away with, and married, her cousin, Esmond Romilly, who had joined the International Brigades in the Spanish Civil War. The Romillys moved to the United States early in 1939; in 1941 Esmond joined the Canadian air force, and was killed in a raid on Hamburg. Remarried in 1943 to an American, Bob Treuhaft, and a member of the Communist Party until 1958, Jessica Mitford won a reputation as a writer with her best-selling *Hons and Rebels* (1960), an account of her upbringing and family, and *The American Way of Death* (1963).[25]

Mitford's fascination with Grace Darling was rooted deep in her childhood. The Grace Darling song was the favourite song of her mother, Sydney, born in 1880, who used to gather her daughters round the piano for family singing. The song stuck in Jessica's head, and in the late 1950s she passed it on to Lou Gottlieb, leader of a folksinging group, the Limelighters, who introduced it, with modifications, to schoolchildren in Berkeley, California – though Jessica vetoed his wish to give Grace a Jewish, rather than an English, heart. Then, in 1985, in discussions about a possible contribution Jessica Mitford might make to a series entitled *Lives of Modern Women*, she rejected ideas for studies of Eleanor Roosevelt or Jackie Onassis. Her publishers, however, were much taken with her husband's suggestion of a study of Grace Darling, the mention of her name triggering in Jessica a rendering of the song. So the idea for the book was born, Jessica Mitford posing much the same question as has underlain this book: 'Why, and how, did the Grace Darling legend originate, and what accounts for its remarkable persistence and longevity?'[26]

It is difficult to avoid the conclusion that Jessica Mitford came to regret her decision to write her book on Grace Darling, or 'Grey Starling' as she came to call her after a transcription error by a Californian printer. Her research assistants and friends overwhelmed her with material. The county archivist for Northumberland, with a fine disregard for professional standards, 'sent me stacks of material'. Her house 'looked like a vast Lost and Found depot – quantities of letters, books, pamphlets, old newspapers Lost by me and Found in a trice' by her assistant. Her American publisher 'never failed to respond to my constant cris de coeur', going over the manuscript 'not once, not twice, not even thrice, but as many times as it took to get it in acceptable shape', and even then it was her English publisher 'who pulled the whole thing together into an actual book'. Besides these two, and her picture researcher, her own contribution seemed to her 'minimal'. Jessica Mitford's name on a book-jacket could be guaranteed to sell copies of almost anything, and it seems that her publishers decided that it was worth putting time and effort into a venture that was in danger of faltering.[27]

Mitford, intrigued that Grace Darling should attain such instant celebrity, devotes part of the book to exploring, with some insight, the media of the early nineteenth century. She also set out with the presupposition that Grace perfectly exemplified what Mitford saw as the typical early Victorian virtues for 'a person of her age, sex, and lowly station in life: chastity, humility, obedience to her parents, devotion to domestic tasks, piety …' The real Grace, Mitford discovered, fitted this stereotype only very roughly. By the end of the book she is simply puzzled, and perhaps irritated, by the responses to Grace of 'the advance guard of the feminist movement, militant young women bent on consciousness-raising and the like'. One of Mitford's correspondents, in her early thirties, blamed Grace for the fact that as a child she was not allowed to run around in wellington boots and trousers, and another, in her early forties, hated her, or rather not her but the version of her that meant that 'generations of young women … would have their hopes and aspirations neatly trimmed by the Appropriate Female Heroine, themselves set out on butterfly pins'. Why, wondered a bemused Mitford, did Grace Darling 'arouse such venomous loathing?' Mitford has no time at all for the Richard Armstrong version of Grace, and even less for Peter Dillon's play. Grace was, she concluded, 'a fairly intelligent girl with a certain sharpness of wit, yet strangely incurious'. Perhaps, in the final words of the book, there was not much more to say about her than that she was 'simply trying to rescue the shipwrecked'. The Grace Darling song had embedded itself deep into Mitford's consciousness in childhood, and she was in a way so entranced by it, that the kind of feminist or politically radical analysis that might have been expected from someone of her reputation never took off. Mitford's Grace Had an English Heart, published to coincide with the 150th anniversary of the deed, certainly helped rescue Grace from disgrace, but the author was simply relieved to be shot of her: 'Grey Starling is about to take wing', she wrote, 'oh the amazing relief'.[28]

Where Jessica Mitford had ducked the feminist challenge posed by Grace, Tony

Benn embraced it. In a series of 'letters to historical figures' for BBC Scotland in 1994, Benn recalled how he had learned about Grace in childhood. Addressing Grace, he told her how 'like every schoolchild I was told about you and your father', and how you 'are remembered as a real heroine ever since'. Grace's heroism, Benn claimed, had a lesson for us: heroes are always thought of as men, but in fact 'women are a lot more gutsy than men'. Think of women in the Blitz in 1940, or the women who protested against nuclear weapons at Greenham Common, or the wives in the miners' strike in 1984–5. Here was courage, moral as much as physical. In Benn's hands, Grace was about to become a founding mother of a tradition of female courage. Moreover, for the first, and perhaps last, time, she was set to become a heroine of the left, someone from whom modern women activists could draw inspiration. How unlike the response of 'the advance guard of the feminist movement' whom Mitford had contacted. Although something of Benn's invocation of female courage is to be found in the books for children written at around the same time, no one else has tried to make Grace a heroine of the left. Benn himself enjoyed the attempt to draw parallels to Grace's deed from the politics of his own lifetime, and was pleased with the outcome. 'I must say', he wrote in his diary, 'the Grace Darling [letter] is excellent. I used the shipping forecast, "South-East Iceland, Faroes, Fair Isle, Viking, Forties, Cromarty, Forth, Dogger, Tyne, Humber" to lead into Grace's lighthouse.'[29]

Tony Benn's broadcast has something of the feel of the collective biographies of women of the nineteenth century: its confident tone comes from the placing of Grace within a history of heroic women. What characterizes most of the other invocations of Grace's deed in the late twentieth and early twenty-first centuries is what might be seen as a postmodern uncertainty. Grace is dehistoricized, and can be anything anyone wants to make her.

Some still think that there is money in her name. In 1983 Robert Elderton produced a medal of Grace, with music on the reverse referring to 'Amazing Grace' and 'You Are My Saving Grace'. It sold for £75–£100. Then, to mark the 150th anniversary of the deed in 1988, Royal Doulton issued an extraordinarily romantic figurine of Grace. With shoulder-length black hair, she looks out to sea, presumably looking for the survivors from the wreck. As Jessica Mitford put it, she was 'transformed into a composite of Elizabeth Taylor and Snow White'. How well it sold is unknown. But certainly anything associated with Grace Darling has a value. When one of her silver medals was auctioned in 1999, it sold for £38,900, nearly double the asking price.[30]

There are also uses of the Grace Darling name and fame with no obvious commercial purpose. Take the Grace Darling Singers, formed in 1990, and based to the south of Manchester, 'a bunch of people who want to sing for the sheer pleasure of singing', with an emphasis on 'neglected but worthwhile "non-masterpieces" for the fun of it'. Why Grace Darling? As their web site explains,

'At the first rehearsals, there was not a great deal of music to choose from. There was the *Gesang der Moorsoldaten*, which the prisoners in German concentration camps sang as they marched to and from their forced labour. There was the Temperance hymn *Throw Out the Life-Line* ... And there was *The Grace Darling Song*. It was certainly different. You would not really call it a masterpiece. Was it worthwhile, though? Well, we do not sing it very often now! But somehow the name stuck.' The Grace Darling Singers' repertoire concentrates on Gallery Music, sacred music heard in churches and chapels from about 1700 to 1850; their name is almost an accident, and one that would not have been adopted had Grace Darling had a less euphonious name.[31]

There are other apparently random uses of Grace Darling's name. A Grace Darling boat for hire at Stratford-on-Avon. An annual Knutsford Royal Mayday ceremony where the Cheshire town is enlivened by sailors pulling Grace Darling and her father through the streets. A Grace Darling potentilla fruticosa, salmon pink with a very pale reverse, stemming from Wooler in Northumberland in the 1950s, to add to the gardening association established by the rose in the nineteenth century. At the Greenwich Festival in September 2003 three black mime artists, Grace and two sailors, dressed up to look like rusty statues that have been in the sea, moving slowly to strike appropriate poses.[32] These invocations of Grace, only distantly, if at all, related by geography or reconstruction to anything in Grace's life, suggest a residual knowledge of her name and deed, but one so residual that it can be turned to any purpose.

In the north east, things are very different. There everyone knows of Grace. She had pride of place in Frank Graham's *Famous Northumbrian Women* (1969). In 2004 she was voted Northumberland's top woman.[33] Songwriters and poets have returned to her story. In 'The Songs of the Hit Parade' (Polystar, 1993), Julian Henry, pictured with Bamburgh in the background, and inspired 'by going on holiday ... and owning old books by dead people', sings of the dying Grace. Harriet Pringle's poems are very simple:

> Heroine
> Yes,
> She
> Was
> One.

And:

> Best
> Oh, Grace,
> You beat the rest,
> You were the best,
> Northern heroine!

And:

> Merchandising
> Tea towels, mugs,
> Postcards, fudge …
> Grace, the Victorian Queen
> Of merchandising.

Pringle allows herself to imagine something that never happened, a Hollywood film. Grace, 197 years old, has the last word:

> You can't grasp
> The Past
> Your Presumption
> Makes me gasp,
> For I was there.[34]

Keith Armstrong, the poet and the coordinator of Northern Voices, has returned to the 'Saving Grace' theme in his poignant tribute to her:

> The Grace Darling League
> Must be one of those 20,000 Leagues Under The Sea.
>
> In your Museum,
> The Flotsam & Jetsam
> Drifts on a becalmed Bamburgh day,
> A sharp sunlight cuts through the church window:
>
> 'Out of the Deep have I called unto Thee'
>
> 'Charity, Faith & Hope'.
>
> These tangled words that make up our lives,
> the tattered wrecks, flaked skins.
>
> I stare in awe at a piece of the Oar you used,
> constructing a jigsaw of your life:
>
> here is a scrap of your dress,
> a throb of your 'English Heart';
>
> here, locked up, a lock of your hair,
> a handbag containing your thoughts;
>
> and 'There's the Girl That I Love Dearly',
> a storm in a teacup,
>
> a National Heroine of Japan

who coughed herself to death

like a seagull choking in oil,

like the bloodshot wreck of a dying Empire:

'Saving Grace',
save our souls:

Sister,
Save Our Souls.[35]

Grace Darling has always been of special importance in the north east, but now the museum, on the itinerary of so many school children, anchors her firmly there. In some ways in recent times Grace Darling has become more of a regional, less of a national, heroine than she once was. Certainly for a time, in the 1960s and 1970s, when Grace Darling seems to have ceased to be a story all children were brought up on, it was in the north east above all that her memory was preserved and something of her reputation sustained.

But if there was a generation of people now adults, aged between about thirty and fifty, who had Graceless childhoods, that is no longer the case. Especially since the 150th anniversary of Grace's deed in 1988, there have been many positive stories and television programmes about her. She is embedded in the Key Stages of the school curriculum; she was, for example, in the autumn 2005 schedule for Channel 4 learning. From the disgrace and oblivion that threatened her, Grace has now recovered.

9

Remembering Grace Darling

The confidence in 1838 that Grace's deed would be remembered to the end of time has so far been justified. There was a blip in the generation that grew up in the 1960s, 1970s and 1980s, but otherwise, in the nearly 170 years since her deed, her name and image have been so imprinted in the minds of the British people that the two words 'Grace Darling' immediately have meaning. Moreover, from the outset, her fame reached out beyond Britain to many parts of the world. What can this story tell us about heroism, about celebrity, and about the processes of remembrance?

Grace Darling's courage had an appeal that made her an inspiration to any human being. She was a heroine not only for the British but also for many people in other lands. Her fame spread rapidly and widely. 'The deed she had done', claimed the *Berwick and Kelso Warder*'s 1843 *Memoir*, 'may be said to have wafted her name over the civilised world, and to have secured its perpetuity through future ages, alongside of those of the most renowned of her sex.'[1] 'Europe' was sometimes substituted for 'the civilised world' in this formulation, but that her name had 'wafted' was a constant: it implied that news of her deed had, as it were, floated overseas on a gentle breeze or on the surface of the ocean, without any human agency. Such courage, such heroism, such goodness, needed no trumpet; they would strike home to the heart of any sensitive (and 'civilised') human being. In practice, of course, human agents did the wafting. News of Grace's deed travelled the trade routes of the early and mid-nineteenth century. Ships, appropriately, were the medium. By sail and by steam, by the word of mouth of sailors and travellers, and by the newspapers they carried with them, the story of Grace's deed percolated to the farthest reaches of the world known to Europeans.

Continental Europe was the nearest and first destination, and the British mercantile communities in ports were the first to respond. Such was the enthusiasm in St Petersburg that in the summer of 1839 a Mr Gordon and his niece made a trip to the Longstone, and presented 'the heroine' with embroidered slippers and 'an elegant silver-wrought cestus'. Gordon also carried with him a miniature of his nephew 'on the understanding that he was to get Grace Darling to kiss it, after which it should not be again touched until the owner received it'. Gordon, reportedly a small man (he must have been very small), evidently had to get on a chair 'to enable him to reach the lips of the reluctant heroine'.[2]

Evidence for a more distinctly European response is, however, distinctly patchy. A trawl through European newspapers would probably unearth reporting of Grace's deed, but without that we have to feed on scraps, mostly from relatively recent times. Take two unlikely morsels of evidence from the middle years of the twentieth century. First, in 1938, the museum received from a Danish periodical something that it was until then lacking, the music of the Grace Darling song. In Denmark, Phipps Hornby claimed in 1961, 'Grace Darling is very highly regarded'. Secondly, in 1958, the annual report of the Grace Darling Museum revealed that the Maritime Museum in Trieste had requested material about Grace for display.[3] They are not much to go on, but they suggest that in two very different parts of Europe there was knowledge of Grace's deed, and a respect for it. Whether it would be possible to trace that knowledge in a continuous line through from the 1830s to the present must remain uncertain, as must the extent of its spread within particular European countries.

There are shards of evidence from other countries. The Irish, apparently, adopted Grace as their own, replacing the 'Grace had an English heart' of the Grace Darling song with 'Grace had an Irish heart'.[4] In India Grace Darling was published with a Bombay imprint in 1960.[5] As to Japan, the Grace Darling League (or more probably Constance Smedley) evidently announced that Grace had been 'the National Heroine of Japan since 1858', but Japanese scholars whom I have consulted are unable to confirm this, on the face of it, implausible claim. The Grace Darling Museum does, however, have incontestable evidence of Japanese interest in Grace, in the shape of stories about her.[6]

We are on firmer ground in tracing the worldwide appeal of Grace if we turn to English-speaking countries. Australia can claim a continuous interest. There was a Grace Darling Hotel in Adelaide in the 1850s – it later became the South Australian Institution for the Blind, Deaf and Dumb. Melbourne's Grace Darling Hotel, a well-known landmark and restaurant, survives to this day, its walls decorated with portraits of the heroine and her family.[7] In the Melbourne Cup horse race in 1885 'Grace Darling' finished second.[8] In Adelaide, a version of the Grace Darling song was known, and being taught to children, in the early twentieth century.[9] Emigrants from Britain carried with them knowledge of the deed, and kept up to date with reportage in the local weekly papers from the towns of their birth. When Grace's reputation was being impugned in the 1890s, a correspondent warned of the possible harmful impact; because the Newcastle Weekly Chronicle was read in all parts of the world, 'many of the rising generation of Northumbrian families in the Antipodes and elsewhere might be led astray'.[10] And it was not only newspapers that crossed the oceans. So also did books. In Miles Franklin's 1902 My Career Goes Bung: Purporting to be the Autobiography of Sybylla Penelope Melvyn, the heroine tries to educate herself through reading biographies: 'I read ardently, nay, furiously would better express the way that one tackles the things one wants to do. Grace Darling, Charlotte Brontë, Joan of Arc and Mrs Fry passed in review, evidently by dull old professors.'[11] Sybylla Penelope Melvyn was not impressed, but her reading is a reminder that children in the empire on which the sun never set encountered the same stories as children in Britain. Perhaps that was true of the middle-aged woman I encountered while undergoing the ritual demanded of those seeking access to the treasures of the Bodleian in Oxford. While I was promising not to deface or otherwise harm the manuscripts, she, spotting my research topic, exclaimed with some delight that she had been brought up on Grace Darling in Perth, and she had assumed as a child that the rescue was mounted in the Pacific. Or perhaps she had run together the stories of Grace Darling and Grace Bussell. In 1876 in Western Australia, Grace Bussell had bravely ridden her horse through roaring breakers to bring assistance to women and children clinging onto a boat after the wreck of the *Georgette*. Quickly she became known as 'the Grace Darling of Australia'.[12]

The lands bordering the Atlantic rather than the Pacific provided the warmest welcome to the story of Grace Darling. North America holds most clues that Grace was 'wafted overseas'. Appropriately enough, the first piece of evidence, in 1854, is the naming of a new clipper from Boston as *Grace Darling*. The *Boston Daily Atlas* could not contain its enthusiasm: 'Who has not read the story of the heroic maiden, whose name adorns this beautiful ship, and who would have a heart that throbbed not with admiration, at the very mention of her name?' Like all too many *Grace Darlings*, it ended up wrecked, in January 1878 off Cape Flattery, bound for San Francisco.[13] Further evidence that America knew of Grace comes from the response to the rescues mounted by Ida Lewis, the daughter of the keeper of the Lime Rock lighthouse in Newport Harbor, Rhode Island. Born in 1842, the year of Grace's death, Ida had taken on her father's duties after he suffered a severe stroke in 1858. Ida, over the years, is said to have rescued at least eighteen people, most of them pleasure-seekers who had got into difficulty with their yachts. Public attention came only in 1869 when two soldiers were rescued, and newspapers picked up on the story. Ida, said the New York *Herald Tribune*, 'performed a deed that places her side by side, in point of self-sacrificing courage, with the Grace Darling of England …' She was 'America's Grace Darling'. Just as in Australia a decade later, the story of Grace's rescue was the point of reference, writers confident that readers would know of her. The American response to Ida's deed was very similar to the British response to Grace's thirty years earlier: money raised, hair much in demand, requests to appear on stage, constant visitors to the lighthouse, and a heroine who had little time for all the fuss. But whereas Grace's fame endured, Ida's did not. She lived to the age of sixty-nine, after a disastrous marriage in her twenties, her failure to complete the heroine's role by an early death perhaps putting her at a disadvantage. Now, beyond an Ida Lewis Yacht Club on the Lime Rock, there is little evidence that she is a popular heroine.[14]

The East Coast boasts further evidence of Grace Darling's popularity in the United States. Pride of place in the carriage section of the Long Island Museum of American Art, History and Carriages at Stoney Brook is given to a 'Grace Darling' carriage. It was built in about 1880 for a livery company that specialized in transporting passengers between the railway stations and the beach, and also offered excursions around the countryside. A large omnibus, it could carry forty-five passengers, pulled by a team of up to six horses. As was the custom, the 'Grace Darling' was elaborately decorated, the letters of the name prominent in gold leaf against a blue background. It was in service until 1904, and between 1925 and 1952 was used by St Paul's School, Concord, New Hampshire, to transport pupils to school events. Then it was donated to the Museum. Its history is evidence that in the later nineteenth century the Grace Darling name had potential publicity value in the burgeoning leisure industry. And today the Museum display keeps alive memory of Grace Darling on the eastern seaboard.[15]

There is other random evidence of the pull of Grace Darling in the United States. In St Augustine, Florida, you can book in to the 'Grace Darling Room' (a favourite for honeymooners) in the Old Powder House Inn, and surround yourself with mementoes of the deed. An early American film star called herself Grace Darling. New Orleans boasts the saxophonist, singer and songwriter, Grace Darling, whose 1997 debut, 'Imaginary Love', was a hit. The American Peony Society promotes a 'Grace Darling Peony', and, to add to the floral theme, there is a 'Grace Darling Neoregelia'. The San Francisco Brewing Company, just to prove that this is not a purely East Coast phenomenon, markets a 'Grace Darling Bock': 'Amber in color, the Grace Darling Lager possesses an extremely smooth, rich malty character. A big, impressive interpretation of bock style.' Just how that connects to Grace Darling is unclear, but somehow an advertising or marketing executive has seen potential and promise in the Grace Darling name. Nor is it clear why there should have been a Grace Darling Putnam Bisque BYE-LO doll for sale on eBay from Tucson, Arizona, in August 2005.[16]

Alongside these snippets of data, there is evidence of a more substantial kind to indicate that Grace Darling was well known and well-loved in North America. It lies in the family trees that Americans post on the web, and in the prevalence of the Grace Darling name. Google 'Grace Darling' on pages from the UK, and you get 29,00 hits; on the web, the hits rise to 90,000, many of them American genealogies. The earliest I have found is a 'Grace Darling Mecomber', born in Maine in 1859, followed by a 'Grace Darling Weeks', born in Connecticut in 1862, and a 'Grace Darling Hutchinson', born in New Hampshire in 1864. In the late nineteenth and early twentieth centuries the name spread south to Louisiana, west to Illinois and Wisconsin, north to Nova Scotia, New Brunswick and Ontario. In the 1930s people named their children after film stars. In an earlier period, Grace Darling was a heroine and celebrity with an alluring name. Not surprisingly, parents gave her name to their daughters, hoping doubtless that they would imbibe some of the admired characteristics of their namesake.

Grace Darling's deed was, and is, remembered across the globe; her appeal is universal. But her name and deed had, and have, most resonance in Britain. What place does Grace Darling hold in the story of the nation? We can perhaps best understand her particular and changing appeal by seeing whom she was compared to. Her deed, we need to remember, was thought from the outset to be 'unexampled in the feats of female fortitude', unique and never to be repeated, but that did not stop contemporaries and later writers trying to place her in her appropriate niche in the pantheon of heroines. The writers who did this were British, and the story they wanted to tell about Grace's heroism was a peculiarly British one.

In the middle years of the nineteenth century, the public imagination was gripped by the memory of the civil wars of the seventeenth century and their aftermath up to the end of the Jacobite threat in 1745. The heroines of those years were those most commonly compared with Grace. Perhaps closest to Grace, because of her youth, was Lady Grisell Baillie, who at the age of eleven was smuggling messages to her father, Sir Patrick Hume, and Robert Baillie in gaol in Edinburgh. She then protected her father after his involvement in 1683 in the Rye House Plot to kill both Charles II and his brother James. Much praise was also given to Charlotte Stanley, Countess of Derby, who in 1644, in her husband's absence, defended Lathom House, near Ormskirk, against Parliamentary forces. Another well-known heroine was Rachel Russell whose husband William was also involved in the Rye House Plot; Rachel's unsuccessful attempts to save his life won much admiration. And then there was Lady Nithsdale who enabled her husband to escape from the Tower of London after his involvement in the 1715 uprising. Finally, in 1745, there was Flora MacDonald who, reluctantly, helped Charles Edward to escape after Culloden by disguising him as her Irish maid, Betty Burke, and assisting him in rowing to safety. The common rowing theme sometimes led to confusion of Grace and Flora. Like Grace, Flora owed some of her fame to a song, in her case Harold Boulton's 'Skye Boat Song' of the 1880s.

How did Grace compare with these heroines of the seventeenth and eighteenth centuries? The answer contemporaries gave was that Grace's heroism was purer than that of her forebears. With the exception of Flora MacDonald, they all had strong family motivation for their actions; nothing wrong with that, but in comparison, Grace's heroism was inspired only by a larger love for humanity. And her deed stood out from these earlier examples of female heroism for two other reasons: for all of them there had been a political element as well as a family one; and they all came from the upper sections of society, many of them being aristocratic. For Grace Darling, there was no political element in her heroism, and she was one of the common people, 'a heroine in humble life', an exemplar of virtues that the nation could celebrate.

Joan of Arc was also one of the common people, and was the person to whom people most frequently turned when they tried to measure the heroism of Grace Darling. Jerold Vernon must take responsibility or credit for first suggesting the parallel. His subtitle, 'The Maid of the Isles', would have reminded readers immediately of the 'Maid of Orleans', and he made the link explicitly. Joan herself was a familiar figure in the nineteenth century, featuring in plays, most famously by Schiller, and operas, by Verdi (1845), Gounod (1873) and Tchaikovsky (1878). A call for her canonization was first made in 1869, a status eventually achieved in 1920 after surmounting the intermediate hurdles of becoming Venerable in 1894 and Blessed in 1909.[17] In the century after her deed, Grace Darling seemed to many to be Britain's Joan of Arc.

What was there in common between this Catholic saint-in-waiting who had lived and been burnt at the stake in the fifteenth century and Grace? Both showed physical courage, and both died young and virgins. In the story of their lives a link was forged between the innocence associated with childhood and virginity, on the one hand, and virtue and courage, on the other. Both were 'children of nature', growing up amidst natural elements and forces that became their teachers, and never losing the essential goodness of their childhood. Both were of the people, not the middle or upper classes. And through their childhoods rooted in the soil, the woods of Domrémy in Lorraine for Joan, the coast of Northumberland for Grace, each became a symbol of her nation. They were ideal icons for nations in which the people, in the shape of republicanism or a slowly emerging democracy, were acknowledged to be a growing force. Over and above this, the lives and deeds of both of them could be represented as simple and instinctive, representing what Marina Warner has called 'the Western attachment to changelessness and our terror of flux'.[18] The similar role played by the two women in the iconography of their nations is driven home by the fact that the goods that were marketed through their names have a remarkable similarity.[19]

The emphasis in this iconography of nationhood was on the courage associated with modesty and maidenhood in the two women. In the anonymous *Jeanne Darc, the Patriot Martyr: and Other Narratives of Female Heroism in Peace and War* (1883), we read how 'the patriot is the focus of all that contributes to the existence and welfare of the nation, and takes highest rank among the great men and women cherished in the memory of a people'. Pride of place was given here to Joan, but Grace is featured along with six other women who had some claim to be ranked with the 'patriot martyr'.[20] Many British writers, however, ranked Grace's heroism above that of Joan. 'Joan of Arc', wrote Eva Hope, 'was a noble girl, full of inspiration and courage; but her deeds were great as the world looks on greatness, and there was much of pomp and show about her achievements.

But this girl [Grace] went out on the angry waters in the grey light of an early morning, with the simple purpose in her heart of saving from drowning those whose lives were in jeopardy ... She must have had the purest motives in what she did, and in this she excelled many women who have been praised.' But the two were equally praised for their response to fame: 'Like Joan of Arc', wrote Marianne Kirlew in 1897, 'amid all the tumults of applause, Grace never forgot the modest dignity which became her maidenhood.'[21] The dream of making Grace a national heroine inspired the Grace Darling League in the 1930s, one aim being that 'Grace Darling should be known and loved of British children as Joan of Arc is loved in France'.[22]

The differences between Grace in Britain and Joan in France were, however, quite as important as what they shared in common. The modern posthumous life of Joan of Arc began in 1841 when Jules Michelet made her the embodiment of the Republican tradition in France. Joan, for Michelet, stood out from the enthusiasts who swayed the masses in what he called 'the ages of ignorance' by her '*bon sens*', her commonsense, a quality that made her intelligible to, and almost a contemporary of, the nineteenth century.[23] Joan's earthy practicality found another exemplar in Grace Darling. So far, so much in common. But in France, 'in every era of French defeat and ensuing discontent with its Republican government, Joan of Arc was invoked most powerfully by the monarchists and other rightist groups'. Michelet's republican heroine struggled to survive; she was appropriated by the church and by right-wing political groups, becoming in the late twentieth and early twenty-first centuries a symbol of a true France for Jean-Marie Le Pen's National Front.[24] Britain, not suffering defeat in the way that France did, for example in the Franco-Prussian War, was perhaps less in need of a warrior heroine who could exemplify the nation: Boudica, the most plausible version of Joan in Britain, never attained her continental rival's significance. But equally important, Britain did not have the distinct political traditions – republican, Bonapartist, monarchist – that shaped France's life. There were, of course, differences between Whigs and Tories, or, later, Liberals, Conservatives and socialists, but that did not lead to hugely variant versions of the national past. Until Tony Benn provided Grace with a progeny of the women's movements of the twentieth century, she lived posthumously, as she had during her life, outside the political sphere. Unlike Joan, she was not easily appropriated for political purposes, even if there had been a wish to do so.

In 1917 it was reported that someone on hearing the name of Florence Nightingale had exclaimed, 'Oh! yes. Didn't she do something with a lifeboat'. It was, evidently, a not uncommon confusion. In 1938 the *Newcastle Weekly Chronicle* reported that a visitor from London had been heard saying, 'Oh yes, the Longstone Lighthouse, the place where Florence Nightingale saved the sailors'.[25] It was in some ways an understandable mistake, for Florence Nightingale and

Grace Darling for many years undoubtedly enjoyed top position in the roll call of nineteenth-century British heroines, their names bracketed together. And their reputations have followed a similar trajectory: they were on a pedestal in the nineteenth century, but were battered and bruised in the twentieth. Florence Nightingale, who lived until 1910, received the standard two-volume biography by Sir Edward Cook in 1913, but then had the misfortune to be one of Lytton Strachey's *Eminent Victorians* in 1918. Strachey's was not a hatchet job: it was in many ways a sympathetic portrait, but his opening paragraph makes it plain that this was going to be no panegyric. 'Every one knows', he wrote,

> the popular conception of Florence Nightingale. The saintly, self-sacrificing woman, the delicate maiden of high degree who threw aside the pleasures of a life of ease to succour the afflicted, the Lady with the Lamp, gliding through the horrors of the hospital at Scutari, and consecrating with the radiance of her goodness the dying soldier's couch – the vision is familiar to all. But the truth was different. The Miss Nightingale of fact was not as facile fancy painted her ... A Demon possessed her. Now demons, whatever else they may be, are full of interest. And it so happens that in the real Miss Nightingale there was more that was interesting than in the legendary one; there was also less that was agreeable.

Florence Nightingale, Strachey was happy to acknowledge, was certainly 'heroic', 'yet her heroism was not of that simple sort so dear to the readers of novels and the compilers of hagiologies – the romantic sentimental heroism with which mankind loves to invest its chosen darlings'. What marked it, rather, was 'the fixed determination of an indomitable will'. And this, her demon, came fully into its own in the years after the Crimea, when from her sickbed she set about reforming the army, nursing, and anything else that attracted her attention, driving many men to distraction and poor Sidney Herbert to his death.[26] Strachey was not alone in challenging the legend. In 1950 Cecil Woodham-Smith's *Florence Nightingale*, a best seller, dissected the heroine's family life, and in 1982 F. B. Smith emphasized 'her talent for manipulation', her 'unyielding, unremitting drive to dominate her associates and opponents', 'her egotism', 'the narcissistic quality of her personality', and her 'habit of deceit'.[27]

Grace Darling's reputation survived unscathed for longer than Florence Nightingale's, but then, as we have seen, from the 1960s, her legend was dismantled. Yet, just as Grace Darling has made a recovery in the late twentieth and early twenty-first centuries, so also has Florence Nightingale. Hugh Small's *Florence Nightingale: Avenging Angel* (1998) brings new light to bear on her post Crimean War breakdown, ascribing it to her guilt in agreeing to the suppression of the evidence that the death rate at the Scutari hospital had been exceptionally high, and in doing so, in the words of a review, 'goes a long way to rehabilitate her'.[28]

Florence Nightingale and Grace Darling were for many years bracketed together as heroines. Nightingale has rightly been seen by historians as by a long way the more significant historical figure, not only for her actions in the Crimean War, but perhaps more for her subsequent achievements in public health. So much so, that it now seems rather absurd to consider them together, just as it seems absurd to compare Grace Darling with Joan of Arc. But we need to remember that Grace Darling was once put on the same pedestal as people who played a significant role in major historical events. How did that happen?

Images have much to do with it. When people think of Grace Darling, they see her in the coble struggling in a tempestuous sea. When they think of Florence Nightingale, they see 'the Lady with the Lamp'. Grace Darling rowing to the rescue and Florence Nightingale ministering to the wounded were, in the nineteenth and for much of the twentieth century, inspiring images of femininity. In a world where women were, at least partially, excluded from so much, from politics, from education, from the professions, these two acts showed that there was a way in which women could play a distinctively feminine role in the saving of life. And if you believed the common story that it was Grace who persuaded her father to go out to the rescue, then women, more than men, seemed to have qualities that led them to self-sacrificing heroism. Both women and men drew inspiration from them. For women, they provided what we might now call role models: ideals of what women, and women alone, could achieve. Men could have their masculinity confirmed by recognizing and idealizing a distinctively feminine role in ministering to humanity: while they went about the manly business of building an empire or making money, with all the unpleasantness that that might involve, women could be imagined as angels, free from the pollution of the world, and the embodiment of all that was good. Simple images, of Grace Darling in her coble and Florence Nightingale with her lamp, were the most powerful way of articulating and justifying these differences between men and women.

The widely disseminated images of Grace Darling and Florence Nightingale were more than images of themselves, or of an idealized femininity: they were also images of the nation. Britain, or its constituent parts, was often seen as masculine. From the later eighteenth century John Bull was a recognizable symbol of the nation, sometimes identified with George III, sometimes a kind of plodding yeoman farmer, sometimes a rather breezy man about town. But whatever his incarnation, he was not exactly an inspiring figure – he was frequently pictured weighed down by taxes, and seems to have always represented the economic interests of the nation, rather than something more elevated. He evoked a kind of wry affection, a sense that he was one of us, but he was hardly a figure to risk life for.[29] The heroes of empire came nearer to doing that. They ranged from missionaries like David Livingstone to the soldiers whose deeds and images so captured the imagination of young and old: Havelock in the 1857 Mutiny, Wolseley, 'Bobs' Roberts and Baden-Powell from the Boer War,

Kitchener of Khartoum (and of the First World War recruiting advertisement), and perhaps with wider appeal than any of them, General Gordon, whose death at Khartoum Kitchener went to avenge.[30] For Gordon was more than a soldier, he was as near as could be a missionary as well, whether in China or Greenwich. Certainly these male heroes cast their spell over boys, but whether they became truly representative of the nation rather than one half of it may be open to doubt.

Girls and women needed someone of their own sex to look up to as an embodiment of the nation. Grace Darling certainly helped fill what was otherwise something of a void. There were, it is true, two other powerful female images of the nation, Queen Victoria and Britannia. The Queen's image in the years after her accession in 1837 was a familiar one. Even when she disappeared from public life after Albert's death, coins and stamps made her well known. Yet it was only in the latter years of her reign, after the 1887 Jubilee, that there were real signs that she was becoming a popular and loved figure. It was then that Oxfordshire cottagers started decorating their front rooms with images of the Queen, and in those years, too, advertisers began to sell their goods to the accompaniment of her pictures.[31] If there were limits to the Queen's status as representative of the nation, even more so was this true of Britannia. She might be familiar to readers of *Punch*, a sometimes stern, sometimes caring, image of the nation, but I know of no evidence that she at any level entered popular consciousness and affection. In short, Britain lacked female icons. Grace Darling and Florence Nightingale filled the gap.

Across the Channel, the situation was very different. The French were spoilt for choice when it came to female icons. First, and enduringly, and something common in all Catholic countries, there was the Madonna; and the Madonna in nineteenth-century France was not simply a religious icon, but also, if contentiously, a national one. Under Napoleon III in the 1850s and 1860s towns competed with one another to raise monuments to the Madonna that were hard to separate from a loyalty to the regime and an opposition to republicanism. France herself (La France) was constantly depicted as female, as were the successive republics. And then there was Marianne. The name derives from opponents of the republic in the 1790s who used it derisively because Marianne or Marie-Anne was a name common among the popular classes. The name lingered on through the empire and the restored monarchy, and in the Second Republic of 1848–50 we find it being used at a popular level in southern France, but now positively: the word was switching from right to left. Marianne became a password within left-wing republican secret societies, breaking out of its southern strongholds. And Marianne was popular. In southern France people had small images of her, and were ready to display them on celebratory occasions. Her future was assured.[32]

Perhaps France needed a panoply of female icons – the Madonna, Marianne, Joan of Arc – because of its divergent and competing political traditions: one for each, as it were. In the more unitary Britain this kind of rivalry of icons was much less in evidence, but it is nevertheless striking how impoverished the British were in visual representations of their nation. Grace Darling and Florence Nightingale were hardly on a par with the female icons of France, but they came to seem representative of what was best in, and peculiarly belonged to, Britain. And there are hints in the iconography of what Grace Darling might have, but never quite, became.

One sign of Grace's potential significance in the national story lay in the attempt to canonize her. Not of course formally as happened to Joan of Arc, but in an understated British way. Take the representation of her in Liverpool. In 1901 it was decided to build an Anglican cathedral in the new diocese, and in 1910 the Lady Chapel was completed. On the stairs are the Noble Women windows where the lives and images of twenty-one women are displayed, the selection designed to show that saintliness 'did not abruptly terminate in the past'. Local women were chosen wherever suitable, but there is a window dedicated to 'Grace Darling and All Courageous Maidens'. The other twenty are a clutch of now mostly-forgotten nineteenth-century missionaries, teachers, doctors and nurses, nearly all of whom had met early deaths brought on by their works of self-sacrifice, Kitty Wilkinson, the local heroine, herself from a poor background, who had helped the poor in the cholera outbreak of 1832, and a rather random selection of more famous figures, including, from the nineteenth century, Elizabeth Fry, Josephine Butler, Queen Victoria, Angela Burdett-Coutts, Christina Rossetti and Elizabeth Barrett Browning. Grace Darling was not only among the great and good, she was also a modern saint. The unstated comparison with Joan of Arc inevitable, it was her maidenhood as well as her courage that the window highlighted.

If there was to be a main shrine to Grace Darling, the modern saint, it had to be in Bamburgh. It is difficult to wander round Bamburgh church and churchyard without sensing in the sculptures and memorials that the groundwork was being laid for a shrine and a place of pilgrimage. And pilgrimages there were. In September 1938 the *Newcastle Chronicle*, under the headline 'Grace Darling's Centenary – Yesterday's Pilgrimage', described how four lifeboats from Holy Island, Boulmer and Seahouses had carried some fifty 'pilgrims' to the Longstone.[33] Anniversaries brought out pilgrims. On the 125th anniversary there was Commander Phipps Hornby, on his own, laying a wreath. Twenty-five years later, perhaps because 150 years seems more important than 125, and perhaps because of the revival in Grace's reputation, the dukes of Atholl, Kent and Northumberland, representing the RNLI, and Viscount Ridley, the Lord Lieutenant, attended a memorial service in the church and laid a wreath near the Big Harcar.[34]

Yet the history of the site is a history of failure and neglect. The wearing away of the Portland stone chosen for the first statue of Grace is somehow symbolic. She was, reported the Diocesan Surveyor, 'reduced to a skeleton'. In the mid-1880s this was replaced by the second statue, with the addition of rails to enclose the tomb, 'which was formerly weedy and grassy'. At the same time the church itself was adorned with the stained glass window.[35] It might seem as if the site of pilgrimage was now once again ready for use. Yet, eleven years later, a visitor found the monument 'in a deplorable state', with some of the rails broken off and the enclosure 'in a filthy state, with animal excreta'. The figure of Grace, said another correspondent, was covered with a 'coating of green vegetable mould'. All this, claimed the vicar, was the result of storm damage some two or three years previously. The fragments broken off had been carefully preserved, but the restoration work awaited 'adequate subscriptions'. Eventually, Sir Walter Besant and others coughed up the necessary amount, less than £200, and the restoration was carried out.[36] But the episode hardly suggests that the site was a place of popular pilgrimage or even affection.

The museum has perhaps replaced the churchyard as a site for proclaiming a modern sainthood. In it are preserved Grace's 'relics', her clothes, her hair, her handwriting and, of course, her coble. Seeing them, 40,000 visitors a year perhaps come away with some sense of reverence.

Were there, in the twentieth century, new national heroines who could rival or supplant their nineteenth-century forebears? Edith Cavell, the nurse in the First World War, who was executed by the Germans, and whose statue in London has a commanding position outside the National Portrait Gallery, looking down on to Trafalgar Square, came nearest to doing so. Yet, in 1972, a letter in *The Times* thought it doubtful that even ten out of a hundred Londoners knew who she was.[37] Perhaps the twentieth century, as *The Times* suggested thirty years previously, in 1942, in the midst of war, and reflecting on the centenary of her death on 'Sisters of Grace Darling', had almost a superfluity of heroines. 'In the reign of George VI any one of us may shake hands any day with a woman as heroic as Grace Darling'.[38]

Yet, in that same year, 1942, there was still a distinctive place for Grace in the national story. Reflecting on what was distinctive about *English Women*, Edith Sitwell found their distinguishing quality lying in 'character, not intellect', and provided pen sketches of nineteen women 'in whom that quintessence of character expressed itself'. Grace was one of them (though we are perhaps more likely to focus on the intellect rather than the character of her immediate companions, Jane Welsh Carlyle, Emily Brontë and George Eliot).[39] Both in her courage, and in her interpretation of the role appropriate to a woman, Grace Darling seemed to be the embodiment of all that was best in our 'island story'.

None of the mid-twentieth-century women whose hand *The Times* leader-writer might have shaken has left a name with as deep a resonance as Grace Darling. We should not, of course, underestimate the power of the name itself. Those contemporaries who said that if she had been a Dorothy Dobbs,[40] we would in all likelihood have soon forgotten about her, are right in at least this respect: there would not have been a Dorothy Dobbs chocolate, or Dorothy Dobbs speculative mining companies, or a Dorothy Dobbs beer, nor would there have been girls who were given the name of Dorothy Dobbs. We might have remembered Dorothy Dobbs's deed of courage, but she would not have become a celebrity in the way that Grace Darling did, able to add value to anything with which her name was associated. Grace herself is reported to have said that if she ever married she wanted to keep her own name.[41] She was fully aware of its resonance.

It is possible that the British, like the Americans, called their daughters 'Grace Darling', but there is no search engine that I know of that can find the answer. There are, however, some examples of Grace Darlings in Britain. At least one of them just happened to have the same name. There are, intriguingly, letters in 1839 and 1840 to and from a Miss Grace Darling in Edinburgh. Was the heroine, after all, tempted to visit that city? No, it is another Grace Darling altogether, renting a property. The most extraordinary Grace Darling was the headmistress of the St Gabriel's school in Rangoon in Burma who drowned in 1894 trying to save the life of a pupil. 'She died worthy of that name', reported the Reverend Thomas Ellis. More prosaically, there was a Mrs Grace Darling Patterson buying derelict cottages in Worcestershire in 1935, and a Miss Grace Darling Southey who died in Worthing in 1980, leaving £487,806 in her will.[42]

But there is more to Grace Darling than her name. She is, in Pierre Nora's term, a *lieu de mémoire*, never stable, always changing. In her first embodiment, Grace Darling was a heroine for the age of romance. In the 1830s and 1840s, and even beyond that, there is no sense that she made a particular appeal, or indeed any appeal at all, to children. She was a heroine for adults of the middle and upper classes, who were captivated by the thought that a young woman of the people, a 'child of nature', could perform an act so 'sublime', and so far removed from what was seen as the domain of women. To make sense of Grace and her deed, they fictionalized her and placed her in fiction – an English Jeannie Deans. In her second and posthumous incarnation, Grace Darling's deed and character were placed in the history of the world, of the nation and of Northumbria. She was seen to exemplify certain admirable character traits that were specifically British – or, more narrowly, Northumbrian. Then, from the 1870s onwards, began a process whereby Grace Darling was turned into a role model for the young of the nation. In one (conservative) interpretation she stood for qualities sadly under threat; her heroism now extended beyond the deed to her whole life and character, and in particular her devotion to home, and her acceptance of her social rank

– 'a heroine in humble life'. In another (more radical) interpretation she was a pioneer of women who sought to break out of the bounds imposed upon them by society. Either way, she was a fit symbol of the nation and of femininity for the age of imperialism. And the appeal was increasingly to children. Once made familiar to all children, she entered popular culture, becoming a figure who could sell goods to adults and add value to speculative ventures.

Constance Smedley in the 1930s tried to make Grace more specifically a national heroine linked to the sea, but she cannot be said to have succeeded. Grace Darling certainly remained in the inter-war period and beyond a heroine with a place in the national story, but Smedley's one-woman effort to link her specifically with the sea never captured the popular imagination. The oak trees in ports across the empire were never planted, and even the small sums necessary to place a roof over the coble proved hard to raise. Constance Smedley enhanced the profile of Grace Darling in the 1930s, but there were probably very few who came to see Grace as the sea heroine of Smedley's dreams.

Smedley's research, and her children's book, and books for children written under the influence of her interpretation, ensured nevertheless that Grace Darling remained a heroine for children into the second half of the twentieth century. Adults who know about Grace Darling know her from childhood. They learnt about her in simple storybooks, in magazines or comics, and in school lessons. As Diana Athill, born in 1917, remembered, Grace Darling 'came into the nursery: nannies and nursery-maids loved to tell her story'. And it was the story of her courage that sent the young Athill in imagination 'up cliffs, down pits, into burning houses, across flooding rivers, to rescue imperilled Denis, or Wilfred the cowman's son'.[43]

From the 1960s for nearly a quarter of a century there was a downturn among the young in knowledge of the heroine. Adults no longer thought her an appropriate role model, and, like nearly all heroes and heroines of the nineteenth century, her reputation was besmirched. But towards the end of the twentieth century and into the twenty-first century children have once again come to know about Grace. Despite the pressures to construct a national story for all children in British schools, Grace no longer plays any overt role in that story. Rather, she is now again on a world stage, fit to be compared with Mahatma Gandhi or Nelson Mandela. She is represented as someone of real flesh and blood whose life and deed can be used to bring children face to face with some of the most important ethical issues they will confront. Grace's heroism was simple and straightforward: anyone could (and can) imagine themselves in her position in the early hours of that September dawn in 1838; and can wonder what they might, or might not, have done. In the simple version of the story, uncomplicated by tales of an over-loving father or the lure of a reward, what faced Grace was, in its starkest form, the most fundamental of ethical issues to face a human being: should I, would

I, risk my life to save others? Grace's instinctive and unquestioning affirmative answer make her an inspirational role model. It is perhaps not so surprising as we might first think that she should have been seen as a modern saint.

Unlike more contemporary heroines, such as Ellen MacArthur, Grace did not put her life at risk in pursuit of a personal goal; she did so to save others. Add to this her youth and her social origins, and she is the perfect example to place before the young. Children across the nation could and can identify with her. Two anecdotal examples from here in Kent, far away from Northumberland. The head-teacher of a primary school tells me that she always does a school assembly on the story of Grace Darling. And a girl in Canterbury, baptized Grace, is nicknamed Darling by her friends: neither she nor they will ever forget it.

Appendix

GRACE DARLING

AMONG the dwellers in the silent fields
The natural heart is touched, and public way
And crowded street resound with ballad strains,
Inspired by ONE whose very name bespeaks
Favour divine, exalting human love;
Whom, since her birth on bleak Northumbria's coast,
Known unto few but prized as far as known,
A single Act endears to high and low
Through the whole land – to Manhood, moved in spite
Of the world's freezing cares – to generous Youth –
To Infancy, that lisps her praise – to Age
Whose eye reflects it, glistening through a tear
Of tremulous admiration. Such true fame
Awaits her 'now'; but, verily, good deeds
Do not imperishable record find
Save in the rolls of heaven, where hers may live
A theme for angels, when they celebrate
The high-souled virtues which forgetful earth
Has witnessed. Oh! that winds and waves could speak
Of things which their united power called forth
From the pure depths of her humanity!
A Maiden gentle, yet, at duty's call,
Firm and unflinching, as the Lighthouse reared
On the Island-rock, her lonely dwelling-place;
Or like the invincible Rock itself that braves,
Age after age, the hostile elements,
As when it guarded holy Cuthbert's cell.
All night the storm had raged, nor ceased, nor paused,
When, as day broke, the Maid, through misty air,
Espies far off a Wreck, amid the surf,
Beating on one of those disastrous isles –

Half of a Vessel, half – no more; the rest
Had vanished, swallowed up with all that there
Had for the common safety striven in vain,
Or thither thronged for refuge. With quick glance
Daughter and Sire through optic-glass discern,
Clinging about the remnant of this Ship,
Creatures – how precious in the Maiden's sight!
For whom, belike, the old Man grieves still more
Than for their fellow-sufferers engulfed
Where every parting agony is hushed,
And hope and fear mix not in further strife.
"But courage, Father! let us out to sea –
A few may yet be saved." The Daughter's words,
Her earnest tone, and look beaming with faith,
Dispel the Father's doubts: nor do they lack
The noble-minded Mother's helping hand
To launch the boat; and with her blessing cheered,
And inwardly sustained by silent prayer,
Together they put forth, Father and Child!
Each grasps an oar, and struggling on they go –
Rivals in effort; and, alike intent
Here to elude and there surmount, they watch
The billows lengthening, mutually crossed
And shattered, and re-gathering their might;
As if the tumult, by the Almighty's will
Were, in the conscious sea, roused and prolonged
That woman's fortitude – so tried, so proved –
May brighten more and more!

True to the mark,
They stem the current of that perilous gorge,
Their arms still strengthening with the strengthening heart,
Though danger, as the Wreck is neared, becomes
More imminent. Not unseen do they approach;
And rapture, with varieties of fear
Incessantly conflicting, thrills the frames
Of those who, in that dauntless energy,
Foretaste deliverance; but the least perturbed
Can scarcely trust his eyes, when he perceives
That of the pair – tossed on the waves to bring
Hope to the hopeless, to the dying, life –

One is a Woman, a poor earthly sister,
Or, be the Visitant other than she seems,
A guardian Spirit sent from pitying Heaven,
In woman's shape. But why prolong the tale,
Casting weak words amid a host of thoughts
Armed to repel them? Every hazard faced
And difficulty mastered, with resolve
That no one breathing should be left to perish,
This last remainder of the crew are all
Placed in the little boat, then o'er the deep
Are safely borne, landed upon the beach,
And, in fulfilment of God's mercy, lodged
Within the sheltering Lighthouse. – Shout, ye Waves
Send forth a song of triumph. Waves and Winds,
Exult in this deliverance wrought through faith
In Him whose Providence your rage hath served!
Ye screaming Sea-mews, in the concert join!
And would that some immortal Voice – a Voice
Fitly attuned to all that gratitude
Breathes out from floor or couch, through pallid lips
Of the survivors – to the clouds might bear –
Blended with praise of that parental love,
Beneath whose watchful eye the Maiden grew
Pious and pure, modest and yet so brave,
Though young so wise, though meek so resolute –
Might carry to the clouds and to the stars,
Yea, to celestial Choirs, GRACE DARLING'S name!

William Wordsworth (1843)

GRACE DARLING

Take, O star of all our seas, from not an alien hand,
Homage paid of song bowed down before thy glory's face,
Thou the living light of all our lovely stormy strand,
Thou the brave north-country's very glory of glories, Grace.
Loud and dark about the lighthouse rings and glares the night;
Glares with foam-lit gloom and darkling fire of storm and spray,
Rings with roar of winds in chase and rage of waves in flight,
Howls and hisses as with mouths of snakes and wolves at bay.
Scarce the cliffs of the islets, scarce the walls of Joyous Gard,
Flash to sight between the deadlier lightnings of the sea:
Storm is lord and master of a midnight evil-starred,
Nor may sight or fear discern what evil stars may be.
Dark as death and white as snow the sea-swell scowls and shines,
Heaves and yearns and pants for prey, from ravening lip to lip,
Strong in rage of rapturous anguish, lines on hurtling lines,
Ranks on charging ranks, that break and rend the battling ship.
All the night is mad and murderous: who shall front the night?
Not the prow that labours, helpless as a storm-blown leaf,
Where the rocks and waters, darkling depth and beetling height,
Rage with wave on shattering wave and thundering reef on reef.
Death is fallen upon the prisoners there of darkness, bound
Like as thralls with links of iron fast in bonds of doom;
How shall any way to break the bands of death be found,
Any hand avail to pluck them from that raging tomb?
All the night is great with child of death: no stars above
Show them hope in heaven, no lights from shores ward help on earth.
Is there help or hope to seaward, is there help in love,
Hope in pity, where the ravening hounds of storm make mirth?
Where the light but shows the naked eyeless face of Death
Nearer, laughing dumb and grim across the loud live storm?
Not in human heart or hand or speech of human breath,
Surely, nor in saviours found of mortal face or form.
Yet below the light, between the reefs, a skiff shot out
Seems a sea-bird fain to breast and brave the strait fierce pass
Whence the channelled roar of waters driven in raging rout,
Pent and pressed and maddened, speaks their monstrous might and mass.
Thunder heaves and howls about them, lightning leaps and flashes,
Hard at hand, not high in heaven, but close between the walls
Heaped and hollowed of the storms of old, whence reels and crashes

All the rage of all the unbaffled wave that breaks and falls.
Who shall thwart the madness and the gladness of it, laden
Full with heavy fate, and joyous as the birds that whirl?
Nought in heaven or earth, if not one mortal-moulded maiden,
Nought if not the soul that glorifies a northland girl.
Not the rocks that break may baffle, not the reefs that thwart
Stay the ravenous rapture of the waves that crowd and leap;
Scarce their flashing laughter shows the hunger of their heart,
Scarce their lion-throated roar the wrath at heart they keep.
Child and man and woman in the grasp of death clenched fast
Tremble, clothed with darkness round about, and scarce draw breath,
Scarce lift eyes up toward the light that saves not, scarce may cast
Thought or prayer up, caught and trammelled in the snare of death.
Not as sea-mews cling and laugh or sun their plumes and sleep
Cling and cower the wild night's waifs of shipwreck, blind with fear,
Where the fierce reef scarce yields foothold that a bird might keep,
And the clamorous darkness deadens eye and deafens ear.
Yet beyond their helpless hearing, out of hopeless sight,
Saviours, armed and girt upon with strength of heart, fare forth,
Sire and daughter, hand on oar and face against the night,
Maid and man whose names are beacons ever to the North.
Nearer now; but all the madness of the storming surf
Hounds and roars them back; but roars and hounds them back in vain:
As a pleasure-skiff may graze the lake-embanking turf,
So the boat that bears them grates the rock where-toward they strain.
Dawn as fierce and haggard as the face of night scarce guides
Toward the cries that rent and clove the darkness, crying for aid,
Hours on hours, across the engorged reluctance of the tides,
Sire and daughter, high-souled man and mightier-hearted maid.
Not the bravest land that ever breasted war's grim sea,
Hurled her foes back harried on the lowlands whence they came,
Held her own and smote her smiters down, while such durst be,
Shining northward, shining southward, as the aurorean flame,
Not our mother, not Northumberland, brought ever forth,
Though no southern shore may match the sons that kiss her mouth,
Children worthier all the birthright given of the ardent north
Where the fire of hearts outburns the suns that fire the south.
Even such fire was this that lit them, not from lowering skies
Where the darkling dawn flagged, stricken in the sun's own shrine,
Down the gulf of storm subsiding, till their earnest eyes
Find the relics of the ravening night that spared but nine.

Life by life the man redeems them, head by storm-worn head,
While the girl's hand stays the boat whereof the waves are fain:
Ah, but woe for one, the mother clasping fast her dead!
Happier, had the surges slain her with her children slain.
Back they bear, and bring between them safe the woful nine,
Where above the ravenous Hawkers fixed at watch for prey
Storm and calm behold the Longstone's towering signal shine
Now as when that labouring night brought forth a shuddering day.
Now as then, though like the hounds of storm against her snarling
All the clamorous years between us storm down many a fame,
As our sires beheld before us we behold Grace Darling
Crowned and throned our queen, and as they hailed we hail her name.
Nay, not ours alone, her kinsfolk born, though chiefliest ours,
East and west and south acclaim her queen of England's maids,
Star more sweet than all their stars and flower than all their flowers,
Higher in heaven and earth than star that sets or flower that fades.
How should land or sea that nurtured her forget, or love
Hold not fast her fame for us while aught is borne in mind?
Land and sea beneath us, sun and moon and stars above,
Bear the bright soul witness, seen of all but souls born blind.
Stars and moon and sun may wax and wane, subside and rise,
Age on age as flake on flake of showering snows be shed:
Not till earth be sunless, not till death strike blind the skies,
May the deathless love that waits on deathless deeds be dead.
Years on years have withered since beside the hearth once thine
I, too young to have seen thee, touched thy father's hallowed hand:
Thee and him shall all men see for ever, stars that shine
While the sea that spared thee girds and glorifies the land.

Algernon Swinburne (1893)

Notes

Notes to Chapter 1: Introduction

1 *Comic Roots*, on BBC2, 2 September 1983; Jessica Mitford, *Grace Had an English Heart* (London, 1988), p. 20.
2 *Newcastle Chronicle*, 15 September 1838.
3 William Howitt, *Visits to Remarkable Places: Old Halls, Battle Fields, and Scenes Illustrative of Striking Passages in History and Poetry, Chiefly in the Counties of Durham and Northumberland* (London, 1842), p. 466.
4 Evelyn Waugh, *Brideshead Revisited* (1945; London, 1981), pp. 41–2; P. D. James, *Innocent Blood* (1980; London, 1989), p. 33.
5 Pierre Nora, *Realms of Memory: Rethinking the French Past*, ed. Lawrence D. Kritzman, 3 vols (New York, 1996–8), i, p. xvii.
6 Ibid., p. xx.

Notes to Chapter 2: Grace's Deed

1 National Archives, BT 107/428
2 *The Loss of the Steamship Forfarshire, Captain Humble, which Struck on the Fern Islands on her Voyage to Dundee, on the Night of 7th September 1838, and the Heroic Conduct of Grace Darling in Venturing Her Life, and Rescuing the Survivors from Destruction* (on internal evidence published in Hull or Newcastle, c. 1842), pp. 20–2; Richard Armstrong, *Grace Darling: Maid and Myth* (London, 1965), p. 95; information on the Reverend John Robb from the *Official Report of the Scottish Parliament*, 8 June 2005, col. 17647.
3 *The Journal of William Darling, Grace Darling's Father; from 1795 to 1860* (London, 1886), p. 22.
4 William Kenefick, 'The growth and development of the Port of Dundee in the nineteenth and early twentieth centuries', in Louise Miskell, Christopher A. Whatley and Bob Harris (eds), *Victorian Dundee: Image and Realities* (East Linton, 2000), pp. 38–50; National Archives, BT 107/428, 98/240; W. M. Phipps Hornby, 'Grace Horsley Darling, 1815–1842: Northumbrian Heroine', *Mariner's Mirror*, 54 (1968), p. 56; Colin Bain, 'A footnote to the story of Grace Darling', *The Scottish Genealogist*, 35 (Sept. 1988), pp. 125–6.
5 W. S. Lindsay, *History of Merchant Shipping and Ancient Commerce*, 4 vols (1874; New York, 1965), iv, pp. 64–5; Philip S. Bagwell, 'Inland Navigation and Coastal Shipping', paper

read at Transport History Conference 1975, pp. 12–16; 'Report on Steam Vessel Accidents', *Parliamentary Papers* (1839), xlvii, pp. 20–7.

6   Constance Smedley, *Grace Darling and Her Times* (London, 1932), pp. 70–1; Phipps Hornby, 'Grace Horsley Darling', p. 56.

7   *Hull Advertiser and Exchange Gazette*, 28 September 1838 (letter from William Just, manager of the Dundee and Hull Steam Packet); Armstrong, *Grace Darling*, p. 96.

8   Armstrong, *Grace Darling*, pp. 98–100.

9   Ibid., pp. 101–6; *Shipping and Mercantile Gazette*, 10 September 1838; *Dundee Courier*, 11 September 1838, letter from James Duncan, mate of the *Forfarshire*; 'Report on Steam Vessel Accidents', pp. 70–1, evidence of James Kelly.

10 'Select Committee appointed to inquire into the Causes of Shipwrecks', *British Parliamentary Papers, Shipping Safety* (Shannon, 1968), ii, pp. iii–iv; 'Report on Steam Vessel Accidents', p. 7.

11 William J. Palmer, *Dickens and New Historicism* (New York, 1997), pp. 49–100, esp. p. 59.

12 James Taylor, 'Private Property, Public Interest, and the Role of the State in Nineteenth-Century Britain: The Case of the Lighthouses', *Historical Journal*, 44 (2001), pp. 749–71.

13 Smedley, *Grace Darling*, pp. 274–5.

14 Lindsay, *Merchant Shipping*, iii, pp. 624–9; Smedley, *Grace Darling*, pp. 285–7.

15 John Bird, *Dorothy and the Forsters of Bamburgh* (Berwick-upon-Tweed, 1982); '23rd Report of the Charity Commissioners', *Parliamentary Papers* (1830), xii, pp. 456–74; 'Lord Crewe's Charity', typescript, NRO, 452.

16 Smedley, *Grace Darling*, p. 30; '23rd Report of the Charity Commissioners', p. 472.

17 '23rd Report of the Charity Commissioners', pp. 456–74; William Howitt, *Visits to Remarkable Places: Old Halls, Battle Fields, and Scenes Illustrative of Striking Passages in History and Poetry, Chiefly in the Counties of Durham and Northumberland* (London, 1842), pp. 450–7; Bird, *Dorothy and the Forsters*, p. 10.

18 http://homepage.ntlworld.com/foxtree/genealogy/darling2.htm; *Journal of William Darling*, p. 6; Smedley, *Grace Darling*, p. 24.

19 http://homepage.ntlworld.com/foxtree/genealogy/darling2.htm; Smedley, *Grace Darling*, pp. 227–8.

20 Smedley, *Grace Darling*, p. 38.

21 Ibid., p. 41; Armstrong, *Grace Darling*, p. 36; 'Report from the Select Committee on the State and Management of Lighthouses', *British Parliamentary Papers, Shipping Safety* (Shannon, 1969), i, pp. vi–vii, 21.

22 Bella Bathurst, *The Lighthouse Stevensons* (London, 1999); Smedley, *Grace Darling*, pp. 41–2.

23 'Select Committee on the State and Management of Lighthouses', appendix 38, p. 359.

24 Richard Woodman and Jane Wilson, *The Lighthouses of Trinity House* (Bradford on Avon, 2002), pp. 96–7; *Journal of William Darling*, pp. 6–8.

25 W. A. Montgomery and M. Scott Weightman, *Grace Darling* (Seahouses, 1987 edn), p. 3.

26 *Journal of William Darling*, pp. 14, 17; for the argument that the *Journal* conceals much income of this kind, Armstrong, *Grace Darling*, pp. 73–4.

27 Smedley, *Grace Darling*, pp. 34–7.

28 Ibid., pp. 36, 51, 54.

29 [Daniel H. Atkinson], *Grace Darling; Her True Story* (London, n.d. [1880]), p. 36.

30 Ibid., pp. 69–72.

31 *Sunderland Herald*, 23 November 1838, quoted in Smedley, *Grace Darling*, p. 111.

32 *Newcastle Weekly Chronicle*, 14 January 1893.

33 Mrs C. Sharp to William Darling and family, 20 December 1838, NRO, SANT/BEQ/14/1.

34 William Darling to Mrs Sharp, 6 February 1838, Gloucestershire Archives, D6919/2/6.

35 Margaret Ker to Thomasin Darling, 26 April 1831, RNLI Archive, E.GD.2.8.

36 Thomasin Darling to her Father and Mother, 1837, RNLI Archive, E.GD.2.18.

37 W. N. Darnell to Mrs Sharp, 25 October 1838, Gloucestershire Archives, D3549/17/4/4.

38 Armstrong, *Grace Darling*, pp. 65–7; Draft letter in NRO, SANT/BEQ/14/2.

39 *Newcastle Weekly Chronicle*, 19 December and 29 October 1892.

40 Smedley, *Grace Darling*, pp. 62–4; Armstrong, *Grace Darling*, pp. 70–2.

41 George Darling to Daniel Atkinson, 10 December 1892, NRO, SANT/BEQ/14/7.

42 Howitt, *Visits to Remarkable Places*, p. 419.

43 F. M. L. Thompson, *English Landed Society in the Nineteenth Century* (London, 1963), pp. 80, 106, 167, 262; *The Greville Memoirs*, 8 vols (London, 1904), i, p. 164; *Times*, 13 February 1847.

44 *Journal of William Darling*, p. 15; Smedley, *Grace Darling*, pp. 43–4.

45 Thomas Dibdin, *A Bibliographical Antiquarian and Picturesque Tour in the Northern Counties of England and in Scotland*, reprinted in *idem*, *Newcastle in 1836* (Newcastle, 1968), pp. 346, 398.

46 Howitt, *Visits to Remarkable Places*, pp. 281, 287, 310, 313, 318; Jack Morrell and Arnold Thackray, *Gentlemen of Science: Early Years of the British Association for the Advancement of Science* (Oxford, 1981), p. 198.

47 Robert Spence Watson, *The History of the Literary and Philosophical Society of Newcastle-upon-Tyne (1793–1896)* (London, 1897); Maurice Milne, 'Strikes and strike-breaking in North-East England, 1815–44: the attitude of the local press', *International Review of Social History*, 22 (1977), pp. 226–7; Richard Welford, *Men of Mark 'Twixt Tyne and Tweed*, 3 vols (London, 1895), i, pp. 323–9; ii, pp. 543–55, quoting p. 548; iii, pp. 199–205; Howitt, *Visits to Remarkable Places*, p. 322.

48 Morrell and Thackray, *Gentlemen of Science*, pp. 186–202.

49 Smedley, *Grace Darling*, p. 54.

50 Hewitson's letters to William Darling in RNLI Archive, E.GD.2.20, 22–7.

51 Smedley, *Grace Darling*, pp. 57–8.

52 RNLI Archive, E.GD.2.15–18, 24–5.

53 Smedley, *Grace Darling*, pp. 124–5; John Hancock to William Darling, 5 November 1838, NRO, SANT/BEQ/14/1.

54 'Report on Steam Vessel Accidents', pp. 8, 20–1, 73.

55 *Shipping and Mercantile Gazette*, 14 September 1838.

56 *Hull Advertiser*, 28 September 1838.

57 *Newcastle Chronicle*, 15 September 1838, quoted in Jerold Vernon, *Grace Darling, The Maid of the Isles* (Newcastle-upon-Tyne, 1839), pp. 209–18.

58 Smedley, *Grace Darling*, pp. 69, 73–4.

59 *Grace Darling; Her True Story*, p. 5.

60 Ibid., p. 5; NRO, SANT/BEQ/14/2/53. 'The Darlings' may have referred to the coble, which bore that name, rather than the family.

61 NRO, SANT/BEQ/14/1.

62 *Grace Darling; Her True Story*, pp. 2–3.

63 Thomasin Darling to Daniel Atkinson, 5 November 1878, NRO, SANT/BEQ/14/6; *Grace Darling; Her True Story*, pp. 24, 67; see also W. N. Darnell to Mrs Sharp, 6 October 1838 on 'the heroism' of Grace's mother: 'think of the pangs of the mother and wife till they returned', Gloucestershire Archives, D3549/17/4/4.

64 Andrew Craig Rutter, *A Seahouses Saga* (Stockport, 1998), p. 70.

65 Armstrong, *Grace Darling*, p. 115.

66 William Darling to T. M. Joy, in Smedley, *Grace Darling*, p. 80.

67 Smedley, *Grace Darling*, pp. 82–5; *Grace Darling; Her True Story*, p. 5.

68 Howitt, *Visits to Remarkable Places*, p. 468.

69 *Journal of William Darling*, p. 23; *Times*, 2 October 1838.

70 Trinity House, Warden's Minutes, 29 October and 13 November 1838, MS 30025, vol. 12, pp. 96–7, 118.

Notes to Chapter 3: *In the Spotlight of the Media*

1 *Gateshead Observer*, 8 September 1838, in *Times*, 11 September 1838; Constance Smedley, *Grace Darling and Her Times* (London, 1932), p. 89.

2 *Berwick and Kelso Warder*, 15 September 1838.

3 *Dundee Courier*, 11 September 1838, in Smedley, *Grace Darling*, pp. 89–90.

4 Smedley, *Grace Darling*, pp. 91–5; 'Report on Steam Vessel Accidents', *Parliamentary Papers*, 1839, xlvii, pp. 69–72.

5 Smedley, *Grace Darling*, pp. 277–85; 'Report on Steam Vessel Accidents', esp. pp. 8, 69–73.

6 *Hull Advertiser and Exchange Gazette*, 28 September 1838; Smedley, *Grace Darling*, p. 105; 'Report on Steam Vessel Accidents', p. 73.

7 *Berwick and Kelso Warder*, 15 September 1838; David Kennedy to William Darling, 15 September 1838, NRO, SANT/BEQ/14/1.

8 *Newcastle Chronicle*, 15 September 1838.

9 NRO, SANT/BEQ/14/1.

10 NRO, SANT/BEQ/14/2.

11 Edmund Burke, *A Philosophical Enquiry into the Origin of Our Ideas of the Sublime and Beautiful*, ed. Adam Phillips (Oxford, 1990), quoting pp. 54, 103, 105–6; Aidan Day, *Romanticism* (London and New York, 1996), pp. 183–6.

12 Walter Scott, *The Heart of Midlothian* (1818; Oxford, 1982), pp. 251, 143–4, 87.

13 E.g. *Times*, 19 September 1838, *Berwick and Kelso Warder*, 15 September 1838.

14 Newspaper cutting, 25 September 1838, NRO, 404/353.

15 *Shipping and Mercantile Gazette*, 20 September 1838.

16 *Berwick and Kelso Warder*, 22 September 1838.

17 John Stewart to J. Marsden, 10 October 1838, NRO, SANT/BEQ/14/1.

18 *Berwick and Kelso Warder*, 6 October 1838.

19 Smedley, *Grace Darling*, p. 122; Richard Ormond, *Early Victorian Portraits*, 2 vols (London, 1973), i, pp. 130–3.

20 Smedley, *Grace Darling*, pp. 126–31.

21 NRO, SANT/BEQ/14/2/47, 48.

22 Smedley, *Grace Darling*, pp. 127–8, 136; Chevalier D'Hardvillier to Grace Darling, 16 November 1838, NRO, SANT/BEQ/14/1.

23 'Henry Perlee Parker or an Artist's Narrative', Bodleian, MS Eng.misc.e.654 (dated 18 March 1871).

24 Richard Welford, *Men of Mark 'Twixt Tyne and Tweed*, 3 vols (London and Newcastle-Upon-Tyne, 1895), iii, p. 251.

25 'Thomas Musgrave Joy', *Oxford DNB*.

26 Smedley, *Grace Darling*, p. 111.

27 William Howitt, *Visits to Remarkable Places: Old Halls, Battle Fields, and Scenes Illustrative of Striking Passages in History and Poetry, Chiefly in the Counties of Northumberland and Durham* (London, 1842), pp. 464–5.

28 H. P. Parker to D. Lucas, Newcastle City Library, L920, D221P.

29 Richard Armstrong, *Grace Darling: Maid and Myth* (London, 1965), p. 80.

30 Jenny Uglow, *Elizabeth Gaskell: A Habit of Stories* (London, 1993), p. 63.

31 Parker to Lucas, Newcastle City Library.

32 Ormond, *Early Victorian Portraits*, i, pp. 130–3; Grace Darling Museum.

33 Smedley, *Grace Darling*, pp. 123, 127, 132–3; see also Armstrong, *Grace Darling*, pp. 79–82; Ormond, *Early Victorian Portraits*, i, pp. 130–3; for a positive view of Hastings's lithographs, and the interest they excited, see the *Spectator*, 17 November 1838, p. 1095.

34 David Cordingly, *Marine Painting in England, 1700–1900* (New York, 1973); William Vaughan, *Romanticism and Art* (London, 1994), quoting p. 163; T. S. R. Boase, 'Shipwrecks in English Romantic Painting', *Journal of the Warburg and Courtauld Institutes*, 22 (1959), pp. 332–46.

35 Christine Riding, '*The Raft of the Medusa* in Britain: Audience and Context', in Patrick Noon (ed.), *Constable to Delacroix: British Art and the French Romantics* (London, 2003), pp. 66–93; Julian Barnes, *A History of the World in 10½ Chapters* (London, 1989), ch. 5.

36 Riding, '*The Raft of the Medusa*', pp. 88–9; John Gage, *J. M. W. Turner: 'A Wonderful Range of Mind'* (New Haven and London, 1987), pp. 229–30.

37 Smedley, *Grace Darling*, pp. 125–6.

38 *Sunderland Pottery*, revised by John C. Baker (Tyne and Wear, 1984).

39 Asa Briggs, *Victorian Things* (Harmondsworth, 1990), pp. 147–55; A. and N. Harding, *Victorian Staffordshire Figures, 1815–1875* (Atglen, Pennsylvania), 3 vols, i, p. 55, iii, p. 36; P. D. Gordon Pugh, *Staffordshire Portrait Figures and Allied Subjects of the Victorian Era* (Woodbridge, 1987), pp. 13, 101, 524–5; Anthony Oliver, *The Victorian Staffordshire Figure: A Guide for Collectors* (London, 1971), esp. pp. 150, 152, 157–9.

40 Smedley, *Grace Darling*, pp. 135–6; Robert Darling to Thomasin Darling, 6 February 1839, RNLI Archive, EGD.2.14.

41 Smedley, *Grace Darling*, pp. 136–7. From the description Smedley gives, I suspect this may have been, not a panorama, but the 'Pictorial and Mechanical Exhibition on the Plan of De Loutherbourg's Eidophusikon', depicting the rescue, described in R. D. Altick, *The Shows of London* (Cambridge, Massachusetts and London, 1978), p. 216. An Eidophusikon was a small stage or box with mechanical devices for moving objects and scenery.

42 Fred. H. Yates to Grace Darling, 27 November 1838, Grace Darling Museum; Edward Stirling, *Grace Darling; or, The Wreck at Sea* (London, n.d. [1838?]); *Spectator*, 8 December 1838, p. 1159.

43 Jerold Vernon to Grace Darling, 10 July 1839, NRO, SANT/BEQ/14/6.

44 Jerold Vernon, *Grace Darling, the Maid of the Isles* (Newcastle-upon-Tyne, 1839), quoting pp. 24, 28, 86, 221.

45 Ibid., quoting pp. 141, 179.

46 Ibid., quoting pp. 402, 479.

47 Smedley, *Grace Darling*, pp. 217–18; Grace Darling to Thomasin Darling, 22 December 1841, NRO, SANT/BEQ/14/2.

48 Draft letter, William Darling to Edward Stamp, NRO, SANT/BEQ/14/2.

49 *Grace Darling; or the Loss of the 'Forfarshire'. A Tale by a Young Lady* (Glasgow, 1840), quoting pp. v, 134, 273. There is a copy of this book in the National Maritime Museum.

50 Ibid., quoting pp. 278, 282, 293, 295, 302.

51 W. H.Ollivier, *Grace Darling, Stanzas Commemorative of the Heroic Bravery of Grace Darling and Her Father on the Occasion of the Disastrous Wreck of the Forfarshire Steam Ship on the –th September 1838* (London, n.d.[1838–9]); Christopher Thomson, *Grace Darling, or the Wreck, Narrative Ballad* (London, n.d. [1838–9]); George Linley, *Grace Darling Ballad* (London, n.d. [1838–39]); see also P. M. Stewart's ballad, in Vernon, *Grace Darling, the Maid of the Isles*, p. 221 where the same themes dominate.

52 Quoted in Smedley, *Grace Darling*, p. 109.

53 NRO, SANT/BEQ/14/2; *Scotsman* quoted in Eva Hope, *Grace Darling, Heroine of the Farne Islands: Her Life and its Lessons* (London, 1875), pp. 242–3.

54 *Spectator*, 17 November 1838, p. 1095.

55 Mrs Octavius Freire Owen, *The Heroines of Domestic Life* (London, 1861), p. 367.

Notes to Chapter 4: The Life and Death of a Heroine

1 NRO, SANT/BEQ/14/8.

2 William Darling to Mrs Sharp, 6 February 1839, Gloucestershire Archive, D6919, 2/6.

3 Grace Darling Museum.

4 [Daniel H. Atkinson], *Grace Darling: Her True Story* (London, n.d.[1880]), p. 45; William Howitt, *Visits to Remarkable Places: Old Halls, Battle Fields, and Scenes Illustrative of Striking Passages in History and Poetry, Chiefly in the Counties of Durham and Northumberland* (London, 1842), p. 466.

5 Constance Smedley, *Grace Darling and Her Times* (London, 1932), pp. 155–61.

6 F. J. Harvey Darton, *Children's Books in England* (2nd edn Cambridge, 1932) p. 225.

7 Quoted in Smedley, *Grace Darling*, pp. 159–60.

8   NRO, SANT/BEQ/14/8.

9   Smedley, *Grace Darling*, pp. 160–2; Letter to William Darling, 21 November 1838, expressing view of Lieutenant Brunton and Captain Hays, both probably employed by the Coast Guard, that Grace should not 'on any account assent to go to Edinburgh', NRO, SANT/BEQ/14/1; Henry Hewitson to William Darling, 2 February 1839, strongly advising his 'dear old friend' to dissuade Grace from going, as was rumoured, to London: 'she would be made a public spectacle', RNLI Archive, E.GD.2.20.

10 A. H. Saxon, *The Life and Art of Andrew Ducrow and the Romantic Age of the English Circus* (Hamden, Connecticut, 1978); Marius Kwint, 'The Legitimization of the Circus in Late Georgian England', *Past and Present*, 174 (2002), pp. 72–115; Brenda Assael, *The Circus and Victorian Society* (Charlottesville and London, 2005).

11 Thomas Frost, *Circus Life and Circus Celebrities* (London, 1881), pp. 97–8; *Scotsman*, 17 and 27 October, 3, 10 and 24 November, 5 December 1838.

12 *Scotsman*, 27 October 1838.

13 *Alnwick and County Gazette*, 5 November 1892.

14 *Fifty Famous Women: Their Virtues and Failings, and the Lessons of Their Lives* (London, n.d. [1864]), p. 132.

15 NRO, SANT/BEQ/14/5.

16 NRO, SANT/BEQ/14/5; letter from R. K. Douglas, *Birmingham Journal*, 16 February 1839, SANT/BEQ/14/1.

17 Letter from Henry Edwards, 10 June 1839, NRO, SANT/BEQ/14/1.

18 Draft letter William Darling to Edward Stamp, NRO, SANT/BEQ/14/2.

19 Letter from Archibald Reid, Joint City Clerk, Perth, 20 March 1839, NRO, SANT/BEQ/14/1; SANT/BEQ/14//3.

20 J. Scafe to William Darling, 19 September 1838, 'I have thought it perfectly proper to represent your courageous and humane conduct to the Duke of Northumberland ...' NRO, SANT/BEQ/14/2/17.

21 Quoted in Smedley, *Grace Darling*, pp. 164–5.

22 Trinity House, Board Minutes, 31, Guildhall Library, MS 30010, p. 228.

23 Trinity House, Court Minutes, 21, Guildhall Library, MS 30004, p. 8.

24 Trinity House, Board Minutes, 32, Guildhall Library, MS 30010, p. 575.

25 Smedley, *Grace Darling*, p. 166.

26 The Glasgow Humane Society sent their medal on 29 September 1838 (NRO, SANT/BEQ/14/2), and the decision of the Edinburgh and Leith Society to send a medal was reported in the press on 1 October 1838 (NRO 404/353).

27 Royal Humane Society, Annual Report, 1838; http://www.royalhumane.org/history/keydates.htm.

28 Benjamin Hawes to Duke of Northumberland, 19 October 1838, Royal Humane Society, Letter Book.

29 Royal Humane Society, Minutes of Committee, 17 October 1838; Minutes of Special General Court, 31 October 1838; NRO, SANT/BEQ/14/1; Hawes to Duke of Northumberland 25 October 1838, Royal Humane Society, Letter Book.

30 Hawes to Duke of Northumberland, 1 November 1838, Royal Humane Society, Letter Book; Minutes of Committee, 22 November 1838.

31 Smedley, *Grace Darling*, pp. 178–9, 186.

32 Ibid., pp. 188–9.

33 Ibid., pp. 201–13; NRO, SANT/BEQ/14/9; Duke of Northumberland to Grace Darling, 10 December 1840, NRO, SANT/BEQ/14/2/27; for offers of marriage, see Howitt, *Visits to Remarkable Places*, pp. 466–7; *Memoir of Grace Horsley Darling: The Heroine of the Farnes* (Berwick-upon-Tweed, 1843), p. 39.

34 Ibid., pp. 205–6.

35 Grace Darling to the Duke of Northumberland, 24 January 1840, Alnwick Archives, DP/D3/5/26; letters quoted in Smedley, *Grace Darling*, pp. 207–13.

36 NRO, SANT/BEQ/14/2/40–4.

37 Royal Archives, VIC\QVJ\1838, 28 September 1838.

38 Royal Archives, VIC\QVJ\1839, 9 and 14 January 1839.

39 Quoted in Smedley, *Grace Darling*, pp. 236–7.

40 Between 1837 and 1871 Queen Victoria donated an average of £8,160 p.a. to individuals, institutions and annual charities, 17 per cent of it (or an average of £1,387 p.a.) to individuals. Frank Prochaska, *Royal Bounty: The Making of a Welfare Monarchy* (New Haven and London, 1995), pp. 77–9.

41 Smedley, *Grace Darling*, p. 148.

42 Howitt, *Visits to Remarkable Places*, p. 465.

43 John Forster, *Walter Savage Landor*, 2 vols (London, 1876), ii, p. 360.

44 NRO, SANT/BEQ/14/1; Smedley, *Grace Darling*, pp. 51, 155.

45 *Memoir of Grace Horsley Darling*, p. 40.

46 Donald Read, *Peel and the Victorians* (Oxford, 1987), pp. 288–94.

47 Newspaper cutting, 29 September 1838, NRO, 404/353.

48 W. N. Darnell to Mrs Sharp, 25 October 1838, Gloucestershire Archive, D3549/17/4/4.

49 Howitt, *Visits to Remarkable Places*, pp. 467–8.

50 *Memoir of Grace Horsley Darling*, p. 39.

51 W. H. Maehl, 'Chartist Disturbances in Northeastern England, 1839', *International Review of Social History*, 8 (1963), pp. 389–414; W. L. Burn, 'Newcastle upon Tyne in the Early Nineteenth Century', *Archaeologia Aeliana*, 34 (1956), pp. 1–13.

52 W. N. Darnell to Mrs Sharp, 25 October 1838, 31 July 1839, Gloucestershire Archives Office, D3549/17/4/4.

53 [Daniel H. Atkinson], *Grace Darling: Her True Story*, p. 35.

54 Rebecca Craggs to Grace Darling, 14 March 1839, 17 February 1841; Mrs Gilchrist to Mr Macgregor 29 March 1841, Ann McGregor to Grace Darling, n.d., W. Lowthorp to Grace Darling, n.d. and draft reply on back dated 27 March 1841, NRO, SANT/BEQ/14/8; Smedley, *Grace Darling*, pp. 195–7.

55 NRO, SANT/BEQ/14/1.

56 Letters from National Swimming Society, 12 September 1839, 5 September 1840, NRO, SANT/BEQ/14/1.

57 http://homepage.ntlworld.com/foxtree/genealogy/darling2.htm; Trinity House, Warden's Minutes, 13 November 1838, MS 30025, vol.12, p. 118.

58 Letters quoted in Smedley, *Grace Darling*, pp. 224, 229. Smedley, however, seems to assume that the George of these letters is Grace's brother.

59 He just might be George Emmerson who in October 1842 left a parcel to be given to Grace, 'only a book' apparently. Kitty Marsden to Thomasin Darling, 7 October 1842, RNLI Archive, E.GD.2.21.

60 NRO, SANT/BEQ/14/7. In 1878 Thomasin gave this verse, and another on the vanity of titles or riches, to Daniel Atkinson's sister.

61 Smedley, *Grace Darling*, pp. 212–13; NRO, SANT/BEQ/14/2/28.

62 [Daniel H. Atkinson], *Grace Darling: Her True Story*, p. 11; Thomasin Darling to Atkinson, 5 November 1878 NRO, SANT/BEQ/14/6.

63 Draft by William Darling, n.d., NRO, SANT/BEQ/14/2; Copy of letter, William Darling to H. Headlam, 22 March 1839, NRO, SANT/BEQ/14/1/11.

64 Howitt, *Visits to Remarkable Places*, pp. 464–7.

65 John S. Roberts, *Grace Darling and the Farne Isles* (London and Newcastle-upon-Tyne, n.d. [1875]), p. 48.

66 Smedley, *Grace Darling*, pp. 126–7.

67 David Dunbar, 7 July 1855, NRO, SANT/BEQ/14/2/45; Grace Darling Museum; Smedley, *Grace Darling*, p. 78; Richard Ormond, *Early Victorian Portraits*, 2 vols (London, 1973), i, pp. 130–1, citing Amy Nordeley. There are allegedly other bits of Grace's dress, see Paton Collection, National Library of Scotland, GB233/MS 3219, fol. 210, and Abbey House Museum, Leeds, LeedM.E.W 1196.

68 Smedley, *Grace Darling*, p. 116; NRO, SANT/BEQ/14/1.

69 The Reverend M. M. Humble to Grace Darling, 14 November 1839, NRO, 3126/3; *Memoir of Grace Horsley Darling*, pp. 22–3.

70 NRO, SANT/BEQ/14/1.

71 Grace Darling to Mrs Sneinton, 15 November 1838, NRO, SANT/BEQ/14/1; Smedley, *Grace Darling*, p. 206.

72 Smedley, *Grace Darling*, pp. 116–17.

73 *Guardian*, 24 August 2005.

74 NRO, SANT/BEQ/14/2/56.

75 NRO, SANT/BEQ/14/2; Grace Darling to Samuel Burton, 22 March 1839, SANT/BEQ/14/1.

76 Pat Jalland, *Death in the Victorian Family* (Oxford, 1996), p. 26.

77 Many have suggested psychological factors as the main or a contributory cause of Grace's death. For what it is worth, her death certificate states that cause of death was 'consumption'.

78 Smedley, *Grace Darling*, pp. 230–2.

79 Ibid., p. 233.

80 Ibid., p. 247.

81 Ibid., p. 248.

82 *Memoir of Grace Horsley Darling*, pp. 38–9.

83 *Berwick Advertiser*, 29 October 1842, quoted in Smedley, *Grace Darling*, p. 250.

Notes to Chapter 5: A Place in History

1   Thomas Arthur, *The Life of Grace Darling, the Heroine of the Farne Isles* (London, n.d. [1885]; 1st edn, 1875), p. 101.

2   Quoted in Elizabeth Nussbaum, *Dear Miss Baird: A Portrait of a 19th-Century Family* (Charlbury, Oxfordshire, 2003), p. 43.

3   Jerold Vernon, *Grace Darling, The Maid of the Isles* (Newcastle-upon-Tyne, 1839), pp. 12, 142–52; William Howitt, *Visits to Remarkable Places: Old Halls, Battle Fields, and Scenes Illustrative of Striking Passages in History and Poetry, Chiefly in the Counties of Durham and Northumberland* (London, 1842), pp. 398–418, quoting pp. 398–9.

4   Arthur, *The Life of Grace Darling*, p. 37; Eva Hope, *Grace Darling, Heroine of the Farne Islands: Her Life and its Lessons* (London, n.d.), p. 148.

5   Constance Smedley, *Grace Darling and Her Times* (London, 1932), p. 254; D. H. Atkinson to Thomasin Darling 11 December 1878 and her undated reply, NRO, SANT/BEQ/14/6.

6   F. M. L. Thompson, *English Landed Society in the Nineteenth Century* (London, 1963), pp. 91–3; *Oxford DNB*.

7   *Memoir of Grace Horsley Darling, The Heroine of the Farnes* (Berwick-upon-Tweed, 1843), pp. 40–1; Smedley, *Grace Darling*, pp. 20–1.

8   *Memoir of Grace Horsley Darling*, p. 44.

9   NRO, SANT/BEQ/14/10.

10 My thanks to Michael Duffy for sending me details of this memorial.

11 Raleigh Trevelyan, *A Pre-Raphaelite Circle* (London, 1978), pp. 16–17; David Cannadine, *G. M. Trevelyan: A Life in History* (London, 1992), p. 4.

12 Trevelyan, *Pre-Raphaelite Circle*, pp. 11–58.

13 Ibid., pp. 67–106.

14 Ibid., pp. 107–8; Robert Spence Watson, *The History of the Literary and Philosophical Society of Newcastle-Upon-Tyne (1793–1896)* (London, 1897), pp. 109, 314; W. Minto (ed.), *Autobiographical Notes of the Life of William Bell Scott*, 2 vols (New York, 1892).

15 Quoted in Trevelyan, *Pre-Raphaelite Circle*, p. ii.

16 Ibid., pp. 115–18.

17 Ibid., p. 120; information at Wallington.

18 *Autobiographical Notes*, ii, pp. 7, 35–6, 38, 43.

19 John Batchelor, *Lady Trevelyan and the Pre-Raphaelite Brotherhood* (London, 2006), pp. 130–41.

20 Scott to Lady Trevelyan, n.d. [1857/8], and 31 May 1859, Trevelyan Papers, WCT 80/27, 74/28; to Sir Walter Trevelyan, n.d. [1859], WCT 80/60.

21 Cecil Y. Lang (ed.), *The Swinburne Letters*, 6 vols (New Haven, 1959–62), i, p. 34; iv, p. 282; vi, p. 36.

22 *Autobiographical Notes*, ii, p. 58.

23 Scott to Sir Walter Trevelyan, 13 July 1860, Trevelyan Papers, WCT 74/47.

24 *Autobiographical Notes*, ii, p. 55.

25 Scott to Lady Trevelyan, 3 September 1860, Trevelyan Papers, WCT 74/51.

26 *Autobiographical Notes*, ii, pp. 55–6; Scott to Lady Trevelyan, n.d. [1860], Trevelyan Papers, WCT 80/32.

27 Quoted in Batchelor, *Lady Trevelyan and the Pre-Raphaelite Brotherhood*, p. 197.

28 Scott to Sir Walter Trevelyan, 30 October [1860], Trevelyan Papers, WCT 80/15.

29 *Autobiographical Notes*, ii, pp. 47–8; Scott to Trevelyan, 7 October 1860, Trevelyan Papers, WCT 74/53.

30 Scott to Trevelyan, 29 June 1861, to Lady Trevelyan, 5 and 8 July 1861, Trevelyan Papers, WCT 75/6, 9, 10; Jeremy Maas, *Gambart, Prince of the Victorian Art World* (London, 1975), pp. 139–42.

31 Scott to Lady Trevelyan, 11 August 1861, Trevelyan Papers, WCT 75/13.

32 Scott to Lady Trevelyan, 23 July, 11 August, 23 August 1861; to Sir Walter Trevelyan, 8 September 1861, Trevelyan Papers, WCT 75/12–15; *Autobiographical Notes*, ii, p. 67; Trevelyan, *Pre-Raphaelite Circle*, p. 172; William E. Fredeman, 'The letters of Pictor Ignotus: William Bell Scott's correspondence with Alice Boyd, 1859–1884', *Bulletin of the John Rylands Library*, 58 (1975–6), p. 80.

33 Quoted in Trevelyan, *Pre-Raphaelite Circle*, p. 195; *Autobiographical Notes*, ii, pp. 11–13.

34 *The Library Edition of the Works of John Ruskin*, 39 vols (London, 1903–12), xxxvi, p. 454.

35 Quoted in Trevelyan, *Pre-Raphaelite Circle*, p. 196.

36 Quoted in Cannadine, *Trevelyan*, p. 2.

37 Swinburne to Edmund Gosse, 5 December 1892, in Lang (ed.), *The Swinburne Letters*, vi, p. 46.

38 *Works of John Ruskin*, xv, pp. 491–4.

39 Alethea Hayter, *The Wreck of the Abergavenny* (London, 2002).

40 Wordsworth to Richard Parkinson, 17 March 1843, in *The Letters of William and Dorothy Wordsworth*, vii, *The Later Years*, part 4, *1840–1853*, ed. Alan G. Hill (Oxford, 1988), p. 401.

41 Wordsworth to Mrs Charles James Blomfield, 23 March 1843, in ibid., pp. 406–7. For further evidence of Wordsworth's distribution of the poem, see, ibid., pp. 399, 402, 404, 407, 410, 411, 422, 427, 433, 436.

42 J. D. Vann, 'The Publication of Wordsworth's "Grace Darling"', *Notes and Queries*, 223 (1978), pp. 223–5.

43 *Letters of William and Dorothy Wordsworth*, vii, part 4, pp. 422, 445–6.

44 *The Poetical Works of William Wordsworth*, 6 vols (London, 1882), iv, pp. 357–60.

45 *Memoir of Grace Horsley Darling*, pp. 19–21, 36.

46 Lucasta Miller, *The Brontë Myth* (London, 2001), pp. 57–79.

47 *Life-boat*, 1 October 1856, pp. 191–4; Arthur, *Life of Grace Darling*, p. 2. For other evidence of this trope in Victorian writing about Grace, R. Chambers (ed.), *The Book of Days*, 2 vols (London, n.d.[1863–4]), ii, p. 475; John S. Roberts, *Grace Darling and the Farne Isles* (London, n.d. [1875]), p. 64; Letter from Robert J. Burn, in *Alnwick and County Gazette*, 21 May 1892.

48 Mrs Octavius Freire Owen, *The Heroines of Domestic Life* (London, 1861; 2nd edn, 1877), p. ix.

49 *Fifty Famous Women: Their Virtues and Failings, and the Lessons of Their Lives* (London, n.d. [1864]), pp. 2–3.

50 Joseph Johnson, *Brave Women: Who Have Been Distinguished for Heroic Actions & Noble Virtues; who have exhibited fearless courage; stout hearts; and intrepid resolve* (Edinburgh and London, n.d. [1875]), pp. iii–vi.

Notes to Chapter 6: The Age of Celebrity

1 David Mayer, 'Billy Purvis: Travelling Showman', *Theatre Quarterly*, 1 (1971), p. 34.
2 Thomas Arthur, *The Life of Grace Darling, the Heroine of the Farne Isles* (London, n.d. [1885]), pp. 2–3, 5, 100, 104–5.
3 Alexander McCallum to Thomasin Darling, 1 December 1875, NRO, SANT/BEQ/14/10.
4 Marianne Farningham, *A Working Woman's Life: An Autobiography* (London, 1907).
5 Ibid., pp. 111–30; see also Linda Wilson, '"Afraid to be Singular": Marianne Farningham and the Role of Women, 1857–1909', in Sue Morgan (ed.), *Women, Religion and Feminism, 1750–1900* (Basingstoke, 2002), pp. 107–21.
6 Farningham, *Working Woman's Life*, pp. 131–2.
7 Ibid., pp. 131–4.
8 Jerold Vernon, *Grace Darling, The Maid of the Isles* (Newcastle-upon-Tyne, 1839), p. 16; Arthur, *Life of Grace Darling*, pp. 17–18; Eva Hope, *Grace Darling, Heroine of the Farne Islands: Her Life, and its Lessons* (London, n.d.), pp. 104–5.
9 Hope, *Grace Darling*, pp. 302, 282.
10 Ibid., pp. 201–3.
11 Ibid., pp. 287–90.
12 Ibid., pp. 293–4.
13 Ibid., pp. 1–15, quoting pp. 2, 15.
14 Ibid., pp. 221–2, 295–6.
15 Farningham, *Working Woman's Life*, pp. 154–8, 170, 203, 278, 241–54.
16 Hope, *Life of Grace Darling*, pp. 14, 198, 143, 278.
17 Ibid. p. 296.
18 Ibid., pp. 160, 279.
19 Ibid., pp. 34, 55, 14, 140–52.
20 NRO, SANT/BEQ/14/5.
21 Elizabeth Nussbaum, *Dear Miss Baird: A Portrait of a 19th-Century Family* (Charlbury, 2003), pp. 53–9.
22 Jeremiah Odman [D. H. Atkinson], *Old Leeds: Its Byegones and Celebrities, by an Old Leeds Cropper* (Leeds, 1868); *An Opportune Rescue*, by the Author of *Grace Darling; Her True Story* (Printed for Private Circulation, 1883); *Ralph Thoresby, the Topographer; His Town and Times*, 2 vols (Leeds, 1885, 1887).
23 Thomasin Darling to Daniel Atkinson, 6 September 1881, 5 November 1878, and n.d., NRO, SANT/BEQ/14/6.
24 NRO, SANT/BEQ/14/6; http://www.artguide.org/museums/.
25 http://www.victoriansilk.com/stevens/pictures/st01-303/st180.html; card game lent to me by Bryan Lewis; http://www.dragonantiques2.co.uk/EBIMAGE/nov00/gracedarling. htm; *The Children's Encyclopedia* (London, n.d.), p. 4846. On stevengraphs, see Asa Briggs, *Victorian Things* (Harmondsworth, 1990), pp. 147–8, 156.
26 For the different versions, see Bodleian Library, Harding Collection B 15 (118a), J. Sharp, Printer; Firth Collection c. 12 (125 and 126); 2806 c. 14 (25); British Library, Crampton Ballads, vol. 4, p. 20; Broadside Ballad, vol. 4, p. 235 (ref: LR 271.a.2); J. S. Bratton, *The Victorian Popular Ballad* (London, 1975), passim, quoting p. 68; see also for the popularity

of ballads, Patrick Joyce, *Visions of the People: Industrial England and the Question of Class 1848–1914* (Cambridge, 1991), pp. 230–55.

27 Jessica Mitford, *Grace Had An English Heart* (London, 1988), p. 16–17, 20.

28 *Catalogue of Printed Music in the British Library to 1980* (London, 1985), xxxvii, pp. 128–37; Roy Palmer (ed.), *The Oxford Book of Sea Songs* (Oxford, 1988), pp. 208–9; Michael Kilgarriff, *Sing Us One of the Old Songs: A Guide to Popular Song, 1860–1920* (Oxford, 1998), p. 483.

29 Bodleian Library, Harding Collection B 13(240), B 11(4158).

30 Constance Smedley, *Grace Darling and Her Islands* (London, n.d. [1934]), p. 150; RNLI Archive; Phipps Hornby to Publicity Secretary for RNLI, 15 August 1961, RNLI Archive.

31 They can be heard in the National Sound Archive in the British Library.

32 Robert Wood, *Victorian Delights* (London, 1967), p. 95.

33 William McGonagall, *Poetic Gems* (1890; London, 1975), pp. 75–7.

34 *He Calls Me His Own Grace Darling*, Written and Composed by Lawrence Barclay (London, n.d.[*c.* 1899]).

35 Mitford, *Grace Had an English Heart*, pp. 11, 137–43, quoting p. 139.

36 Lori Anne Loeb, *Consuming Angels: Advertising and Victorian Women* (Oxford, 1994).

37 National Archives, BT 98/240.

38 Grace Darling museum for the lifeboats; *Times*, 20 December 1848, 6 May 1852, 2 March 1874, 17 September 1910, 8 September 1911, 20 December 1919; west-penwith.org.uk/jts/stives3.htm (1853 schooner); Lancashire Record Office, CBP 70/24 (1895 smack).

39 Papers of Lord Armstrong and Family, DF.A/4/15, Tyne and Wear Archives; National Archives, FS 15/1552; *Times*, 29 July and 26 August 1910.

40 Grace Darling (Broken Hill) Silver Mines Ltd, National Archives, BT 31/4611/30248; Grace Darling Purchase Syndicate Ltd, National Archives, BT 31/7566/53946.

41 National Archives, BT 31/26944/178599.

42 *Newcastle Daily Chronicle*, 7 September 1888; see also *Newcastle Weekly Courant*, 31 August 1888.

43 William Donaldson, *Popular Literature in Victorian Scotland: Language, Fiction and the Press* (Aberdeen, 1986), pp. 77–100; David Pae, *Grace Darling, the Heroine of the Longstone Lighthouse; or, The Two Wills. A Tale of the Loss of the 'Forfarshire'* (Dundee & London, n.d. [1888]), quoting p. 425.

44 *Echo*, 25 October 1892; *Shipping World*, 1 November 1892, press cuttings in NRO, SANT/BEQ/14/10.

45 *Newcastle Daily Chronicle*, 20 October 1892, press cutting in NRO, SANT/BEQ/14/10.

46 *Alnwick and County Gazette*, 22 October 1892.

47 *Newcastle Weekly Chronicle*, 29 October 1892.

48 Ibid., 5 and 11 November 1892.

49 Ibid., 31 December 1892.

50 Ibid., 12 November 1892.

51 Ibid., 24 December 1892, 7 January 1893.

52 Ibid., 31 December 1892, 7 January 1893.

53 George Darling to Daniel Atkinson, 8 November 1892, 10 and 19 December 1892, 14 February 1893, NRO, SANT/BEQ/14/7.

54 Donald Thomas, *Swinburne: The Poet in His World* (1979; Chicago, 1999), pp. 8–9.
55 Ibid., p. 14.
56 Cecil Y. Lang (ed.), *The Swinburne Letters*, 6 vols (New Haven, 1959–62), iv, p. 282; vi, pp. 36, 66.
57 *The Poems of Algernon Charles Swinburne*, 6 vols (London, 1909), vi, pp. 164–9.
58 Rikky Rooksby, *A.C. Swinburne: A Poet's Life* (Aldershot, 1997), pp. 270–1; Lang, *Swinburne Letters*, vi, p. 30.
59 Mitford, *Grace Had an English Heart*, p. 146.
60 Arthur, *Life of Grace Darling*, p. 9; *Grace Darling: A Story of Shipwreck and Heroism* (London, n.d. [1896]), p. 10.
61 *Longmans' New Readers, Standard IV* (London, 1886), pp. 11, 39–47. For teaching methods in elementary schools, see Stephen Heathorn, *For Home, Country, and Race: Constructing Gender, Class, and Englishness in the Elementary Schools of Victorian England, 1880–1914* (Buffalo, NY and London, 2000).
62 *Simple Stories from English History for Young Readers* (London, 1893), pp. 176–8, 183, 186.

Notes to Chapter 7: 'Our National Sea-Heroine'

1 Constance Smedley, *Grace Darling and Her Times* (London, 1932), pp. 262–3; Thomas Arthur, *The Life of Grace Darling, the Heroine of the Farne Isles* (London, n.d. [1885]; 1st edn, 1875), pp. 89–90; *Life–Boat* (October 1938), p. 532; George Darling to John Scott, 20 May and 12 August 1873, RNLI Archive.
2 George Darling to John Scott, 28 June and 15 July 1873, RNLI Archive.
3 *Life-Boat* (October 1938), p. 532.
4 Press cutting, RNLI Archive.
5 George Darling to John Scott, 6 and 12 April, 1 and 22 May 1883, RNLI Archive; Grace Darling Museum for the receipt. Ten years later Buck helped to scotch the worst allegations in the newspaper dispute over Grace's deed. George Darling to D. H. Atkinson, 14 February 1893, NRO, SANT/BEQ/14/8.
6 Smedley, *Grace Darling*, p. 263.
7 Ibid., p. 263; *Times*, 21 January 1913.
8 *Life-Boat* (November 1930), pp. 165–8.
9 *Times*, 26 October 1929.
10 http://www.theheritagetrail.co.uk/notable%20houses/cragside.htm; *Times*, 17 October 1941; *Who Was Who, 1941–1950*.
11 A. D. Farr, *Let Not the Deep: The Story of the Royal National Lifeboat Institution* (Aberdeen, 1973), pp. 47–52.
12 *Life-Boat*, 1 October 1856, pp. 191–4; 1 August 1893, pp. 501–2.
13 Vince to W. J. Oliver, 6 October 1932; Oliver to Vince 10 October 1932; Oliver to Satterthwaite 15 November 1932, RNLI Archive.
14 Satterthwaite to Oliver, 14 November 1932; note by Satterthwaite, 26 May 1933 after meeting with Armstrong, RNLI Archive.

15 *Times*, 26 March 1933.

16 Constance Smedley, *Crusaders: The Reminiscences of Constance Smedley* (London, 1929), quoting pp. 6–7, 37, 144, 147; *Oxford DNB*; Jessica Mitford, *Grace Had an English Heart* (London, 1988), p. 172; Duchess of Northumberland to Mrs Williams-Wynn, 25 February 1932, Alnwick Castle Archives, DP/D8/II/87.

17 Smedley, *Crusaders*, pp. 3, 54–74, 191.

18 Ibid., pp. 96–9, 196–9, 222–4, 250; *Oxford DNB*; Nicola Gordon Bowe, 'Constance and Maxwell Armfield: An American Interlude, 1915–1922', *Journal of Decorative and Propaganda Arts*, 14 (1989), pp. 6–27.

19 Constance Smedley's diaries, 27 January, 9 February, 3 March, 17 July to 9 August 1930; Maxwell Armfield's diaries, 14 November to 3 December 1931.

20 Marchioness of Aberdeen to Duchess of Northumberland, 12 November 1931, Alnwick Castle Archives, DP/D8/II/87; Smedley, *Grace Darling*, p. 15.

21 Smedley to Duchess of Northumberland, 14 and 18 April 1932, Alnwick Castle Archives, DP/D8/II/87.

22 Maxwell Armfield to Satterthwaite, 11 April 1941, RNLI archive; Constance Smedley's diaries, 19 May 1932, where the publisher tells her that the book as it stands 'is unusable … It slightly stuns me …'

23 Smedley to Oxberry, 27 March 1932, NRO, SANT/BEQ/14/10; David Cannadine, *The Decline and Fall of the British Aristocracy* (London, 1996), pp. 322, 336, 546.

24 Smedley to Duchess of Northumberland, 25 April 1932, Alnwick Castle Archives, DP/D8/II/87.

25 Smedley, *Grace Darling*, pp. 180–5, 268–9.

26 Smedley to Duchess of Northumberland, 8 March 1933, Alnwick Castle Archives, DP/D8/II/87.

27 Constance Smedley, *Grace Darling and Her Islands* (London, n.d. [1934]), p. 190; for King-Hall, *Oxford DNB*.

28 Smedley to Oxberry, 15 November 1932, NRO, SANT/BEQ/14/10.

29 Constance Smedley's diaries, 3 August 1930; Smedley, *Grace Darling*, p. 18.

30 Ibid., pp. 268–9.

31 Smedley to Oxberry, 27 March 1932, NRO, SANT/BEQ/14/10.

32 Smedley to Duchess of Northumberland, 3 May and 21 September 1932; to Miss Macdonagh, 10 May and 14 September 1932; J. H.Cleet to Miss MacDonagh, 30 September 1932, Alnwick Castle Archives, DP/D8/II/87; *Times*, 3 October 1932.

33 For example, *Times Literary Supplement*, 10 November 1932, quoted in Mitford, *Grace Had an English Heart*, pp. 159–60; *Times*, 22 November 1932; *Sunday Times*, 27 November 1932.

34 Constance Smedley's diaries, 2 November 1933.

35 Constance Smedley's diaries, 1933, esp. 21 April, 24 August, 20 September, 2 and 7 November.

36 Armfield to Satterthwaite, 11 April 1941, RNLI Archive.

37 Constance Smedley, *Grace Darling and Her Islands* (London, n.d. [1934]), p. 191.

38 Ibid.; *The Times*, 26 March 1933.

39 Smedley to Charles Vince, Publicity Secretary, RNLI, 18, 21 and 25 February 1933; Vince to Smedley, 28 February 1933, RNLI Archive.

40 Smedley to Vince, 1 March 1933, Vince to Smedley, 8 March 1933, Smedley to Vince 9 March 1933, RNLI Archive.

41 Smedley to Satterthwaite, 27 March 1933, RNLI Archive.

42 Satterthwaite's notes on the meeting, 7 April 1933, Smedley to Satterthwaite, 8 April 1933, RNLI Archive.

43 Smedley to Satterthwaite, 3 and 7 July 1934, Satterthwaite to Smedley, 9 July 1934, RNLI Archive.

44 Smedley to Satterthwaite, 18 October 1934, 9 February 1935, RNLI Archive.

45 Smedley to Satterthwaite, 9 February 1935, RNLI Archive.

46 Smedley to Satterthwaite, 28 August, 23 September 1937, RNLI Archive.

47 *Life-Boat* (February 1935), pp. 422–3.

48 *Times*, 22 July 1949.

49 National Archives, ED32/1691.

50 *Daily Telegraph*, 10 September 1938.

51 Smedley to Vince, 23 September 1937, Maxwell Armfield to Satterthwaite, 3 October 1937, RNLI Archive.

52 Vince to Miss Connell, 4 October 1935, Satterthwaite to P. S. Farrant, 8 May 1935, RNLI Archive.

53 Oliver to Vince, 6 September 1937, Vince to R. W. Ascroft, 8 September 1937, RNLI Archive.

54 Smedley to Vince, 1 March 1933, press cutting 23 April 1933, RNLI Archive.

55 Smedley to Satterthwaite, 20 December 1934, RNLI archive. There is not a mention of any of this in the parish council minutes, which deal mainly with scavenging, the disposal of a dead dog, and the possibility of electric lighting and a public convenience coming to the village. The only sign of dispute with Lord Armstrong was over the siting of a telephone kiosk. Berwick Record Office.

56 Smedley to Satterthwaite, 18 October 1934, RNLI Archive.

57 Armstrong to Satterthwaite, 16 March 1935 and 20 April 1935, RNLI Archive.

58 Oliver, 16 September 1933, Satterthwaite to Armstrong, 18 October 1934, Armstrong to Satterthwaite, 21 October 1934, RNLI Archive.

59 Gardiner to Satterthwaite, 4 January 1935, Smedley to Satterthwaite, 11 January 1935, RNLI Archive.

60 Armstrong to Satterthwaite, 28 December 1934, RNLI Archive.

61 Armstrong to Satterthwaite 28 December 1934, Satterthwaite to Armstrong, 29 December 1934, Gardiner to Satterthwaite 4 January 1935, Satterthwaite to Gardiner 12 January 1935, Satterthwaite to Smedley, 13 February 1935, RNLI Archive.

62 *Berwick Journal*, 7 November 1935; Oliver to Satterthwaite 18 December 1935, RNLI Archive.

63 Forster to Satterthwaite, 25 and 29 November 1935, Oliver to Satterthwaite 18 December 1935, RNLI Archive.

64 Oliver to Satterthwaite, 28 December 1935, RNLI Archive; Grace Darling Museum for the appeal leaflet.

65 Oliver to Satterthwaite, 28 December 1935, RNLI Archive; reminiscences of Joan Graham and Brenda Knight.

66 Oliver to Satterthwaite, 13 October 1936, RNLI Archive.

67 Satterthwaite to Forster, 9 January and 17 September 1936, Oliver to Vince, 14 January 1936, and 12 March 1937, RNLI Archive.

68 Vince to Oliver 27 August 1937, to R. W. Ascroft, 27 August 1937, Oliver to Vince, 11 September 1937, RNLI Archive.

69 Oliver to Smedley, 1 September 1937, Armfield to Satterthwaite, 3 October 1937, RNLI Archive.

70 Smedley to Vince, 22 November 1937, RNLI Archive.

71 Satterthwaite to Oliver, 22 June 1938, RNLI Archive.

72 *Life-Boat* (October 1938), pp. 530–3.

73 Ibid., pp. 532–6; *Newcastle Weekly Chronicle*, 10 September 1938; *Newcastle Daily Chronicle*, 8 September 1938.

74 *Newcastle Weekly Chronicle*, 3 September 1938; *Newcastle Daily Chronicle*, 8 September 1938.

75 *Times*, 17 July 1939; NRO, SANT/BEQ/14/10; BBC Archives.

76 *Times*, 7 September 1938, 5 October 1942.

77 *Manchester Guardian*, 7 September 1938; *Daily Telegraph*, 10 September 1938.

78 Constance Smedley's diary, 13 April 1933; John M. Mackenzie, 'David Livingstone: the Construction of the Myth', in Graham Walker and Tom Gallagher (eds), *Sermons and Battle Hymns: Protestant Popular Culture in Modern Scotland* (Edinburgh, 1990), pp. 24–42.

79 Press cutting, NRO, SANT/BEQ/14/10; Basil Dean, *Mind's Eye: An Autobiography, 1927–1972* (London, 1973).

80 Smedley to Vince, 1 March 1933, Smedley to Satterthwaite, 8 April 1933 and 22 September 1937; Satterthwaite's notes re Women's International Film Association, 13 June 1934, RNLI Archive; Smedley to Duchess of Northumberland, 12 January and 6 February 1933, Duchess of Northumberland to Smedley, 16 January 1933, Mrs Sheldon Wilkinson, Founder of the Women's International Film Association, to Duchess of Northumberland, 9 September 1933, Alnwick Castle Archives, DP/D8/II/87.

81 Smedley, *Grace Darling*, p. 6.

82 *Hutchinson's Story of the British Nation*, 4 vols (London, n.d.), iii, p. 1561.

83 *Girl Guiding: A Handbook for Brownies, Guides, Rangers, and Guiders* (1938), pp. 55–6.

84 J. A. W. Hamilton, *Twelve Clever Girls* (London, n.d. [1937]), pp. 81–7; http://digital.lib.msu.edu

Notes to Chapter 8: Disgrace and Recovery

1 District Organizer to RNLI, 5 June and 17 July 1963, RNLI Archive.

2 *Times*, 22 November 1932.

3 Jim Mackenzie, 'A Man of Mystery', *The Northumbrian*, undated cutting.

4 *The Journal of William Darling, Grace Darling's Father; from 1795 to 1860* (London, 1886), p. 3.

5 Richard Armstrong, *Grace Darling, Maid and Myth* (London, 1965), pp. 13, 38–41, 73–4.

6 Ibid., pp. 119–20, 124.

7   Ibid., p. 50.

8   Ibid., pp. 70, 76–8.

9   Ibid., pp. 200–9.

10 Peter Dillon, *Grace* (Cullercoats, North Shields, 1984), quoting pp. 4, 18.

11 Jill Paton Walsh, *Grace* (London, 1991), quoting pp. 254–6, 13.

12 W. J. Oliver to Vince, 12 September 1945, RNLI Archive.

13 RNLI Archive.

14 Phipps Hornby to Dunn, 8 July 1969, Berwick Record Office.

15 Correspondence in Berwick Record Office, quoting Phipps Hornby to RNLI, 27 June 1969.

16 These reports can be studied in the City of Newcastle Library. At the time of my research the Grace Darling Museum was unable to locate copies of the annual reports.

17 BBC Archives. Programmes broadcast on 1 June 1959, 21 September 1963, and 13 October 1971.

18 BBC Archives. Programmes broadcast on 18 May 1965, 31 March 1989, and, for the *Look North* programmes, on 11 May 1989, 19 September 1990, 16 November 1999, 4 May 2000, 28 July 2000.

19 BBC Archives. Programmes broadcast on 19 July 1965 and 18 April 1968.

20 BBC Archives. Programmes broadcast on 10 March 1966, 6 June 1988, 21 October 1996.

21 Joanna Dessau, *Amazing Grace* (London, 1980).

22 Helen Cresswell, *The Story of Grace Darling* (London, 1988), quoting pp. 42, 62–8, 70.

23 Jenny Lloyd, *Grace Darling* (Devon County Council, 1996); Clare Chandler, *Grace Darling* (Hove, 1995); Christine Moorcroft and Magnus Magnusson, *Grace Darling 1815–1842* (London, 1998); see also, Maureen Hazelhurst, *The Story of Grace Darling* (London, 1996) for children grades 3–4.

24 Tim Vicary, *Grace Darling* (1991; Oxford, 2000); Margaret Nash, *Grace to the Rescue!* (Hemel Hempstead, 1995).

25 Mary S. Lovell, *The Mitford Girls: The Biography of an Extraordinary Family* (London, 2001); *Oxford DNB*.

26 Jessica Mitford, *Grace Had an English Heart* (London, 1988), pp. 19–26.

27 Ibid., pp. 20, 171–5; Lovell, *Mitford Girls*, p. 514.

28 Mitford, *Grace*, pp. 24, 103, 169–70; Lovell, *Mitford Girls*, p. 514.

29 Tony Benn, 'Grace Darling', BBC Radio Scotland, September 1996; *idem, Free at Last! Diaries 1991–2001* (London, 2002), p. 270.

30 http://www.christophereimer.co.uk/single/8106.html; Mitford, *Grace*, between pp. 64–5; news.bbc.co.uk/1/hi/uk/538239.stm.

31 http://www.gracedarlingsingers.org.uk.

32 Ibid.; webmaster @marcliff.net; www.rhs.org.uk/plants/documents/Potentilla; information from Dr John Gardiner.

33 *Woman's Hour*, 14 October 2004.

34 Harriet Pringle and Babington White, *Grace Darling and Other Poems and Handsome is as Handsome Does* (Hastings, 1998), pp. 14, 16, 19, 27.

35 My thanks to Keith Armstrong for sending me his poem. The 'saving grace' theme also runs through the Strawbs' 'Grace Darling' in their 'Old School Songs' (http://www.strawbsweb.co.uk/lyrics/halcukly.asp).

Notes to Chapter 9: Remembering Grace Darling

1   *Memoir of Grace Horsley Darling, The Heroine of the Farnes* (Berwick, 1843), p. 36.
2   Ibid., p. 36; *Times*, 23 August 1839.
3   Phipps Hornby to Howarth, Publicity Secretary for RNLI, 15 August 1961; Grace Darling Museum, Annual Report 1958, RNLI Archive.
4   Roy Palmer (ed.), *The Oxford Book of Sea Songs* (Oxford, 1988), pp. 208–9, citing J. Ranson, *Songs of the Wexford Coast* (Wexford, 1948 and 1975).
5   My thanks to Louis James for this information.
6   W. A. Montgomery and M.Scott Weightman, *Grace Darling* (Seahouses, 1974; revised, 1987), p. 20; email correspondence with Masahiro Kawamoto; Grace Darling Museum.
7   www.townsendhouse.com.au; my daughter, Kirsty Cunningham, kindly supplied me with photos of the Melbourne hotel.
8   www.melbournecup.co.au/previous.php.
9   Ron Edwards, *The Overlander Song Book* (London and Adelaide, 1972), pp. 284–6.
10 *Newcastle Weekly Chronicle*, 12 November 1892.
11 Miles Franklin, *My Career Goes Bung: Purporting to be the Autobiography of Sybylla Penelope Melvyn* (1946; London, 1981), p. 28. Completed in 1902, the book was potentially too libellous to be published.
12 http://www.abc.net.au/backyard/shipwrecks/wa/georgette.htm.
13 www. bruzelius.info/Nautica/News/BDA/BDA (1854-05-29).html; www.cinms.nos.noaa.gov/shipwreck/dbase/ocnms/gracedarling.html.
14 Jessica Mitford, *Grace Had an English Heart* (London and New York, 1988), pp. 127–36.
15 http://freepages.genealogy.rootsweb.com/~bfhs/art10.html; http://www.offbeattravel.com/carriage.html.
16 www.oldpowderhouse.com/inn_bnb_rooms; Mitford, *Grace*, p. 172 and www.imdb.com; Yahoo!Music; American Peony Society; www.febs.org/pictures/Neo.htm; www.ratebeer.com.
17 Jerold Vernon, *The Maid of the Isles* (Newcastle-upon-Tyne, 1839), pp. 479–80; Marina Warner, *Joan of Arc: The Image of Female Heroism* (London, 1981).
18 Ibid., pp. 241–54, 267.
19 Michel Winock, 'Joan of Arc', in Pierre Nora, *Realms of Memory: Rethinking the French Past*, ed. Lawrence D. Kritzman, 3 vols (New York, 1996–8), iii, p. 442.
20 *Jeanne Darc, the Patriot Martyr: and other Narratives of Female Heroism in Peace and War* (London, 1883), quoting p. 6.
21 Eva Hope, *Grace Darling, Heroine of the Farne Islands: Her Life and its Lessons* (London, 1875), p. 301; Marianne Kirlew, *Twelve Famous Girls* (London, n.d. [1897]), p. 51.
22 NRO, SANT/BEQ/14/10.
23 Stephen Bann, *The Clothing of Clio: A Study of the Representation of History in Nineteenth-Century Britain and France* (Cambridge, 1984), pp. 50–1; Nadia Margolis, 'Rewriting the Right: High Priests, Heroes and Hooligans in the Portrayal of Joan of Arc (1824–1945)', in Dominique Goy-Blanquet (ed.), *Joan of Arc, A Saint for All Reasons: Studies in Myth and Politics* (Aldershot, 2003), pp. 59–63.
24 Margolis, 'Rewriting the Right', pp. 59–104, quoting p. 103.

25   *British Journal of Nursing*, 17 March 1917, p. 195 (rcnarchive.rcn.org.uk/data); *Newcastle Weekly Chronicle*, 3 September 1938.

26   Lytton Strachey, *Eminent Victorians* (London, 1918), pp. 117–79, quoting pp. 119, 137.

27   Cecil Woodham-Smith, *Florence Nightingale, 1820–1910* (London, 1950); F. B. Smith, *Florence Nightingale: Reputation and Power* (London and Canberra, 1982), pp. 11, 12, 21, 22, 201.

28   Hugh Small, *Florence Nightingale, Avenging Angel* (London, 1998); review by Jane Ridley in the *Spectator*.

29   Tamara L. Hunt, *Defining John Bull: Political Caricature and National Identity in Late Georgian England* (Aldershot, 2003), esp. pp. 121–69; Miles Taylor, 'John Bull and the Iconography of Public Opinion in England c. 1712–1929', *Past and Present*, 134 (1992), pp. 92–128.

30   See, e.g., Graham Dawson, *Soldier Heroes: British Adventure, Empire, and the Imagining of Masculinities* (London, 1994); Keith Surridge, 'More than a Great Poster: Lord Kitchener and the Image of the Military Hero', *Historical Research*, 74 (2000), pp. 298–313.

31   Flora Thompson, *Lark Rise to Candleford* (London, 1954), pp. 261–71; Lori Anne Loeb, *Consuming Angels: Advertising and Victorian Women* (Oxford, 1994), pp. 85–95.

32   Maurice Agulhon, *Marianne into Battle: Republican Imagery and Symbolism in France, 1789–1880* (Cambridge and Paris, 1981); for the later history of Marianne, see *idem*, *Marianne au pouvoir, l'imagerie et la symbolique républicaines de 1880 à 1914* (Paris, 1989), and *Métamorphoses de Marianne, l'imagerie et la symbolique républicaines de 1914 à nos jours* (Paris, 2001).

33   *Newcastle Chronicle*, 8 September 1938.

34   *Life-boat*, winter 1988/89, p. 44.

35   Papers of Lord Armstrong and Family, Tyne and Wear Archives, DFA/4/15, 32; *Times*, 25 July 1885.

36   *Times*, 2 June 1896, 5 June 1896, 9 June 1896, 13 June 1896.

37   Quoted in Richard Weight, *Patriots: National Identity in Britain, 1940–2000* (London, 2002), p. 530.

38   *Times*, 5 October 1942.

39   Edith Sitwell, *English Women* (London, 1942), esp. pp. 33–4.

40   *Spectator*, 17 November 1838, p. 1095.

41   [Daniel H. Atkinson], *Grace Darling; Her True Story. From Unpublished Papers in the Possession of her Family* (London, n.d. [1880]), p. 11.

42   William Pitcairn papers, GD1/675/115, National Archives of Scotland; *Times*, 25 May 1894, 18 April 1980; Nevill papers, ABE/73B2, East Sussex Record Office.

43   Diana Athill, *Yesterday Morning* (London, 2002), p. 142.

Bibliography

1. MANUSCRIPT SOURCES

ALNWICK CASTLE ARCHIVES

Letters to Duke of Northumberland, DP/D3/5/26
Constance Smedley correspondence, DP/D8/II/87
Correspondence about the opening of the museum, DP/D9/I/40

BODLEIAN LIBRARY, OXFORD

Catalogue of Ballads, Harding B 11 (4158), B 13 (240), B 15 (118a); Firth c.12
    (125, 126); 2806 c.14 (25)
Henry Perlee Parker, or An Artist's Narrative, MS Eng, misc.e.654

BBC WRITTEN ARCHIVES CENTRE

Script of *The Fame of Grace Darling*

GLOUCESTERSHIRE ARCHIVES

Papers of Lloyd-Baker family, D3549/17/4/4
Papers of Browne/Murray-Browne family and related families of Lloyd-Baker
    and Sharp, D6919/2/6

GRACE DARLING MUSEUM

The Museum has been undergoing a major modernization programme, and
    when it reopens in 2007 its holdings are likely to be different to those I
    examined in 2003/4. It will, however, undoubtedly remain a major source for
    the study both of the Darling family and of the loss of the *Forfarshire*.

GUILDHALL LIBRARY

Trinity House, Court Minutes, MS 30004

Trinity House, Board Minutes, MS 30010
Trinity House, Warden's Minutes, MS 30025

NATIONAL ARCHIVES

BT 31/4611/30248, Grace Darling (Broken Hill) Silver Mines Ltd
BT 31/7566/53946, Grace Darling Purchase Syndicate Ltd
BT 31/26944/178599, Grace Darling Hosiery Company Ltd
BT 98/240, contains details of some of the Forfarshire's voyages and crew
BT 107/428, registration document of Forfarshire
COPY 1/364/425-31, Photographs of Grace Darling Boat at International
    Fisheries Exhibition
ED 32/1691, Grace Darling Special School, Battersea
FS 15/1552, Grace Darling Lodge, Ancient Free Gardeners

NEWCASTLE CITY LIBRARY

Letter, H. P. Parker to D. Lucas, 1839, L920 D221P
Grace Darling Museum, newsletters

NEWCASTLE UPON TYNE UNIVERSITY, ROBINSON LIBRARY

Trevelyan papers, WCT, 72-80

NORTHUMBERLAND RECORD OFFICE (NRO):

Berwick
Bamburgh Parish Council, Minute Book, 1930s
Documents from Murton White House, BRO 17/12, 12b, 13
Gosforth
Manuscript letters, notes and newspaper cuttings, SANT/BEQ/14/1-11
Papers relating to Grace Darling, 1826–63, SANT/BEQ/14/2/1-59
Newspaper cuttings, 404/353

PRIVATE

Nicola Gordon Bowe, Dublin: Diaries of Constance Smedley and Maxwell
    Armfield, 1930–6

ROYAL ARCHIVES
Queen Victoria's Journal, RA, VIC/QVJ/1838

ROYAL HUMANE SOCIETY ARCHIVE
Annual Reports
Minutes of Committee
Minutes of General Court
Letter Book

ROYAL NATIONAL LIFE-BOAT INSTITUTION ARCHIVE, POOLE
Darling family letters, E.GD.2.1-31
Papers relating to the foundation of the museum

TYNE AND WEAR ARCHIVES
Papers of Lord Armstrong, DFA/4/15, DFA/4/32

2. PRINTED SOURCES

A. GRACE DARLING

Armstrong, Richard, *Grace Darling: Maid and Myth* (London, 1965)
Arthur, Thomas, *The Life of Grace Darling, the Heroine of the Farne Isles* (1875; London, n.d. [1885])
[Atkinson, Daniel H.], *Grace Darling: Her True Story. From Unpublished Papers in Possession of her family* (London, n.d. [1880])
Chandler, Clare, *Grace Darling* (Hove, 1995)
Cresswell, Helen, *The Story of Grace Darling* (London, 1988)
Dessau, Joanna, *Amazing Grace* (1980, Bath, 1982)
Dillon, Peter, *Grace* (North Shields, 1984)
Grace Darling: A Story of Shipwreck and Heroism (London n.d. [1896])
Grace Darling; or the Loss of the 'Forfarshire'. A Tale by a Young Lady (Glasgow, 1840)
Hazelhurst, Maureen, *The Story of Grace Darling* (London, 1996)
Hope, Eva, *Grace Darling, Heroine of the Farne Islands: Her Life and its Lessons* (London, 1875)
http://homepage.ntlworld.com/foxtree/genealogy/darling2.htm
Linley, George, *Grace Darling, Ballad* (London, n.d.)

Lloyd, Jenny, *Grace Darling* (Devon County Council, 1996)

McGonagall, William, 'Grace Darling: or the Wreck of the *Forfarshire*' in *Poetic Gems* (1890; London, 1975)

Memoir of Grace Horsley Darling, the Heroine of the Farnes (Berwick-upon-Tweed, 1843)

Mitford, Jessica, *Grace Had an English Heart* (London and New York, 1988)

Montgomery, W. A. and Weightman, M. Scott, *Grace Darling* (Seahouses, 1974)

Moorcroft, Christine and Magnusson, Magnus, *Grace Darling, 1815–1842* (London, 1998)

Nash, Margaret, *Grace to the Rescue!* (Hemel Hempstead, 1995)

Ollivier, W. H., *Grace Darling: Stanza Commemorative of the Heroic Bravery of Grace Darling and Her Father on the Occasion of the Disastrous Wreck of the Forfarshire Steam Ship on the _th September 1838* (London, n.d.)

Pae, David, *Grace Darling, the Heroine of the Longstone Lighthouse; or, The Two Wills. A Tale of the Loss of the 'Forfarshire'* (Dundee and London, n.d. [1888])

Paton Walsh, Jill, *Grace* (London, 1991)

Phipps Hornby, W. M., 'Grace Horsley Darling, 1815–1842: Northumbrian Heroine', *Mariner's Mirror*, 54 (1968), 55–68.

Pringle, Harriet and White, Babington, *Grace Darling and Other Poems and Handsome Is as Handsome Does* (Hastings, 1998)

Reynolds, G. W. M., *Grace Darling; or, the Heroine of the Fern Islands. A Tale* (London, 1839)

Roberts, John S., *Grace Darling and the Farne Isles* (London, n.d. [1875])

Smedley, Constance, *Grace Darling and Her Islands* (London, n.d. [1934])

Smedley, Constance, *Grace Darling and Her Times* (London, 1932)

Smith, C. Fox, *The Story of Grace Darling* (London, 1940)

Stirling, Edward, *Grace Darling; or, The Wreck at Sea, a Drama in Two Acts* (London, n.d.)

Swinburne, Algernon Charles, 'Grace Darling', in *The Poems of Algernon Charles Swinburne*, 6 vols, 6, 164–70 (London, 1909)

Thomson, Christopher, *Grace Darling, or the Wreck, Narrative Ballad* (London, n.d.)

Vernon, Jerold, *Grace Darling, the Maid of the Isles* (Newcastle-upon-Tyne, 1839)

Vicary, Tim, *Grace Darling* (1991, Oxford, 2000)

Wordsworth, William, 'Grace Darling', in *The Poetical Works of William Wordsworth*, 6 vols (London, 1882), 4, 357–60

B. COLLECTIVE WORKS THAT INCLUDE GRACE DARLING

Bigland, Eileen, *The True Book About Heroines of the Sea* (London, 1958)

A Book of Golden Deeds of All Times and All Lands (London, 1864)

Bruce, Charles (ed.), *The Book of Noble Englishwomen: Lives Made Illustrious by Heroism, Goodness, and Great Attainments* (London and Edinburgh, 1875)

Carey, Rosa Nouchette, *Twelve Notable Good Women of the Nineteenth Century* (London, 1899)

Chambers, R. (ed.), *The Book of Days*, 2 vols (London, n.d. [1863–4])

The Complete History Readers: Standard I: A First Book of Stories from History (London, 1904)

Craig, Annie, *Golden Deeds Told Anew* (London, n.d. [1897])

Cross, F. J., *Beneath the Banner: Being Narratives of Noble Lives and Brave Deeds* (London, n.d. [1894])

Edwards, Ron, *The Overlander Song Book* (London and Adelaide, 1972)

Everyday Heroes: Stories of Bravery During the Queen's Reign 1837–1888 (London, n.d.[1889])

Farrance, E. H., *Twelve Wonderful Women* (London, 1936)

Fifty Famous Women: Their Virtues and Failings, and the Lessons of Their Lives (London, n.d.[1864])

Girl Guiding: A Handbook for Brownies, Guides, Rangers, and Guiders

Hamilton, J. A. W., *Twelve Clever Girls* (London, n.d. [1937?])

Hutchinson's Story of the British Nation, 4 vols (London, n.d.)

Jeanne Darc, the Patriot Martyr: and Other Narratives of Female Heroism in Peace and War (London, 1883)

Johnson, Joseph, *Brave Women: Who Have Been Distinguished for Heroic Actions & Noble Virtues; who have exhibited fearless courage; stout hearts; and intrepid resolve* (Edinburgh and London, n.d.[1875])

Kirlew, Marianne, *Twelve Famous Girls* (London, n.d. [1897])

Longmans' New Readers, Standard IV (London, 1885)

Macmillan's New History Readers (London, 1905)

Mee, Arthur, *The Children's Encyclopedia*

Owen, Mrs Octavius Freire, *The Heroines of Domestic Life* (London, 1861)

Palmer, Roy (ed.), *The Oxford Book of Sea Songs* (Oxford, 1988)

Simple Stories from English History for Young Readers (London, 1893)

Sitwell, Edith, *English Women* (London, 1942)

Spaulding, George L., *Women in History, Vocal or Instrumental* (Philadelphia, 1919)

Starling, Elizabeth, *Noble Deeds of Women* (3rd edn, London, 1848)

C. HEROES AND HEROINES

Agulhon, Maurice, *Marianne into Battle: Republican Imagery and Symbolism in France, 1789–1880* (Cambridge and Paris, 1981)

Bann, Stephen, *The Clothing of Clio: A Study of the Representation of History in Nineteenth-Century Britain and France* (Cambridge, 1984)

Dawson, Graham, *Soldier Heroes: British Adventure, Empire, and the Imagining of Masculinities* (London, 1994)

Hunt, Tamara L., *Defining John Bull: Political Caricature and National Identity in Late Georgian England* (Aldershot, 2003)

Loeb, Lori Anne, *Consuming Angels: Advertising and Victorian Women* (Oxford, 1994)

Mackenzie, John M., 'David Livingstone: the Construction of the Myth', in Graham Walker and Tom Gallagher (eds), *Sermons and Battle Hymns: Protestant and Popular Culture in Modern Scotland* (Edinburgh, 1990), 24–42

Margolis, Nadia, 'Rewriting the Right: High Priests, Heroes and Hooligans in the Portrayal of Joan of Arc, 1824–1945', in Dominique Goy-Blanquet (ed.), *Joan of Arc, A Saint for All Reasons: Studies in Myth and Politics* (Aldershot, 2003)

Miller, Lucasta, *The Brontë Myth* (London, 2001)

Nora, Pierre, *Realms of Memory: Rethinking the French Past*, 3 vols, ed. Lawrence D. Kritzman (New York, 1996–8)

Small, Hugh, *Florence Nightingale: Avenging Angel* (London, 1998)

Smith, F. B., *Florence Nightingale: Reputation and Power* (London and Canberra, 1982)

Strachey, Lytton, *Eminent Victorians* (London, 1918)

Surridge, Keith, 'More than a great poster: Lord Kitchener and the image of the military hero', *Historical Research*, 74 (2001), 298–313

Taylor, Miles, 'John Bull and the Iconography of Public Opinion in England *c.* 1712–1929', *Past and Present*, 134 (1992), 92–128

Vicinus, Martha, 'Models for public life: biographies of "Noble Women" for girls', in Claudia Nelson and Lynne Vallone (eds), *The Girls' Own: Cultural Histories of the Anglo-American Girl, 1830–1915* (Athens, Georgia and London, 1994), 52–68

Warner, Marina, *Joan of Arc: The Image of Female Heroism* (London, 1981)

Woodham-Smith, Cecil, *Florence Nightingale, 1820–1910* (London, 1950)

D. NORTHUMBERLAND

[Atkinson, Daniel H.] (ed.), *The Journal of William Darling, Grace Darling's Father; from 1795 to 1860* (London, 1886)

Batchelor, John, *Lady Trevelyan and the Pre-Raphaelite Brotherhood* (London, 2006)

Bird, John, *Dorothy and the Forsters of Bamburgh* (Berwick-upon-Tweed, 1982)

Burn, W. L., 'Newcastle upon Tyne in the Early Nineteenth Century', *Archaeologica Aeliana*, 34 (1956), 1–13

Cannadine, David, *G. M. Trevelyan: A Life in History* (London, 1992)

Colls, Robert and Lancaster, Bill (eds), *Newcastle Upon Tyne: A Modern History* (Chichester, 2001)

Dibdin, Thomas, *A Bibliographical Antiquarian and Picturesque Tour in the Northern Counties of England and in Scotland*, reprinted in idem, *Newcastle in 1836* (Newcastle, 1968)

Fredeman, William E., 'The letters of Pictor Ignotus: William Bell Scott's correspondence with Alice Boyd, 1859–1884', *Bulletin of the John Rylands Library*, 58 (1975–6), 66–111, 306–52

Graham, Frank, *Famous Northumbrian Women* (Newcastle-upon-Tyne, 1969)

Howitt, William, *Visits to Remarkable Places: Old Halls, Battle Fields, and Scenes Illustrative of Striking Passages in History and Poetry, Chiefly in the Counties of Durham and Northumberland* (London, 1842)

Lang, Cecil Y. (ed.), *The Swinburne Letters*, 6 vols (New Haven, Connecticut, 1959–62)

McCord, Norman, 'The making of modern Newcastle', *Archaeologica Aeliana*, 5th series, 9 (1981), 333–46

Maehl, W. H., 'Chartist Disturbances in Northeastern England, 1839', *International Review of Social History*, 8 (1963), 389–414.

Milne, Maurice, 'Strikes and strike-breaking in North-East England, 1815–44: the attitude of the local press', *International Review of Social History*, 22 (1977), 226–40

Minto, W., (ed.), *Autobiographical Notes of the Life of William Bell Scott*, 2 vols (New York, 1892)

Nussbaum, Elizabeth, *Dear Miss Baird: A Portrait of a 19th-Century Family* (Charlbury, 2003)

Rutter, Andrew Craig, *A Seahouses Saga* (Stockport, 1998)

Surtees, Virginia (ed.), *Reflections of a Friendship: John Ruskin's Letters to Pauline Trevelyan 1846–66* (London, 1979)

Thompson, F. M. L., *English Landed Society in the Nineteenth Century* (London, 1963)

Trevelyan, Raleigh, *A Pre-Raphaelite Circle* (London, 1978)

Watson, Robert Spence, *The History of the Literary and Philosophical Society of Newcastle-upon-Tyne (1793–1896)* (London, 1897)

Welford, Richard, *Men of Mark 'Twixt Tyne and Tweed*, 3 vols (London and Newcastle-upon-Tyne, 1895)

E. LIGHTHOUSES, SHIPWRECK, AND LIFESAVING

Bain, Colin, 'A footnote to the story of Grace Darling', *Scottish Genealogist*, 35 (Sept. 1988), 125–6

Barnes, Julian, *A History of the World in 10½ Chapters* (London, 1989), ch. 5

Bathurst, Bella, *The Lighthouse Stevensons* (London, 1999)

Boase, T. S. R., 'Shipwrecks in English Romantic Painting', *Journal of the Warburg and Courtauld Institutes*, 22 (1959), 332–46

Cameron, Ian, *Riders of the Storm: The Story of the RNLI* (London, 2002)

Farr, A. D., *Let Not the Deep: The Story of the Royal National Lifeboat Institution* (Aberdeen, 1973)

Hayter, Alethea, *The Wreck of the Abergavenny* (London, 2002)

http://www.abc.net.au/backyard/shipwrecks/wa/georgette.htm

Lindsay, W. S., *History of Merchant Shipping and Ancient Commerce*, 4 vols (1874; New York, 1965)

The Loss of the Steamship Forfarshire, Captain Humble, which Struck on the Fern Islands on her Voyage to Dundee, on the Night of 7th September 1838, and the Heroic Conduct of Grace Darling in Venturing Her Life, and Rescuing the Survivors from Destruction (on internal evidence published in Hull or Newcastle, *c.* 1842)

McGregor, Sir Duncan, *Loss of the Kent, East Indiaman*, new edn (London, 1834)

Narrative of the Total Loss of the Rothesay Castle Steam Vessel, on the Dutchman's Bank, August 17, 1831, on her Passage from Liverpool to Wales, 2nd edn (London, 1831)

Palmer, William J., 'Dickens and Shipwreck', ch. 3 in *Dickens and New Historicism* (New York, 1997)

Parliamentary Papers:

'23rd Report of the Charity Commissioners', 1830 (462), xii, 456–74 (on Lord Crewe's charity)

'Report from the Select Committee on the State and Management of Lighthouses', 1834 (590), in *British Parliamentary Papers, Shipping Safety*, vol. 1 (Shannon, 1968)

'Select Committee appointed to inquire into the Causes of Shipwrecks', 1836 (567), in *British Parliamentary Papers, Shipping Safety*, vol. 2 (Shannon, 1968)

'Report on Steam Vessel Accidents', 1839, xlvii

Riding, Christine, '*The Raft of the Medusa* in Britain: Audience and Context', in Patrick Noon (ed.), *Constable to Delacroix: British Art and the French Romantics* (London, 2003), 66–93

Taylor, James, 'Private Property, Public Interest, and the Role of the State in Nineteenth-Century Britain: The Case of the Lighthouses', *Historical Journal*, 44 (2001), 749–71

Woodman, Richard and Wilson, Jane, *The Lighthouses of Trinity House* (Bradford on Avon, 2002)
www.bruzelius.info/Nautica/News/BDA/BDA (1854-05-29).html
www.cinms.nos.noaa.gov/shipwreck/dbase/ocnms/gracedarling.html

F. CULTURAL CONTEXTS

Assael, Brenda, *The Circus and Victorian Society* (Charlottesville and London, 2005)
Athill, Diana, *Yesterday Morning* (London, 2002)
Briggs, Asa, *Victorian Things* (Harmondsworth, 1990)
Burke, Edmund, *A Philosophical Enquiry into the Origin of Our Ideas of the Sublime and Beautiful*, ed. Adam Phillips (Oxford, 1990)
Cordingly, David, *Marine Painting in England, 1700–1900* (New York, 1973)
Donaldson, William, *Popular Literature in Victorian Scotland: Language, Fiction and the Press* (Aberdeen, 1986)
Farningham, Marianne, *A Working Woman's Life: An Autobiography* (London, 1907)
Franklin, Miles, *My Career Goes Bung: Purporting to be the Autobiography of Sybylla Penelope Melvyn* (1946; London, 1981)
Frost, Thomas, *Circus Life and Circus Celebrities* (London, 1881)
Harding, A. and N., *Victorian Staffordshire Figures, 1815–1875*, 3 vols (Atglen, Pennsylvania)
Heathorn, Stephen, *For Home, Country, and Race: Constructing Gender, Class, and Englishness in the Elementary Schools of Victorian England, 1880–1914* (Buffalo, New York and London, 2000)
Hill, Alan G., *The Letters of William and Dorothy Wordsworth*, vii, *The Later Years*, part 4, 1840–1853 (Oxford, 1988)
http://christopherreimer.co.uk/single/8106.html
http://digital.lib.msu.edu
http://www.dragonantiques2.co.uk/EBIMAGE/nov00/gracedarling.htm
http://freepages.genealogy.rootsweb.com/~bfhs/art10.html
http://www.gracedarlingsingers.org.uk
http://offbeattravel.com/carriage.html
http://www.strawbsweb.co.uk/lyrics/halcukly.asp
http://www.victoriansilk.com/stevens/pictures/st01-303/st180.html
Jalland, Pat, *Death in the Victorian Family* (Oxford, 1996)
James, P. D., *Innocent Blood* (1980; London, 1989)
Kilgarriff, Michael, *Sing Us One of the Old Songs: A Guide to Popular Song, 1860–1920* (Oxford, 1998)

Kwint, Marius, 'The Legitimization of the Circus in Late Georgian England', *Past and Present*, 174 (2002), 72–115

Lovell, Mary, *The Mitford Girls: The Biography of an Extraordinary Family* (London, 2001)

Miskell, Louise, Whatley, Christopher A. and Harris, Bob (eds), *Victorian Dundee: Image and Realities* (East Linton, 2000)

Oliver, Anthony, *The Victorian Staffordshire Figure: A Guide for Collectors* (London, 1971)

Ormond, Richard, *Early Victorian Portraits*, 2 vols (London, 1973)

Prochaska, Frank, *Royal Bounty: The Making of a Welfare Monarchy* (New Haven and London, 1995)

Pugh, P. D. Gordon, *Staffordshire Portrait Figures and Allied Subjects of the Victorian Era* (Woodbridge, 1987)

Saxon, A. H., *The Life and Art of Andrew Ducrow and the Romantic Age of the English Circus* (Hamden, Connecticut, 1978)

Scott, Walter, *The Heart of Midlothian* (1818; Oxford, 1982)

Smedley, Constance, *Crusaders: The Reminiscences of Constance Smedley* (London, 1929)

Sunderland Pottery, revised by John C. Baker (Tyne and Wear, 1984)

Sussman, Peter Y., *Decca: The Letters of Jessica Mitford* (London, 2006)

Vann, J. D., 'The Publication of Wordsworth's "Grace Darling"', *Notes and Queries*, 223 (1978), 223–5

Waugh, Evelyn, *Brideshead Revisited* (1945; London, 1981)

Weight, Richard, *Patriots: National Identity in Britain, 1940–2000* (London, 2002)

Wilson, Linda, '"Afraid to be Singular": Marianne Farningham and the Role of Women, 1857–1909', in Sue Morgan (ed.), *Women, Religion and Feminism, 1750–1900* (Basingstoke, 2002), 107–21

Wood, Robert, *Victorian Delights* (London, 1967)

www.imdb.com

www.melbournecup.co.au/previous.php

www.oldpowderhouse.com/inn_bnb_rooms

www.ratebeer.com

www.rhs.org.uk/plants/documents/Potentilla

www.townsendhouse.com.au

Index